"Christians are united in proclaiming that 'J... tradition and Scripture offer different narrative... understand what that means. Witt and Scandrett are wise, charitable, brilliant, and passionate guides to the scriptural, theological, and historical questions that compose atonement theology. This approachable introduction will help everyone who wants a deeper understanding of what we mean when we confess that Christ lived, died, rose again, and ascended into heaven 'for us and for our salvation.'"

—**Tish Harrison Warren**, Anglican priest and author
of *Liturgy of the Ordinary* and *Prayer in the Night*

"Thoughtful Christians looking for guidance on the doctrine of the atonement are flooded with almost too much information. Witt and Scandrett's *Mapping Atonement* brings wonderful clarity to the field. Their choice of figures for discussion is excellent, and their constructive approach to the topic is theologically balanced and insightful. I look forward to using this book in my own teaching."

—**Joseph Mangina**, Wycliffe College, University of Toronto

"*Mapping Atonement* is a major theological accomplishment. It offers a remarkably comprehensive overview of the history of atonement theology. With attention to detail and generosity of interpretation, Witt and Scandrett faithfully map the doctrine of atonement. Rightly arguing that Christ's mission doesn't just illustrate but in fact constitutes atonement, Witt and Scandrett carefully chart their own theological path. This is the textbook on Christ's salvific work that many have been waiting for."

—**Hans Boersma**, Nashotah House Theological Seminary

"*Mapping Atonement* serves admirably both as a contribution to theology and as an introduction for students. It expands the vista offered to earlier generations by Aulén, even as it offers a grammar, rooted in Scripture and composed of history and ontology, to evaluate all proposals. Throughout, and especially in the conclusion (culminating in an 'critical realist' account of T. F. Torrance), Witt and Scandrett understand the urgency of atonement's retrieval in our confused time. I highly recommend it to a wide audience."

—**The Right Rev. George Sumner**, Bishop of
the Episcopal Diocese of Dallas

"With the lucidity and penetration characteristic of their teaching and writing, Witt and Scandrett have provided us a superb survey of atonement theology.

Written from a classical perspective that is respectful of the variety of views on the topic, yet responsibly critical in the application of scriptural and metaphysical demands on the material, the book covers a broad range of reflection on the atonement from the early church to the present, culminating in a careful commendation of T. F. Torrance's work. The volume wears its scholarship lightly but is informed by a mastery of the tradition. This will prove an essential introduction to the topic."

—**Ephraim Radner**, Wycliffe College, University of Toronto

MAPPING ATONEMENT

• • •

The Doctrine *of* Reconciliation
in Christian History *and* Theology

WILLIAM G. WITT
and JOEL SCANDRETT

B

Baker Academic

a division of Baker Publishing Group
Grand Rapids, Michigan

Published by Baker Academic
a division of Baker Publishing Group
PO Box 6287, Grand Rapids, MI 49516-6287
www.bakeracademic.com

Printed in the United States of America

Library of Congress Cataloging-in-Publication Data
Names: Witt, William G., 1955– author. | Scandrett, Joel, author.
Title: Mapping atonement : the doctrine of reconciliation in Christian history and theology /
    William G. Witt and Joel Scandrett.
Description: Grand Rapids, Michigan : Baker Academic, a division of Baker Publishing Group,
    [2022] | Includes bibliographical references and index.
Identifiers: LCCN 2021057336 | ISBN 9780801030680 (paperback) | ISBN 9781540965684
    (casebound) | ISBN 9781493436910 (ebook) | ISBN 9781493436927 (pdf)
Subjects: LCSH: Atonement—History of doctrines.
Classification: LCC BT263 .W58 2022 | DDC 232/.3—dc23/eng/20220112
LC record available at https://lccn.loc.gov/2021057336

22   23   24   25   26   27   28   7   6   5   4   3   2   1

To our students, past and present, at Trinity School for Ministry:
may you be faithful ministers of God's reconciliation
of all things in Jesus Christ

Contents

Acknowledgments

This book is the result of our shared conviction of the need for such a book. Having both taught courses in atonement theology—Bill at Trinity School for Ministry and Joel (previously) at Trinity Evangelical Divinity School—we were surprised to discover no single book that offered a comprehensive survey and analysis of atonement paradigms and their representative theologians throughout the epochs of the Christian tradition. While many comparative texts of atonement paradigms exist, only a few are comprehensive, and most champion a particular paradigm at the expense of others. Moreover, few if any of these texts offer a theological method by which to evaluate the relative strengths and weaknesses of historic paradigms that is not already committed to a particular paradigm. We believe this book is distinctive in that it (1) considers the major atonement paradigms and their respective theologians from the ancient church to the present, and (2) employs an integrated, multilevel set of theological criteria by which to evaluate them. This means of assessment was developed by Bill in a previously published essay.[1]

At the same time, we remain indebted to the scholarship of others in the field of atonement theology. Several works stand out in particular. We found the *T&T Clark Companion to Atonement*, edited by Adam Johnson, to be an excellent resource. Peter Schmiechen's *Saving Power: Theories of Atonement and Forms of the Church* served as a model for us, though our book diverges from that work in vital respects. And though it is both dated and flawed in its argument, the impact of Gustaf Aulén's *Christus Victor* upon the study of the doctrine of atonement can clearly be seen in these pages.

1. Witt, "He Was Crucified under Pontius Pilate."

We are grateful to Trinity School for Ministry for the generous provision of sabbaticals for the completion of this project, and to our colleagues, with whom it is a true joy to labor. We express our appreciation to Trinity student Elizabeth Ames for creating the author index. We are grateful to our spouses, Jennie Johnstone and Karen Scandrett, for their love and support. We are grateful to our students, who continually press us to refine and sharpen our thinking. And we are especially grateful to Bob Hosack at Baker Academic, who patiently waited and occasionally prodded as we sought to bring the book to completion through many delays.

William Witt
Joel Scandrett
Ambridge, Pennsylvania
September 2021

Abbreviations

General

art(s).   article(s)
d.   died
q(q).   question(s)

New Testament Apocrypha

Gos. Nic.   *The Gospel of Nicodemus*

Greek and Latin Works

C. Ar.	Athanasius, *Against the Arians (Contra Arianos)*
C. Gent.	Athanasius, *Against the Pagans (Contra gentes)*
Cels.	Origen, *Against Celsus (Contra Celsum)*
Comm. Jo.	Origen, *Commentary on the Gospel of John (Commentarii in evangelium Joannis)*
Comm. Matt.	Origen, *Commentary on the Gospel of Matthew (Commentarii in evangelium Matthaei)*
Dem. ev.	Eusebius of Caesarea, *Demonstration of the Gospel (Demonstratio evangelica)*
Ep. fest.	Athanasius, *Festal Letters (Epistulae festales)*
Epid.	Irenaeus, *Demonstration of the Apostolic Preaching (Epideixis tou apostolikou kērygmatos)*
Fid. orth.	John of Damascus, *An Exact Exposition of the Orthodox Faith (De fide orthodoxa)*
Haer.	Irenaeus, *Against Heresies (Adversus haereses)*

Inc.	Athanasius, *On the Incarnation* (*De incarnatione*)
Or. Bas.	Gregory of Nazianzus, *Orationes* (*Oratio in laudem Basilii*)
Or. Catech.	Gregory of Nyssa, *The Great Catechism* (*Oratio Catechetica Magna*)
ScG	Aquinas, *Summa contra Gentiles*
Serap.	Athanasius, *The Letters of Athanasius Concerning the Holy Spirit* (*To Serapion*)
ST	Aquinas, *Summa Theologiae*
Syn.	Athanasius, *De Synodis* (*On the Councils of Ariminum and Seleucia*)
Tract. ep. Jo.	Augustine, *Homilies on the First Epistle of John* (*In epistulam Johannis ad Parthos tractatus*)
Trin.	Augustine, *On the Trinity* (*De Trinitate*)

Modern Works

ANF	*The Ante-Nicene Fathers*. Edited by Alexander Roberts and James Donaldson. 10 vols. New York: Christian Literature, 1885–96. Reprint, Peabody, MA: Hendrickson, 1994.
CD	Karl Barth. *Church Dogmatics*. Translated by G. W. Bromiley and T. F. Torrance. 13 vols. Edinburgh: T&T Clark, 1956–75.
CV	Gustaf Aulén. *Christus Victor: An Historical Study of the Three Main Types of the Idea of the Atonement*. Translated by A. G. Herbert. Rev. ed. New York: Macmillan, 1969.
DS	Gustaf Aulén. *The Drama and the Symbols: A Book on Images of God and the Problems They Raise*. Translated by Sydney Linton. Philadelphia: Fortress, 1970.
FCC	Gustaf Aulén. *The Faith of the Christian Church*. Translated by Eric H. Wahlstrom. Philadelphia: Fortress, 1960.
Inst.	John Calvin. *Institutes of the Christian Religion*. Edited by John T. McNeill. Translated by Ford Lewis Battles. 2 vols. Philadelphia: Westminster, 1960.
NPNF[1]	*A Select Library of Nicene and Post-Nicene Fathers of the Christian Church*. Edited by Philip Schaff. 1st series. 14 vols. New York: Christian Literature, 1886–90. Reprint, Peabody, MA: Hendrickson, 1995.
NPNF[2]	*A Select Library of Nicene and Post-Nicene Fathers of the Christian Church*. Edited by Philip Schaff and Henry Wace. 2nd series. 14 vols. New York: Christian Literature, 1890–1900. Reprint, Peabody, MA: Hendrickson, 1995.

Introduction

What Is Atonement?

If one were to summarize the heart of the Christian faith in the fewest words possible, the phrase "Jesus saves" could suffice. To say that "Jesus saves" is to say that the person and work of Jesus Christ creates a salvation that is found nowhere else and accomplished by no one else. This salvation is the solution to a specific problem: the problem of human sin and its consequences. This salvation is of universal import for all human beings because all human beings have sinned. This salvation has cosmic implications, for it entails both the restoration of fallen creation and the promise of an eschatological new creation. This salvation is the work of God, for God who is the Father of Jesus Christ has acted in the person and work of his incarnate Son to bring it about. This salvation is also the work of the Holy Spirit, who imparts it to human beings within the redeemed community of the church. And this salvation is accomplished through the life, death, and resurrection of Jesus in fulfillment of God's original covenant promises to Israel. Thus, the expression "Jesus saves" touches on every area of Christian theology: the doctrines of the Trinity, creation, anthropology, election and covenant, ecclesiology, and eschatology, not to mention soteriology!

That "Jesus saves" has been at the heart of Christian faith from its very beginning because it is at the heart of the New Testament. In Mark, which is generally considered to be the earliest written Gospel, Jesus says of himself, "For the Son of Man came not to be served but to serve, and to give his life a ransom for many" (Mark 10:45). In Luke's account of the earliest preaching of the apostolic church, Peter proclaims: "Repent, and be baptized every one of you in the name of Jesus Christ so that your sins may be forgiven; and you will receive the gift of the Holy Spirit" (Acts 2:38). John's Gospel, regarded as

1

one of the latest of the New Testament writings, contains perhaps the most familiar verse of the entire New Testament: "For God so loved the world that he gave his only Son, so that everyone who believes in him may not perish but may have eternal life" (John 3:16). In what biblical scholars believe to be an echo of one of the earliest formulations of Christian faith, Paul writes, "For I handed on to you as of first importance what I in turn had received: that Christ died for our sins in accordance with the scriptures" (1 Cor. 15:3). Earlier in the same letter Paul writes: "For I decided to know nothing among you except Jesus Christ, and him crucified" (2:2). In Romans, Paul affirms that Jesus was "handed over to death for our trespasses and was raised for our justification" (Rom. 4.25). This witness to the salvation accomplished in Jesus's incarnation, life, death, and resurrection is found throughout the New Testament writings.

The early church continued to proclaim the saving work of Christ as the heart of the Christian message. Clement of Rome (d. 99) encourages his readers: "Let us fix our eyes on the blood of Christ and let us realize how precious it is to his Father, since it was poured out for our salvation and brought the grace of repentance to the whole world."[1] Ignatius of Antioch (d. 110) writes of "Jesus Christ's way, who for our sakes suffered death that you might believe in his death and so escape dying yourselves."[2] In his summary of the early Christian "Rule of Faith," Irenaeus of Lyons (ca. 130–ca. 202) affirms that the church had received from the apostles the belief "in one Christ Jesus, the Son of God, who became incarnate for our salvation."[3]

This language also appears throughout the church's later ecumenical creeds and doctrinal statements. The Nicene Creed (381) confesses: "For us and for our salvation he came down from heaven. . . . For our sake he was crucified under Pontius Pilate; he suffered death and was buried." The Chalcedonian Definition (451) states: "We all with one accord teach men to acknowledge one and the same Son, our Lord Jesus Christ, at once complete in Godhead and complete in manhood, truly God and truly man . . . as regards his manhood begotten, for us men and for our salvation."

Following the patristic era, the saving life, death, and resurrection of Jesus Christ continued to remain central to the faith of the undivided church, both in the East and in the West. In the East, John of Damascus (ca. 675–749) writes:

> Every action, therefore, and performance of miracles by Christ are most great and divine and marvelous: but the most marvelous of all is his precious cross. For no other thing has subdued death, expiated the sin of the first parent, despoiled

1. Clement of Rome, *1 Clement* 7.4.
2. Ignatius of Antioch, *To the Trallians* 2.
3. Irenaeus of Lyons, *Haer.* 1.10.1 (*ANF* 1:330).

Hades, bestowed the resurrection, granted the power to us of contemning the present and even death itself, prepared the return to our former blessedness, opened the gates of Paradise, given our nature a seat at the right hand of God, and made us the children and heirs of God, except the cross of our Lord Jesus Christ.[4]

In the West, Thomas Aquinas (1225–74) writes in the *Summa Theologiae*, "Christ's Passion is the proper cause of the forgiveness of sins. . . . Christ's Passion causes forgiveness of sins by way of redemption. For since He is our head, then, by the Passion which He endured from love and obedience, He delivered us as His members from our sins."[5]

Despite the divisions resulting from the Protestant Reformation, the historic Western churches continued to affirm the centrality of Jesus Christ's saving work as the heart of Christian faith. The Roman Catholic Council of Trent (1545–63) in its "Decree Concerning Original Sin" affirms that "the merit of the one mediator, our Lord Jesus Christ, who has reconciled us to God in his own blood, made unto us justice, sanctification, and redemption" is the only remedy for sin.[6] The Lutheran Augsburg Confession (1530) affirms faith in the "one Christ, truly God and truly human, being born of the Virgin Mary, who truly suffered, was crucified, died, and was buried that he might reconcile the Father to us and be a sacrifice not only for original guilt but also for all actual sins of human beings."[7] The Anglican Thirty-Nine Articles of Religion (1571) states that there is "one Christ, very God, and very Man; who truly suffered, was crucified, dead, and buried, to reconcile his Father to us, and to be a sacrifice, not only for original guilt, but also for actual sins of men." And further: "The offering of Christ once made is that perfect redemption, propitiation, and satisfaction, for all the sins of the whole world, both original and actual; and there is none other satisfaction for sin, but that alone."[8] The Reformed Heidelberg Catechism (1563) opens by asking, "What is your only comfort in life and death?" The appropriate reply is: "That I, with body and soul, both in life and in death, am not my own, but belong to my faithful Savior Jesus Christ, who with His precious blood has fully satisfied for all my sins, and redeemed me from all the power of the devil."[9] If there is a single ecumenical confession that could be considered to reside at the

4. John of Damascus, *Fid. orth.* 4.11 (NPNF[2] 9:80).

5. Aquinas, *ST* III.49.1.

6. *Canons and Decrees of the Council of Trent*, 5th Session, Decree Concerning Original Sin, 3.

7. Augsburg Confession, art. 3, in *Book of Concord*, 39.

8. Thirty-Nine Articles of Religion, arts. 2, 31.

9. Heidelberg Catechism, q. 1.

heart of Christian faith, that is affirmed by the apostolic church in Scripture and repeated throughout Christian history, it is the affirmation that "Jesus saves"—that in Jesus Christ's incarnation, life, death, and resurrection, God has saved his people from sin and its consequences.

The Subject Matter of Atonement Theology

Three overlapping areas of theology have traditionally dealt with the subject matter of the person and work of Jesus Christ. *Christology* focuses on the person of Christ: *who Jesus is*. Christology seeks to understand what it means that Jesus Christ is God become human. In the terminology of the Definition of Chalcedon, Jesus is one divine person with two natures: one divine and one human—"truly God and truly Man." The doctrine of the *atonement* focuses on the "work" of Christ: *what Jesus does*. Atonement deals with Jesus's incarnate mission and earthly life, his crucifixion, resurrection, ascension to and session (seating) at the right hand of God, his second coming, and how all of this accomplishes the reconciliation of sinful human beings to God. *Soteriology* focuses on *how Jesus saves us*. Soteriology seeks to explain how the person and work of Christ are made present by the Holy Spirit to human beings in the church and includes the theology of grace (justification and sanctification), ecclesiology (the nature of the church), and the sacraments.

These three overlapping theological distinctions (Christology, atonement, soteriology) are illustrated by the subject matter of the second and third articles of the Nicene Creed. The first part of the second article speaks of the subject matter traditionally associated with Christology: "one Lord Jesus Christ, the only Son of God, eternally begotten from the Father, God from God, light from light, true God from true God, begotten, not made, of one being with the Father." The second part of the second article focuses on the work of Christ: "who for us and for our salvation came down from heaven: by the power of the Holy Spirit he became incarnate from the Virgin Mary, and was made man. He was crucified under Pontius Pilate; he suffered death and was buried. . . . He rose again. . . . He ascended to heaven and is seated at the right hand of the Father. He will come again in glory. . . . His kingdom will have no end." Finally, the third article focuses on soteriology with its profession of "the Holy Spirit," "one holy Catholic and apostolic church," and "one baptism for the forgiveness of sins." While atonement theology is broadly related to and inseparable from both Christology and soteriology, it focuses primarily on the second half of the second article: how Jesus's mission—life, death, and resurrection—accomplishes the salvation of human beings.

Challenges Raised by the Doctrine of the Atonement

Despite all Christians universally affirming Christ's atonement, this doctrine raises several theological challenges. These challenges are our primary reason for writing this book. *First, there is no ecumenical consensus as to how the atonement was accomplished.* As shown above, the affirmation that "Jesus saves" has been a central affirmation of Christian faith from its beginning. Historically, Christians have considered the person and work of Jesus to uniquely constitute atonement. Jesus is not simply a good example for others to follow, nor is he one savior among many. Nonetheless, while the church catholic has an official Christology, which was expressed at the ecumenical councils of Nicaea and Chalcedon, no similar official theology of atonement exists beyond the basic affirmation that the person and work of Jesus Christ are uniquely constitutive of human salvation. The historic churches have affirmed that only Jesus saves, but no ecumenical council or creed has ever embraced a single understanding of exactly *how* the person and work of Jesus redeems sinners from their sin. The theologically uneducated (especially in the West) might be surprised to learn that some version of the satisfaction model of Anselm of Canterbury (1033/34–1109) has never officially been embraced by the church as a whole. This crucially distinguishes the doctrine of the atonement from other doctrines, such as doctrines of the Trinity and Christology. While there is an ecumenical understanding of the triune God and the person of Jesus Christ, no such ecumenical consensus exists for the doctrine of the atonement.

Instead, a number of paradigms or models of atonement have been put forward in various epochs of the church. Some have had more influence at times than others, but none have ever been officially endorsed by the whole church. During the patristic era, incarnational approaches tended to dominate, reflecting a primary understanding of salvation as incorporation into Christ and expressed in the patristic dictum that "what is not assumed is not redeemed." In the medieval West, following the rise of scholasticism, variations on Anselm's satisfaction model dominated. The Reformation saw the rise of penal and forensic models, and modern theology has often focused on understandings of Jesus as revealer or liberator. Meanwhile in the Christian East, the incarnational model has continued to predominate to this day. While readers might assume that the model most familiar to them is preferable, church history reveals that different eras—including our own—favor different models for different theological reasons, and that different Christian traditions continue to be defined by their preference for particular models.

Second, the language used to describe the saving work of Jesus in the New Testament is varied, metaphorical, and symbolic. Jesus is described in the sacrificial metaphor of the "Lamb of God." However, biblical writers also use the military language of "conquest" of sin, and the forensic imagery of judgment, pardon, and acquittal. They also employ transactional economic language in describing Jesus's death and resurrection, such as the "payment" of a debt, a "ransom," and a "redemption."

What is the relationship between the metaphorical language of Scripture and specific models of the atonement, which invariably elevate one or more biblical metaphors over others? Is Jesus a sacrificial lamb, a conquering hero, or a legal advocate? Theologians have not always adequately explained how the metaphorical language of Scripture relates to various atonement models, models that are often expressed in *non*-metaphorical language. For example, while the biblical metaphor of redemption refers to someone purchasing a slave's liberty—and is used by biblical authors to refer to the price paid by Jesus for our salvation—some theologians also use the term "redemption" more generally to refer to the whole of Christ's atoning work. Is such language faithful not only to the metaphorical dimension of Scripture but also to the *variety* of images used to describe the significance of Jesus's life, death, and resurrection for our salvation?

Furthermore, what is the relationship between this metaphorical language and the earthly Jesus, Jesus of Nazareth, who lived in first-century Judea? We cannot be content to leave atonement language at the metaphorical level because such language is inherently referential—it offers insight into the nature of something else. While atonement language speaks of what God in Christ has done for us, it refers primarily not to us but to Jesus Christ, in whom salvation has been accomplished. Jesus is the one to whom the metaphors refer. Consequently, if atonement language is not to be dismissed as pious mythology, ideology, or projection, it must be meaningfully related to the real, earthly Jesus of Nazareth. And if there is no correlation between the Jesus who saves me now and the Jesus who lived in the first century—the Jesus to whom the Gospel narratives bear witness—then the claim that it is Jesus who saves me is difficult to maintain.

Unfortunately, traditional Western atonement theology has often tended to divorce in just such a manner the Jesus who saves me from the earthly Jesus of the first century. Metaphors that speak of divine judgment on sin, priestly sacrifice for sin, or victorious conquest over sin and death often have not been meaningfully related to the Jesus whom we know from the Gospel narratives—a Jesus who never held judicial or military office, who certainly was neither a Levitical priest nor a wool-bearing, four-legged animal. How are we to make sense of such metaphors in a way that remains faithful to what they signify while also remaining faithful to the biblical account of the life, death, and resurrection of Jesus of Nazareth?

Here we face the danger of imposing onto a metaphor or symbol in the biblical text an interpretation found *outside* the text itself. The text centers on Jesus's identity as God's Son and the constitutive significance of Jesus's crucifixion and resurrection for our salvation. To read the Gospels in light of the incarnation, death, and resurrection of Jesus is to read them in accord with their intent. But the symbols and metaphors themselves must be understood in light of Jesus's identity and mission, not vice versa. Otherwise, we are inclined to select a metaphor or symbol to which we assign our own preferred significance and then project that significance onto the text. However, it is the actual life, death, and resurrection of Jesus that provides the normative context for interpreting the symbols, not the symbols that impose a normative significance for deciding who Jesus is and what he does. Only in light of the life, death, and resurrection of Jesus do we see the biblical metaphors and types fulfilled.

The narrative structure of the Gospel texts tells the story of Jesus's life, death, and resurrection, and these texts must provide the context for rightly understanding the relation between the earthly Jesus and the doctrine of the atonement. By listening to the referential, testimonial, and narrative content of the canonical Gospel texts, we discover the constitutive significance of Jesus's life, death, and resurrection. At the level of symbol, this does not mean that the biblical atonement metaphors are merely projections—they can be understood to constitute salvation. However, these constitutive symbols must be controlled by the narrative elements and the identity of the chief protagonists in the canonical story. For example, we learn what it means for God to judge our sins in Jesus or to deliver us from sin not by a preconceived notion of law or omnipotence (whether an uncritically endorsed notion or an uncritically rejected notion) but by listening to the canonical story of Jesus.

Furthermore, atonement language speaks not only about us and our salvation and about Jesus who saves but also about the God who has saved us in Jesus Christ. The metaphorical and symbolic language about God's salvation in Christ also raises questions about God, God's relation to the world and fallen human beings, God's relation to Jesus, God's intentions in bringing salvation, and how the life, death and resurrection of this first-century Jew can have universal significance for all human beings, for all times.

One of the major insights of twentieth-century theology was the realization by Swiss Reformed theologian Karl Barth (1886–1968) that there must be a correlation between God's revelation in history and God's own nature: God is in himself who he is in his revelation.[10] A similar observation was made by Roman Catholic theologian Karl Rahner (1904–84) in his dictum that the economic Trinity *is* (that is, is rooted in or reflects) the immanent Trinity.[11] While not all agree with the details of Barth's or Rahner's formulations, their basic insight is correct. In a similar way, the saving work of Jesus Christ must be rooted in his identity as God become human—in a biblical Christology. Atonement theology thus has an ontological dimension (what things are in themselves) that considers the relation between Jesus's works and Jesus's being. The economic atonement reflects or is rooted in the immanent union of Jesus's divine and human natures. Thus, if Jesus's personal identity is that of God's incarnate Word (John 1:1) and Son (Heb. 1:1–3), then it is indeed correct to affirm that God himself suffered and died on the cross and that Jesus's word of forgiveness to those who "know not what they do" is God's own word of forgiveness. It may be possible and necessary to distinguish in theory between the person and work of Jesus Christ, but in reality they are inextricably related. What Jesus does reveals who Jesus is. What Jesus does points to his identity as the Word of God incarnate.

How are we to correlate these aspects of metaphor, history, and ontology, all of which are necessary to make sense of Jesus's atoning work? Here theology offers a helpful classic distinction between the orders of knowing (*ordo cognoscendi*) and of being (*ordo essendi*), which reveals that the structure of the Christian faith can be grasped at three different levels. As formulated in the doctrine of the atonement, the first level of knowing is the level of narrative and symbol. Christianity is a story whose central character is a God who speaks and acts. The story is about God, creation, and humanity and has several key chapters: creation, fall, covenant, redemption, and eschatology. Its key plot is that "Jesus saves" through his incarnation, life, death, resurrection, and second coming. The story is communicated through both narratives and symbols. Christian living is a matter of being part of a community (the church) that lives out this story, that patterns its life within the parameters of the story's plotlines. Christians "inhabit" the story through reading Scripture, through worship, through prayer, through living lives that exemplify the story.

The second level is the level of history. As noted above, the narrative and symbolic character of the Christian story refers beyond itself to actual historical events—specifically, God's covenant with Israel and the life of the earthly Jesus. The story includes events that are claimed to have happened but that transcend ordinary historical causality—for example, Israel's exodus from

10. Barth, *CD* I/1.
11. Rahner, *Trinity*.

Egypt, God's giving of the law at Sinai, and the resurrection of Jesus from the dead. At the level of history, the doctrine of the atonement presupposes that God has acted uniquely to save fallen humanity in and through the incarnation, life, death, and resurrection of Jesus Christ.

With the third level we arrive at the level of being or ontology, the *ordo essendi*. The biblical story is referential not only of God's saving acts in history but also of God's being in himself (*in se*). The story assumes that the God who is revealed in history is in himself who he is in his revelation. The God who is revealed as Father, Son, and Holy Spirit in the history of Israel, in the life, death, and resurrection of Jesus, and in the church (the economic Trinity) is the tripersonal reality of Father, Son, and Holy Spirit in himself, from all eternity (the immanent Trinity). God is triune, three distinct relational persons in one Being.

In terms of ontology, the relation between God and creation is unique. God transcends creation yet is immediately present to it. All created being is real (because it receives its being from God), contingent (because it does not have to exist), and orderly (because God creates through his Word and is not arbitrary). In terms of ontology, humanity (anthropology) is characterized as being created in God's image (oriented toward union with God), fallen (no longer in union with God), and redeemed (restored to union with God).

Regarding Jesus's ontology (Christology), the incarnation of God in Christ means that Jesus Christ is a single divine person with a divine and human nature (hypostatic union)—fully divine and fully human (Nicaea and Chalcedon). The relation between Jesus's person and work in the atonement means that Jesus Christ's death and resurrection are *constitutive*, not merely *illustrative*, of salvation.

All three levels are integrally related and depend on one another. The three different levels can be approached from the direction of either knowledge or being. In the *ordo cognoscendi* (narrative and symbol), the source of knowledge is, first, Scripture and, second, the creeds, preaching, the worship of the church, tradition, and so on (level 1). In terms of history (level 2), the fundamental Christian claim is that God is in himself who God is in his revelation. The God who revealed himself as Father, Son, and Holy Spirit in the history of Israel, in the incarnation, life, death, and resurrection of Jesus Christ, and in the Spirit's presence in the church is the triune God who in himself is Father, Son, and Holy Spirit. In the *ordo essendi* (level 3), the triune reality is first. God reveals himself as Father, Son, and Holy Spirit in history because God is first Father, Son, and Holy Spirit (in himself) from all eternity.

Why is this important? Because any adequate discussion of the atonement needs to take all three levels of knowing and being into account and must show how narrative and symbol, the history of the earthly Jesus, and the ontology of divine and created realities are integrated in Jesus's atoning work. Any good account of what it means to say that "Jesus saves" will do this well, whereas a poor account will tend to focus more exclusively on only one of the three levels of knowing and being. Thus, accounts that focus exclusively on the metaphorical language of atonement often reduce Jesus to a good example among others. Accounts that focus exclusively on ontology can reduce atonement to a timeless eternal transaction between the Father and the Son—as in some variations of the satisfaction theory. Accounts that focus solely on the historical Jesus fail to explain why this one man's death should be significant for all people in all times. Various atonement models also omit the significance of God's covenant with Israel or focus narrowly on one aspect of the history of the earthly Jesus: the incarnation simply as an event (some incarnational models), Jesus's life and teaching as an example (some moral example or influence models), and Jesus's death on the cross to the exclusion of his earthly mission and his resurrection (some satisfaction models). However, keeping all three levels of theological knowledge in view illuminates points of connection or disconnection by which to judge whether a given model of atonement does justice to the whole of atonement theology.

Third, a deeply divisive contemporary theological issue concerns constitutive and illustrative understandings of atonement. The above references—first to Scripture and then to the history of theology—have shown that, from the beginning, the Christian tradition has understood the expression "Jesus saves" to mean that Jesus actually creates a salvation that sinful human beings are unable to provide for themselves. Thus, both Jesus's personal identity and his mission are unique and have universal significance for all human beings. If Jesus Christ saves sinful human beings, then no one else does, and anyone who is saved is saved by Jesus and Jesus alone. This understanding of Jesus's person and work as constitutive for salvation has been characteristic of the universal catholic and evangelical tradition of the church.

However, in the last few centuries a new understanding has arisen. The position that Jesus's mission is illustrative rather than constitutive of atonement has become the dominant understanding in much of modern theology since Friedrich Schleiermacher. That is, much modern theology does not interpret atonement language to mean that Jesus uniquely creates our salvation from sin, death, and judgment but rather takes such language to be an illustration or example of a salvation that can be found elsewhere or perhaps even everywhere. Proponents talk about Jesus as "a way" of salvation or Jesus as Savior "for Christians" but suggest that there are other paths of salvation for those of other religions or perhaps of no religion at all. As we will see, this is a crucial issue in any contemporary discussion of the atonement: Is the life, death, and resurrection of Jesus *constitutive* of a salvation found nowhere else, or is it *illustrative* of a salvation that may also be found elsewhere?[12]

To further muddy the waters, many contemporary theological discussions confuse this issue by identifying some particular model of constitutive atonement—often a variation of the satisfaction or penal substitution models—as the only possible "objective" model, thus implying that the only options for atonement theology are those between "objective" satisfaction/penal substitution and "subjective" liberal exemplarism or the like. One of the purposes of this book is to make clear that there have been (and continue to be) a number of ways of speaking objectively and constitutively about atonement in the history of Christian theology.

Structure of the Book

Each of the following chapters focuses on a particular atonement paradigm: its historical origin and development, its central assumptions and reasoning, its significance for one or more Christian traditions, and its relative strengths and weaknesses. Each paradigm is identified as belonging to one of three basic types, corresponding broadly to the three types of atonement summarized in Gustaf Aulén's classic work *Christus Victor*, which we will discuss in subsequent chapters.

Type 1 includes models that are broadly incarnational and ontological, focusing on the incarnation and the hypostatic union. Such models tend toward a *theōsis/deification* soteriology that emphasizes participation in (or ontological union with) Christ.

The first subset of Type 1 models falls under the category of incarnation/recapitulation and focuses on the assumption of human nature by the divine Logos in the person of Jesus Christ as the central locus of atonement (chap. 1). Primary representatives include Irenaeus of Lyons, Athanasius of Alexandria, and Cyril of Alexandria. Later Western examples include sixteenth-century Anglican divines Richard Hooker and Lancelot Andrewes, as well as nineteenth- and twentieth-century Anglicans. More contemporary examples include Thomas F. Torrance and Hans Urs von Balthasar.

The second subset of Type 1 models includes the Christus Victor model and focuses on Jesus's defeat of the powers of sin, death, and Satan, both in his earthly ministry and ultimately in his resurrection and ascension (chap. 2).

---

12. The distinction between a constitutive and an illustrative understanding of the atonement is made by Vernon White in *Atonement and Incarnation*.

This is the model often associated with Gustaf Aulén's well-known book by that name. Historical examples include Irenaeus (again), Origen, Gregory of Nyssa, Gregory the Great, and Rufinus. Aulén names Martin Luther as the primary Reformation example of Christus Victor, though this is disputed. Aulén himself remains the primary modern example. Contemporary Mennonite theologian J. Denny Weaver employs a version of the Christus Victor model, as does Gregory Boyd.

Type 2 includes models that focus specifically on the death of Christ and are broadly concerned with questions of forgiveness of sin, judgment, and guilt. The soteriology of Type 2 models tends to be substitutional or forensic, focusing on the manner in which Christ's death functions to restore relationship between God and human beings.

A first subset of Type 2 models are satisfaction models, which focus principally on Jesus's death as a satisfaction of God's honor/justice. Anselm of Canterbury is the foremost historic advocate of this model (chap. 3). Thomas Aquinas was its most articulate medieval exponent but differs from Anselm in significant ways (chap. 5). Contemporary examples include Roman Catholic Walter Kasper and Lutheran Wolfhart Pannenberg.

A second subset of Type 2 models are substitution models that focus on forensic justice and justification. Substitution models focus on Jesus's death in place of sinners. This theme appears in the Reformation in Luther's notion of the "great exchange." We will focus on John Calvin as the primary Reformation example (chap. 6). Karl Barth both incorporated and modified a forensic model in his essay "The Judge Judged in Our Place" in *Church Dogmatics* IV/1 (chap. 8). In the modern theology of Protestants such as Charles Hodge and later evangelical theologians, the substitution model modifies into penal substitution. Penal substitution arguably contains satisfaction and forensic themes as well.

Type 3 includes models that are principally exemplarist and moral, focusing primarily on the notion of Christ as an example or primary representative of salvation. The soteriological scope of this type is subjective rather than ontological or forensic. While Type 1 and 2 models are variations on constitutive understandings of atonement, Type 3 models incline toward what we have called illustrative understandings of the atonement. Insofar as they include constitutive themes from the previous two types, some Type 3 models attempt to balance the objectivity of Type 1 and 2 models with a focus on God's love in Christ toward redeemed sinners and on subjective human responses of love and gratitude.

The first subset of Type 3 models would be moral influence. The moral influence approach emphasizes the atonement as the revelation or operation of God's love and the human response of love of God and neighbor that it engenders in those who are reconciled to God. Peter Abelard is the classic medieval example of this approach (chap. 4). Modern figures who focus on God's love revealed in Christ include John and Charles Wesley, George MacDonald, C. S. Lewis, and among Roman Catholics, Karl Rahner. The Wesleys, MacDonald, and Lewis show that a moral influence model need not necessarily be merely subjectivist.

A second subset of Type 3 would be moral example. The moral example approach tends to view Jesus as a moral figure to be imitated. Liberal Protestantism has tended to embrace this model. Examples include Friedrich Schleiermacher, Horace Bushnell, Hastings Rashdall, Adolf von Harnack, and some recent liberation and feminist theologians (chap. 7). This model comes closest to understanding Jesus's role as illustratively providing one example among others and to understanding the salvation God offers as being available not only in Jesus but wherever human beings engage in the kind of self-sacrificial behavior that Jesus models. Other examples of Type 3 atonement arguably would include the metaphor of Jesus Christ as "perfect penitent," found in Robert Moberley's *Atonement and Personality*. Some have suggested that nineteenth-century Scottish theologian John McLeod Campbell is an example of Type 3 theology.[13] However, Campbell endorses an ontological exemplarism that echoes patristic incarnational models.

Religious pluralism exemplifies an illustrative model of atonement taken to an extreme. Its most articulate modern proponent would be John Hick. Hick has argued that traditional understandings of incarnation and atonement are inadequate for a modern age in which Christians are more aware of the existence and moral significance of other religions. Rather than being understood as a unique savior, Jesus should be understood to represent one path to salvation, a path followed by Christians but neither demanded nor expected of those who practice other faiths.

After providing an overview of historical and contemporary models of the atonement, the book closes with a final chapter addressing atonement today. The chapter will begin with a discussion of the current controversy among evangelical theologians concerning penal substitution. A discussion of the atonement theology of Thomas F. Torrance will provide both comparison and contrast. The chapter will conclude with our own reflections and recommendations for what it means to say "Jesus saves."

---

13. Campbell, *Nature of the Atonement*.

1

. . .

Atonement as Incarnation

Irenaeus and Athanasius

D id the early church have a doctrine of atonement? An argument could be made to the contrary. While the church fathers used language and images of Jesus's reconciling work largely borrowed from Scripture, they did not explain in detail their understanding of these metaphors and images. Unlike the controversies over the doctrines of the incarnation and the Trinity, which occasioned the ecumenical councils and formulations of the Nicene Creed and the Chalcedonian Definition, atonement was not a subject of controversy. The closest thing to an ecumenical affirmation would be the simple statement of the Council of Nicaea regarding the incarnate Christ: "who, for us and our salvation, came down from heaven," and "for our sake he was crucified under Pontius Pilate."[1]

However, the language of worship of the early church refers regularly to atonement. The liturgical hymn "Gloria in Excelsis Deo" prays, "Lord God, Lamb of God, who takes away the sins of the world, have mercy on us."[2] Liturgies of the ancient church contain within the eucharistic prayer (*anaphora*) (1) an institution narrative, which recites Jesus's words at the Last Supper referring to his body "given for you" and his blood "shed for you and for many for

1. The Chalcedonian Definition does not speak of the purpose for which the Word became incarnate.
2. Cobb, "Liturgy of the Word in the Early Church," 183.

the forgiveness of sins" and (2) a call to remember (*anamnēsis*) Jesus's deeds in his words, "Do this in remembrance of me," referring to Jesus's crucifixion, resurrection, ascension, and second coming. These and other writings of the early church also refer to Jesus's death as a "sacrifice."[3] Catechetical instruction given to converts also addressed the significance of Jesus's "being crucified for us" and "dying for our sins" without providing theological theories or explanations.[4] A collective assessment of these approaches might be called an "affirmation" rather than an "explanation" of atonement.[5]

There is thus no single model of atonement in the early church but rather a rich variety of images and metaphors.[6] Nonetheless, early Christian discussions of atonement tended to be oriented around what we will call an "incarnational" approach. Modern theologians have often dismissed this approach as "physical" and the related Christus Victor model as "mythological."[7] However, the incarnational model would be more accurately designated "ontological" or "onto-relational" and is associated positively with key patristic concepts of salvation such as "re-creation" and "deification."

Accordingly, this chapter will focus on two major patristic theologians: Irenaeus of Lyons and Athanasius of Alexandria. Both were involved in controversy with heretical understandings of Christianity: Irenaeus with Gnosticism and Athanasius with Arianism. Both responded to these inadequate understandings with theologies that focused on the incarnation, especially on the unity of the person of Christ in the incarnation. However, while focusing on the incarnation, their primary concern was soteriological. They believed that it was vital to understand who Jesus is in order to understand what it means that "Jesus saves." Controversy prompted them to articulate a theology that included an incarnational understanding of atonement: Why did God become human?

Irenaeus

Irenaeus of Lyons (c. 130–c. 202) can be credited with a number of firsts: he was the author of the "first comprehensive Christian theology."[8] He was arguably the Christian church's first "biblical theologian." He developed a

3. See Daly, *Christian Sacrifice*; Daly, *Christian Doctrine of Sacrifice*.

4. See especially Cyril of Jerusalem, *Catechetical Lectures* 13 (NPNF[2] 7:82–93).

5. Kelly, *Early Christian Doctrines*, 163; similarly, Pelikan, *Emergence of the Catholic Tradition*, 141–42.

6. Turner, *Patristic Doctrine of Redemption*, 11–28.

7. Harnack, *History of Dogma*, 2:236–94; Rashdall, *Idea of Atonement*, 240–48.

8. Osborn, "Irenaeus of Lyons," 122.

comprehensive theology based on a reading of the Hebrew Scriptures (in the Greek Septuagint) and the apostolic writings of the Gospels and Epistles as one Bible composed of Old and New Testaments.[9] And he was the first theologian to develop a comprehensive theology of creation, fall, and reconciliation.[10]

In what follows we will see that "unity" is the theme that holds Irenaeus's theology together. Irenaeus's gnostic opponents were dualists who focused on discontinuity: a discontinuity between spirit and matter; a divide between divine and physical realities bridged through a chain of emanations; a divided reading of Scripture in which the Creator God of the Old Testament was a different entity from God the Father of Jesus; a divided canon in which some books (especially the Old Testament) were rejected and other books (gnostic gospels) added; a "divided" hermeneutic by which the Scriptures were read through the lens of dualist gnostic speculation; and a division between the elite, "more spiritual" gnostics and the ordinary, "less spiritual" unenlightened.

Over against this gnostic dualism, Irenaeus focused on unity: the unity of the Creator God and God the Father of Jesus Christ; the unity of creation and the economy of salvation; the unity of the covenant people of the Old Testament, the apostles, and the post-apostolic church as the people of God; the unity of the Scriptures as a single canon composed of Old and New Testaments; the unity of God and humanity in the incarnation of God in Christ; the unity of the atonement as the re-creation and union of humanity with Christ through the indwelling Holy Spirit; and the unity of human beings and their material bodies in the original creation, in reconciliation, and in the resurrection. For Irenaeus, "redemption is essentially an at-one-ment."[11] Indeed, Irenaeus's entire approach to theology can be read as an "at-one-ment."[12]

The One Economy of Salvation: The Rule of Faith

The hermeneutical key that Irenaeus uses to summarize the essential subject matter of Christian belief is the "Rule of Faith" or "Canon of Truth"—an early outline of Christian belief that also appears in the writings of church fathers such as Tertullian of Carthage and Clement of Alexandria. Variations

9. On Irenaeus's reading of Scripture, see Greer, "Christian Bible and Its Interpretation," 163–76; Young, "Interpretation of Scripture," 24–27; Holsinger-Friesen, *Irenaeus and Genesis*; Behr, *Way to Nicaea*, 111–33; Behr, *Irenaeus of Lyons*.
10. Turner, *Patristic Doctrine of Redemption*, 74–77.
11. Hochban, "Irenaeus on the Atonement," 548.
12. See Greer, *Early Biblical Interpretation*, 163; Young, "Interpretation of Scripture," 25; Hochban, "Irenaeus on the Atonement," 526; Donovan, *One Right Reading?*, 71; Osborn, *Irenaeus of Lyons*, 9; Boersma, "Redemptive Hospitality in Irenaeus," 208.

of Irenaeus's following statement of the Rule appear several times in his two works *Against Heresies* and *Demonstration of the Apostolic Preaching*:

> The Church, though dispersed through out the whole world, even to the ends of the earth, has received from the apostles and their disciples this faith: [She believes] in one God, the Father Almighty, Maker of heaven, and earth, and the sea, and all things that are in them; and in one Christ Jesus, the Son of God, who became incarnate for our salvation; and in the Holy Spirit, who proclaimed through the prophets the dispensations of God, and the advents, and the birth from a virgin, and the passion, and the resurrection from the dead, and the ascension into heaven in the flesh of the beloved Christ Jesus, our Lord, and His [future] manifestation from heaven in the glory of the Father "to gather all things in one," and to raise up anew all flesh of the whole human race.[13]

Note that the Rule has a threefold trinitarian structure and is simultaneously a narrative, a history, and an ontology. It provides a summary of the Christian story, refers to certain crucial historical events, and presumes a trinitarian ontology of creation, incarnation, and reconciliation. Note also that there is a reciprocal relationship between the Rule and Scripture. The Rule is both a summary of the key themes of the biblical narrative and an indispensable hermeneutical tool by which to read that narrative correctly. The Rule contrasts sharply with the way the gnostics read the Scriptures, which Irenaeus famously compares to someone disassembling the stones of a beautiful mosaic of a king, reassembling those stones into an ugly mosaic of a fox, then claiming that this is the portrait of the king. The Rule and the gnostic hermeneutic do not amount to different but equally valid ways of reading Scripture. The Rule's reading is derived from Scripture, while the gnostic interpretation is an alien imposition upon it (*Haer.* 1.8.1). Frances Young aptly summarizes, "The problem with the heretics was that, in their wild speculations, they had lost the plot."[14]

The One God: Trinity in Unity

Against the gnostic affirmation of numerous "emanations" forming a descending chain of being from the divine to the material realm, Irenaeus repeatedly emphasizes the unity of God (*Haer.* 2.1.2). There is one God, the Creator of heaven and earth and especially of humanity, who has revealed himself in his covenant with Israel and especially in Jesus Christ, and who will

13. Irenaeus, *Haer.* 1.10.1 (*ANF* 1:330–31).
14. Young, "Interpretation of Scripture," 25.

finally bring creation to its original intended conclusion in the eschaton (2.1.1; 2.16.3; 3.10.5; 3.11.7; 3.12.11; 4.1.1). This one God created the entire universe freely from nothing (2.10.4); he did not create because he was incomplete or needed anything besides himself to complete his being. One of the chief distinctions between God and creatures is that God is without beginning or end and needs nothing (2.2.4, 5). Whatever else exists does so because God has granted it existence. All creatures thus have a beginning, can cease to exist, and are dependent on God (3.8.3). God is the omnipotent Creator of all that is, including matter. There is no second God (2.16.3; 2.28.7; 2.30.9).

However, this one God who created the world is not a monad. From eternity, God is triune; the Son and the Holy Spirit are God's Word and Wisdom, the "two hands" through whom God makes all things and in whose image he has created human beings (*Haer.* 2.28.5; 3.6.1; 3.18.1; 4.Preface.4; 4.20.1; 4.20.3). The Word and Spirit are not only the "two hands" by which God creates but also those through whom God speaks in the Scriptures and saves the world. God's wisdom is manifested through the Son in creation; God's love is manifested through the Spirit in salvation. Through the Son and the Holy Spirit, God's goodness is demonstrated in creation, in reconciliation, and in salvation as participation in the triune life. The triune God is known especially through his acts, specifically his covenant with Israel and his salvation in Jesus Christ. Because God is love, we know God through the love revealed by the incarnate Word in atonement, not through abstract speculation (2.30.9; 3.6.2; 3.6.4; 3.12.11; 3.15.3; 3.18.1; 4.1.1; 4.20.1, 4, 6).

Humanity Created in the Image of God

The same theological principles governing the general creation apply in Irenaeus's discussion of the creation of humanity. Like other creatures, human beings are the direct creation of God's "two hands," the Son and the Spirit. God did not create humanity because he needed us to complete his purposes. He has always possessed the Son and the Spirit, by whom he "freely and spontaneously" made all things, including humanity (*Haer.* 4.20.1). Human beings are thus a "subset of a wider created order."[15] At the same time, human beings are distinct from the rest of creation insofar as humanity has been created "in the image of God." Irenaeus understands the image of God in humanity to have a trinitarian form: "For by the hands of the Father, that is, by the Son and the Holy Spirit, man, and not [merely] a part of man, was made in the likeness of God" (5.6.1). In creation, "the Word of the Father and the

---

15. Holsinger-Friesen, *Irenaeus and Genesis*, 115.

Spirit of God, having become united with the ancient substance of Adam's formation, rendered man living and perfect, receptive of the perfect Father" (5.1.3). As such, humanity is "conformable to and modeled after [God's] own Son." Contrary to gnostic matter/spirit dualism, Irenaeus understands human being to be a unity, a composite of soul and spirit united to a "fleshly nature." However, it is the presence of the Holy Spirit that makes the human being complete: soul, spirit, and body are not "humanity" but aspects of humanity. Importantly, Irenaeus frequently distinguishes between the "image" and the "likeness" of God.[16] Without the Spirit, the "image" composed of "soul" and "flesh" is "imperfect." It is the presence of the Spirit that makes the human being "perfect," now existing not only in the image of God but also in his likeness (5.6.1; cf. 5.9.3; 5.12.2).

Here we see one of the distinctive characteristics of Irenaeus's understanding of creation in bringing together protology and eschatology. The human being is teleological: both creation and salvation are seen as *a process with a goal*. At creation, the human being was not yet complete but needed to progress toward completion. Indeed, Irenaeus suggests that Adam and Eve were created as children, not yet fully mature (*Haer.* 4.38.1). While God himself is perfect and does not change, creatures need to advance toward perfection (4.38.3).

Crucial to this notion of progress in perfection are the notions of "free will" and "persuasion." God made the human being so that humanity could obey the commands of God voluntarily, not by compulsion (*Haer.* 4.4.3). Freedom of will is part of what it means to be created in the image of God, since God has free will. God always acts without coercion, exercising a good will toward all. Human beings are capable of obeying and of disobeying God (4.37.1, 2, 4; 4.38.1; 4.39.1). Insofar as our first parents disobeyed, they interrupted this process of growth and introduced death into the world. Humanity continued to exist in the image of God but lost the presence of God's Spirit and thus God's "likeness." Humanity without the Spirit of God is "dead" (5.9.3). As God is good and obedience to God is life, to disobey God is evil and leads to death. "Death" is not an extraneous punishment for sin; rather, sin is its own intrinsic and deadly punishment: "Those who fly from the eternal light of God, which contains in itself all good things, are themselves the cause to themselves of their inhabiting eternal darkness" (4.39.4).

The fall of humanity led to spiritual death (loss of the Holy Spirit), which resulted in physical death. Consequently, the descendants of Adam and Eve

16. Sometimes, however, Irenaeus writes as if image and likeness are identical. See Holsinger-Friesen, *Irenaeus and Genesis*, 109–11.

inherited both the image of God and the consequences of their sin. God had compassion, however, not only on Adam and Eve's posterity but on Adam and Eve as well. They were driven from paradise because God pitied them and wanted to prevent their sin from continuing forever. Death was a blessing, putting an end to sin so that humanity could die to sin and live to God (*Haer.* 3.23.1–8). If, in humanity's original creation, the way toward completion was a gradual process of perfection, the restoration of humanity in atonement is similar. God restores humanity to liberty through a gradual historical process of persuasion. The gradual path of reconciliation began in the covenant with God's Old Testament people and is eventually fulfilled in the new covenant of the incarnation of the Son of God (4.9.3).

Incarnation

Why, according to Irenaeus, did God become human in Jesus Christ? Why did the Word become flesh? Irenaeus's basic answer is that we—humanity—needed salvation but that we are unable to save ourselves. Only God can save us, and he does this personally by the Son of God becoming incarnate as Jesus Christ (*Haer.* 3.18.2; 3.20.3). Irenaeus summarizes the purpose of the incarnation (and atonement) in language that anticipates the later patristic dictum that *God became human, so that humanity might become divine*: "For it was for this end that the Word of God was made man, and He who was the Son of God became the Son of man, that man, having been taken into the Word, and receiving the adoption, might become the son of God" (3.19.1). "The only true and steadfast Teacher, the Word of God, our Lord Jesus Christ . . . did, through His transcendent love, become what we are, that He might bring us to be even what He is Himself" (5.Preface).

It is because the incarnate Jesus Christ is both fully God and fully human that he is able to act as mediator between God and humanity, joining together God and humanity in himself, creating a new friendship and harmony between them, presenting humanity to God and revealing God to humanity. Because he is God, Jesus securely possesses salvation, and can give it freely. Because he is human, Jesus is able to join humanity to God, enabling us to participate in immortality as God intended. And as the incarnate God, through the process of "recapitulation" (which we will discuss below), Jesus passes through every stage of human life, reversing Adam's failure and restoring humanity to communion with God (*Haer.* 3.18.7), thus setting humanity back on the path of progress toward Godlikeness.

Thus, in contrast to gnostic dualism, Irenaeus emphasizes the unity of Jesus Christ as the Word made flesh, the unity of Jesus as the Second Person of the Trinity (the Son of God incarnate) with God, and the unity of Christ's person and work in the economy of salvation. Irenaeus emphasizes both the complete deity and the complete humanity of Jesus Christ as the Word of God incarnate. The only-begotten Word, who is always present with humanity, "united to and mingled with His own creation" and "is Himself Jesus Christ our Lord, who did also suffer for us, and rose again on our behalf, and who will come again in the glory of His Father." Accordingly, Jesus Christ is also in every respect human, having taken humanity into himself. As the Word incarnate, Jesus Christ is "the invisible becoming visible, the incomprehensible being made comprehensible, the impassible becoming capable of suffering, and the Word being made man, thus summing up all things in Himself" (*Haer.* 3.16.6; cf. 3.11.5; 5.18.3).

As human, Jesus Christ is everything that we are, having "a body taken from the earth, and a soul receiving spirit from God." In becoming human, the Word recapitulated his own handiwork, and thus is rightly called "Son of man" (*Haer.* 3.22.1). As the humanity that was lost and needed saving had "flesh and blood," so the incarnate Word himself took on "flesh and blood": "The righteous flesh has reconciled that flesh which was being kept under bondage in sin, and brought it into friendship with God" (5.14.2). Jesus Christ is both the one true human being (the prototype of Adam in whose image humanity was created) and also the one in whom the lost image of God is restored. While humanity is said to have been created after the image of God, the Word incarnate actually "shows" the image of God. The eternal Word is the invisible image who, by becoming visible, restores humanity to that image (5.16.2).

Also as human, Jesus underwent the complete range of human experience. He was baptized and he celebrated the Passover in Jerusalem as did Jews of his time. He did not merely seem to be human (in a docetic fashion) but was that which he appeared to be. As we will see below, he sanctified human experience by living through the complete span of human life: infancy, childhood, youth, and adulthood. Finally, he experienced death itself (*Haer.* 2.22.4).

Since Adam had lost the presence of the Holy Spirit (and so the "likeness" of the divine image), it was necessary that Jesus be anointed with the Spirit at the time of his baptism in order to restore the divine image to human being. Jesus's anointing with the Spirit should not be understood in an adoptionist manner, however. "Christ" did not descend upon Jesus as upon a separate person—as if "Christ" and "Jesus" were two separate individuals. Rather, the Word of God, who is personally identical with Jesus, took on human flesh and was anointed with the Spirit by the Father, in order that fallen humanity might be saved through participation in Jesus's anointing by the Holy Spirit

(*Haer.* 3.9.3). Thus, the name "Jesus Christ" points to the triune unity: it is the Father who anoints, the Son who is anointed, and the Holy Spirit who is the divine unction with which the Son is anointed (3.18.3).

One of the primary functions of the Word of God is to reveal God the Creator. He does this first by means of the created order itself, which declares that it has the Lord as its maker; second, in the creation of humanity; and third, through the history of salvation. The Word preached both himself and his Father through the Old Testament prophets. In becoming incarnate, the Word has made himself visible: "All saw the Father in the Son: for the Father is the invisible of the Son, but the Son the visible of the Father" (*Haer.* 4.6.6). The Son administers all things for the Father, and it is only through the Son that human beings can come to know God: "For the Son is the knowledge of the Father; but the knowledge of the Son is in the Father, and has been revealed through the Son; and this was the reason why the Lord declared: 'No man knoweth the Son, but the Father; nor the Father, save the Son, and those to whomsoever the Son shall reveal [Him]'" (4.6.7).

Thus, for Irenaeus one of Jesus's primary tasks as the Word incarnate was that of teacher. Human beings could learn about their Creator only by seeing their teacher, hearing his voice with their own ears, imitating both his words and his works, and so having communion with the Word who existed prior to creation (*Haer.* 5.1.1). There are similarities between Irenaeus's understanding of Jesus's task as teacher and the later "exemplarist" models of the atonement. However, in Irenaeus's understanding of atonement, the incarnate Jesus Christ did more than provide an example for others to follow. Jesus Christ's reconciling work is not merely pedagogical; it accomplishes something ontologically. Jesus's incarnate life, death, and resurrection are constitutive, not merely illustrative, of atonement.

Recapitulation

However, the purpose of the incarnation is not merely ontological in the sense that the incarnation alone might save human beings. The incarnation is also reparative, restorative, and redemptive. The Word became incarnate to defeat sin and death.[17] The word that Irenaeus characteristically uses to describe Christ's atoning work is "recapitulation" (Latin *recapitulatio* from Greek *anakephalaiōsis*). Derived from Romans 13:9 and especially Ephesians 1:10, the word means to "regather" or "sum up."[18] The notion here is that Jesus Christ has *joined again to himself those who have been separated by*

17. Boersma, "Redemptive Hospitality in Irenaeus," 214.
18. Irenaeus cites Eph. 1:10 in *Haer.* 1.10.1; 3.16.6; *Epid.* 30.

sin. Christ is the "head" (*kephalē*) of the communion between God and humanity (Eph. 1:22). For Irenaeus, the main idea is that in the incarnation, Jesus Christ has "regathered" or brought into unity that which has become separated, restoring humanity to its intended unity. As the second Adam, Jesus brings reconciliation by "recapitulating" the human condition. Where Adam failed, Jesus has succeeded. He has undergone every aspect of human life, accomplishing atonement through his incarnation, death, and resurrection.[19] Recapitulation "corrects and perfects mankind; it inaugurates and consummates a new humanity."[20] What follows is an overview of some of the key themes in Irenaeus's discussion of recapitulation.

Irenaeus's main use of recapitulation is not simply to contrast Adam with Christ (following Paul's discussion in Rom. 5) but to present Jesus Christ as the "second Adam" who "undoes" Adam's disobedience by undergoing a complete human experience, constantly yielding obedience rather than disobedience, at every stage succeeding where Adam had failed. As death and sin came through Adam's disobedience, so salvation comes through Jesus's obedience. As Adam was formed from the dust of the earth without a human father, so the Word was born of the Virgin Mary without a human father. Christ was not formed from the dust of the earth but was born of a human mother because he was not a completely new being; rather, he recapitulated the same humanity that Adam had possessed (*Haer.* 3.21.10; 3.22.1). As sin came into the world through a tree (the tree of temptation in Eden), so salvation came through another tree (the cross of Christ) (5.17.3; 5.19.1). In his famous parallel between Mary and Eve, Irenaeus suggests a kind of parallel recapitulation to that involving Christ and Adam. As sin came into the world through a disobedient virgin (Eve), so salvation came into the world through the obedience of another virgin (Mary the mother of Jesus) (3.22.4; 5.19.1).

The two most significant parallels between Adam and Jesus drawn by Irenaeus concern the temptation narratives and Jesus's death on the cross.[21] While Adam succumbed to temptation in the garden, Jesus resisted Satan's temptations in the desert (*Haer.* 5.21–23). Likewise, through Jesus's obedience concerning a tree, his death on the cross did away with Adam's disobedience concerning a tree (5.16.3). Jesus's death "summed up" and reversed the death of Adam and his descendants as an essential aspect of recapitulation (5.22.2).

19. Lawson, *Biblical Theology of Saint Irenaeus*, 140–44.
20. Osborn, *Irenaeus of Lyons*, 97.
21. Boersma, "Redemptive Hospitality in Irenaeus," 218; Wingren, *Man and the Incarnation*, 118–19.

Ireneaus employs another image to speak of recapitulation—that of Jesus Christ as the "new man." As humans were brought into bondage and made subject to death by the disobedience of our first parents, so we have been "cleansed," "washed," and come to share in God's life through the "new man" Jesus (*Haer.* 4.22.1).

Irenaeus also speaks of atonement as "communion," a restoring of the Holy Spirit and a sharing in Jesus's death and resurrection: "The Lord thus has redeemed us through His own blood, giving His soul for our souls, and His flesh for our flesh, and has also poured out the Spirit of the Father for the union and communion of God and man, imparting indeed God to men by means of the Spirit, and, on the other hand, attaching man to God by His own incarnation, and bestowing upon us at His coming immortality durably and truly, by means of communion with God" (*Haer.* 5.1.1).

Referring to Jesus's death and resurrection, Irenaeus uses the language of "persuasion." The fall into sin had enslaved humanity by violence, but the Word incarnate saves us by the nonviolent means of the "persuasion" of the cross. Although willingly the victim of others' violence in the crucifixion, the all-powerful God does not himself use violent means to accomplish his ends in redemption (*Haer.* 5.1.1).

Irenaeus also uses the language of forgiveness and reconciliation. By disobeying God's commandments, we have become his enemies, but through Christ's incarnation, he has made us his friends. By taking on human flesh and "redeeming us by his blood," Jesus has reconciled those who were formerly enemies (*Haer.* 5.14.3). When Jesus pronounced forgiveness of sins to those whom he healed, he showed not only that he had the authority to forgive sins but further that it was he who had been sinned against in the beginning. By forgiving sins, Jesus not only healed people but made clear who he was, since only God can forgive sin (5.17.1–3; 5.14.3).

Irenaeus refers to Christ having "died for us" (*Haer.* 3.16.9) and having "redeemed us by his blood" (3.16.9; 4.20.2; 5.1.1; 5.2.1–2; 5.14.1–3), making clear that the incarnation alone is not enough to save sinful humanity but that the cross has a special significance. However, in Irenaeus's understanding of "redemption," the cross does not stand apart from Jesus's incarnation, life, teaching, and resurrection. When Irenaeus writes of redemption through Christ's blood, he mentions the incarnation and the resurrection in the same context (3.16.9; 4.20.2; 5.2.1).

A crucial issue of concern for Irenaeus's interpreters is what to make of this language of Christ dying for us and redemption through his blood. Did Irenaeus understand Jesus's death in ways comparable to later models of the atonement: as a substitution, a judicial or penal satisfaction, a sacrifice?

Irenaeus clearly understood recapitulation to mean that God himself has taken on our lot in the incarnation; that, in Christ, God himself has undergone the full extent of human existence; and that through the incarnation, life, crucifixion, and resurrection, Jesus reversed the consequences of human sin and has delivered humanity from sin and death. By contrast, commentators tend to deny any notion of satisfaction or penal substitution in Irenaeus's atonement theology.[22] Irenaeus does use the language of "propitiation" in one passage (*Haer.* 4.8.2); however, "such references do remain sparse."[23]

One more atonement image appears regularly in Irenaeus: the military language of battle and the defeat of sin, death, and the devil that has become associated with the Christus Victor model of atonement. This is a central theme in Irenaeus's theology, but it will be the topic of a separate chapter.

Concluding Reflections on Irenaeus

Our discussion of Irenaeus concludes with some summary reflections. First, the incarnation of God in Jesus Christ is central to Irenaeus's understanding of atonement, but Irenaeus does not reduce atonement to incarnation—as some writers have mistakenly claimed.[24] Rather, Irenaeus has an integrated understanding of the relation between the incarnation and atonement that is directly related to his understanding of what it means that Jesus saves.

Second, Irenaeus's understandings of incarnation and soteriology repeat the same themes and are closely related to the rest of his theology. His doctrines of creation, of the economy of salvation, and of the Scriptures find their unity in and point to Christ. As christological themes regularly appear in other aspects of his theology, so the above themes set the stage for his discussion of Christology and atonement.

Third, atonement and salvation are directly related to Irenaeus's doctrine of creation. Christology and atonement are primarily about the re-creation of humanity in the image of God, as becomes evident in Irenaeus's repeated references to "recapitulation."[25]

Fourth, as Irenaeus understands creation to be a teleological process, so he understands atonement to be a process.[26] Accordingly, the atonement is not restricted to a specific moment in the life of Jesus, whether the birth of Christ or the death of Christ. Rather, it is Jesus Christ's entire personal mission—

---

22. Oxenham, *Catholic Doctrine of the Atonement*, 128; Lawson, *Biblical Theology of Saint Irenaeus*, 193.

23. Boersma, "Redemptive Hospitality in Irenaeus," 220.

24. Wingren refers to this misreading in *Man and the Incarnation*, 82.

25. Wingren, *Man and the Incarnation*, 84.

26. Wingren, *Man and the Incarnation*, 81.

incarnation, life, death, resurrection, and second coming—that constitutes atonement and salvation.

Fifth, this means that Jesus's humanity is central to Irenaeus's understanding of atonement. While Jesus Christ's personal identity as the Son of God and Second Person of the Trinity is crucial to soteriology—only God can save—God must restore humanity from within. The Son of God restores humanity by acting as a human.[27]

Sixth, Irenaeus understands atonement as an entirely gracious move from God to humanity—that is, atonement is not necessary because of a "demand" or "need" on God's part for either satisfaction or justice. Rather, humanity, because of our fallen sinfulness, needs atonement and must be re-created in order to be rescued and restored from sin and death.

Finally, while Irenaeus focuses primarily on an "incarnational" model of the atonement, less prominent themes connected with other atonement models appear in his work as well: exemplar (Christ as exemplar and teacher), Christus Victor (victory over Satan, death, and sin), and even some aspects of substitution or propitiation.

Athanasius

Like Irenaeus, Athanasius of Alexandria (ca. 297–373) forged his theology amid theological controversy. His contention with fellow Christian Arius (also of Alexandria) led to the first ecumenical council at Nicaea and remained at the center of Athanasius's career as bishop and theologian. The theological background to Arianism arose from unresolved ambiguities in early Christology, especially those introduced by the great third-century Alexandrian theologian, Origen (ca. 184–ca. 253). On the one hand, Origen affirmed the eternal generation of the Son from the Father; on the other hand, he affirmed that the Son was in some sense subordinate to and of a lesser being than the Father. Origen also seems to have taught that creation itself is eternal.[28] In addition, the second-century apologists (especially Justin Martyr) tended to speak of the Word (*logos*) as a mediatory figure between God and creation. The apologists focused on Proverbs 8:22—"The LORD created me at the beginning of his work, / the first of his acts of long ago"—as a description of the Word's role in creation, while at the same time affirming the Word's eternity and co-existence with the Father.[29]

27. Lawson, *Biblical Theology of Saint Irenaeus*, 153.
28. Anatolios, *Athanasius* (2004), 7–8; Leithart, *Athanasius*, 2; R. Williams, "Origen," 132–42.
29. Kelly, *Early Christian Doctrines*, 95–101.

Given a clear understanding of the doctrine of creation from nothing (*creatio ex nihilo*), it became necessary to resolve ambiguities about the Son's ontological status in relation both to the Father and to creation. On what side of the divide does the Son stand? Is the Son Creator and eternal or a creature and created from nothing? Arius endorsed the latter, thus setting the terms of the controversy. He embraced Origen's subordinationism: the Son/Word is a creature—"There was a time when he was not." Athanasius endorsed the former: the Son is Creator, fully God, and thus always Son.

God and Creation

Athanasius's theology belongs to the same theological tradition as Irenaeus's. Both closely connect creation and atonement.[30] The distinction between Creator and creature is fundamental. There is one God, who is Creator and Lord of everything that exists. God is self-existent, simple and immaterial, enclosing all things without being enclosed. He creates all contingent things from nothing. Created nature, because it is created from nothing, is finite, contingent, and subject to dissolution and a return to nonexistence.[31]

As with Irenaeus, the creation of the human being in the "image of God" plays a crucial role in Athanasius's theology.[32] His understanding of creation "from nothing" is central. God's motive for creation is love, and the radical dependency of creatures upon God's will for existence leads Athanasius to describe creation itself as a "mercy." He reads God's salvation of sinful humanity back into the original creation, thus emphasizing the continuity between creation and salvation.[33] Emphasizing creation's radical contingency, Athanasius speaks of the creation of humanity using the linguistic distinction between "nature" (φύσις, *physis*) and "grace" (χάρις, *charis*). "Nature" reflects the tendency of creation toward dissolution to "nothingness," while "grace" points to God's love and care for creation and is closely related to Athanasius's notion of participation. While all creation participates in existence, humanity as created in the "image of God" is granted a special "participation" in the "power of the Word," and is called to enter into this participation consciously and actively. Humanity is thus created to share consciously in the Word's own "rationality" and love (*C. Gent.* 41; *Inc.* 3).[34]

30. Anatolios, *Athanasius* (2004), 50.
31. Athanasius, *C. Gent.* 40–41 (NPNF[2] 4:25–26).
32. There are differences. E.g., Athanasius makes no distinction between the "image" and the "likeness" of God.
33. Athanasius, *Inc.* 3 (NPNF[2] 4:37–38).
34. Athanasius's distinction between "nature" and "grace" should not be confused with the later medieval distinction. See Anatolios, *Athanasius* (1998), 55–56, and Leithart, *Athanasius*, 100–116.

For Athanasius, the fall into sin is related to the distinctive connection between humanity and embodiment. In creation, the human being is originally oriented toward union with God. In sin, however, the human being turns to that which is most immediately present—the body—embracing self-indulgence rather than transcendence. For Athanasius, idolatry is the classic portrayal of sin because it is an inversion of the human being's proper orientation to God.[35] The consequence of this fall into sin is that the human being is now drawn toward corruption and nothingness. Sin reverses the order of creation from "grace" toward "nature"—a process of "de-creation."[36] The human being is mortal by nature, having been made from nothing. Through the grace of and participation in the Word, humanity received incorruptible life, but the fall into sin introduced not only corruption but ultimately death (*Inc.* 4–5). Thus, the consequences of sin are not an extrinsic punishment but are logically intrinsic to sin's nature. If life and incorruption are the consequences of union with the Word, corruption and death are the inevitable consequences of the separation that results from sin.[37]

Incarnation and Salvation

Athanasius's understanding of salvation coheres with his understanding of creation and the fall. If sin is a "de-creation," then salvation requires a "re-creation."[38] If the image of God in creation was a union with the divine Word leading to life and incorruption and the fall into sin is the loss of that union—leading to corruption and death—then atonement is a restoration of that lost union with a consequent restoration to incorruption and life.

The Son of God, who is by nature one with God, has become one with humanity in the incarnation so that the humanity of Christ, which is not proper to the Word by nature, has graciously become the "proper" humanity of the Word for our salvation. Through our union with the humanity of the incarnate Word, we who are human by nature (and not divine) have come to share by participation in the divine nature of the Word. There is thus a "rhetoric of reversal," as the God who is our "maker" by nature, and essentially Father of the eternal Word, becomes our Father by grace as the maker of the incarnate Word. "For by partaking of Him, we partake of the Father; because the Word is the Father's own."[39]

35. Anatolios, *Athanasius* (2004), 45, 48. This is a central theme of the *Contra Gentes*.
36. Anatolios, *Athanasius* (1998), 53–67; Anatolios, *Athanasius* (2004), 40–48.
37. Anatolios, *Athanasius* (2004), 48.
38. Anatolios, *Athanasius* (2004), 51.
39. Athanasius, *Syn.* 51 (*NPNF²* 4:477–78); Anatolios, *Athanasius* (1998), 129, 134, 146.

The incarnation manifests the same attributes of divine strength and love as were involved in creation. As the fall into sin is itself a "descent" into corruption and death, the incarnation is a descent culminating in Christ's death, an act of loving divine solidarity with human lowliness that leads to a reversal of human fallenness, and a restoration to life and incorruptibility through the resurrection.[40] As Athanasius says in the best-known statement of his theology: "He was made man that we might be made God" (*Inc.* 54).

Athanasius's two-volume work *Against the Pagans/On the Incarnation* is an apologetic focused on the issue of the "scandal of the cross."[41] Throughout the work, Athanasius argues for the "fittingness" of atonement through the incarnation, death, and resurrection of Christ (*Inc.* 22, 26). According to Athanasius, the entire purpose of the incarnation was so that Jesus Christ might die to save the fallen human race (4, 21). In a manner that anticipated Anselm of Canterbury's *Why God Became Man* (*Cur Deus Homo*), Athanasius suggested that the fall of humanity created a divine dilemma. On the one hand, it would have been "unworthy" of the goodness of God and "unfitting" for God to allow his work to be undone and for humanity to continue on the path of sin and corruption.[42] On the other hand, God could not go back on his word that death would follow from sin. If the only problem was the transgression of a command, then human repentance might have been sufficient. But repentance could neither restore humanity from a state of corruption nor restore the grace of its creation in the image of God. Only God's Word, through whom God had made all things from nothing, could restore corruption to incorruption (*Inc.* 7). Moreover, since the Word is the original image of God, it was appropriate that the Word should restore the corrupted image in humanity (13). Although the Word had been present in the original creation, he now entered the world in a new way: "He took pity on our race, and had mercy on our infirmity, and condescended to our corruption, and, unable to bear that death should have the mastery—lest the creature should perish, and His Father's handiwork in men be spent for nought—He takes unto Himself a body, and that of no different sort from ours" (8).

The incarnation of God in Christ is thus a *re-creation*: the original Word who brought humanity into existence entered his own creation by himself becoming a human being, taking on a human body. As sin came into existence because human beings abandoned transcendence and turned to created realities, thus sinning through embodiment, so the Word brought salvation

40. Anatolios, *Athanasius* (2004), 51.
41. Anatolios, *Athanasius* (1998), 67.
42. Leithart, *Athanasius*, 189n6.

through embodiment, using his body as an "instrument" to be present to fallen humanity (*Inc.* 8, 17, 44). The Word, who by nature does not have a body "proper" to his deity, took on a body, which became "proper" to him as human,[43] in order to enable embodied sinners to perceive their Creator through a body: "To this end the loving and general Saviour of all, the Word of God, takes to Himself a body, and as Man walks among men and meets the senses of all men half-way, to the end, I say, that they who think that God is corporeal may from what the Lord effects by His body perceive the truth, and through Him recognize the Father" (15).

Atonement

The rationale for Athanasius's concern with Christology is thus entirely soteriological. Athanasius is concerned about who Jesus is because of what it means for our salvation. Everything that the Word does, he does "for us." In the incarnation, God humbles himself so that we might be elevated (*C. Ar.* 1.40; 3.51, 52).[44] Athanasius's understanding parallels the incarnational model already seen in Irenaeus.

A key theme of Athanasius's understanding of atonement is that God did not bring about salvation through mere external command but rather through an intrinsic transformation from "within" the human being. God brought into being from nothing a creation external to himself, but the corruption brought into being through sin was something internal to the human being. It was therefore "fitting" or appropriate for God to bring about salvation from "within," by the Word becoming human and effecting salvation from the "inside," as it were (*Inc.* 43–44).[45]

This notion of atonement as an "inside job" appears in Athanasius's account of one of the two main purposes of the incarnation: Christ as teacher (*Inc.* 14). Athanasius states that God had provided four ways in which humanity could be taught about God. First, through being created in the image of God, human beings are made to know and love God. Second, after humanity had fallen, God could still be perceived through creation. Third, God sent the law and the prophets of the Old Testament so that humanity could have instruction "near at hand." However, fourth, when even this proved insufficient, the Word became incarnate, coming down to our own level and meeting us "half-way" (15).

43. Athanasius, *C. Ar.* 3.34 (*NPNF*² 4:412–13).
44. Leithart, *Athanasius*, 134, 153.
45. Anatolios, *Athanasius* (2004), 64; Anatolios, *Athanasius* (1998), 130; Leithart, *Athanasius*, 115; Weinandy, *Athanasius*, 99.

However, it is not only Jesus's teaching that reveals God. Since the incarnate Christ is the Word through whom creation was made, God is also revealed in his works. As the visible Word of God, he makes the invisible Creator known. Through his body, we can perceive the mind of the invisible Father. Through his death, immortality is known. Through his humiliation, he healed our suffering (*Inc.* 54).[46] Athanasius thus anticipates a central theme of later so-called "exemplarist" or "moral influence" theories of the atonement: Christ in his incarnate person reveals God. However, this revelation of God was only part of the reason for the Word's incarnation. The primary reason was salvation obtained through the cross.

Athanasius's discussion of atonement includes the following themes, which appear repeatedly. First, as noted above, creation and atonement are closely connected. The atonement is a divine act of re-creation. Because the Word is the original image of God in whose image humanity was created, the incarnate Word is able to restore the image corrupted through sin (*Inc.* 13).

Second, this re-creation takes place through the union of the Word with humanity. In the incarnation, the Word takes on a human nature in order to restore it. Athanasius repeatedly describes the Word as assuming a nature like our own: "And thus He, the incorruptible Son of God, being conjoined with all by a like nature . . ." (*Inc.* 9); "The body, then, as sharing the same nature with all, for it was a human body, though by an unparalleled miracle it was formed of a virgin only, yet being mortal . . ." (20).

Third, sin, death, and corruption are closely connected. Although the Word is incorruptible in himself, by taking on a human body capable of death and dying on a cross, the Word is able to reverse the process of corruption and death (*Inc.* 13; cf. 8, 9, 10, 20, 21).

Fourth, neither the incarnation alone nor death on a cross alone effects atonement. Further, Athanasius never discusses the cross without mentioning resurrection in the same context. The incarnation, crucifixion, and resurrection of Jesus taken together as a whole accomplish atonement. The incarnation of Jesus was necessary in order that Jesus might restore humanity in the divine image. On the cross, Jesus took on himself the death that was the consequence of sin. However, the resurrection reverses the process of death and corruption, resulting in new life and incorruptibility. While at some points Athanasius states that the purpose of the incarnation was that Christ might die, at others he states that it was the resurrection (*Inc.* 8, 22).

There is, then, an atoning "exchange" of relations because of the incarnation: those characteristics that belong to the Word now belong to fallen and

46. Anatolios, *Athanasius* (1998), 37.

restored humanity, and those characteristics that belong to sinful humanity become the possession of the incarnate Word. The immortal Word, who cannot die, underwent our death on the cross. Through the incorruption of his eternal life as the divine Word, he restores perishing humanity to incorruption. Through his death, he abolishes human death, and through their union with his human nature, those who were clothed with corruption receive the promise of resurrection (*Inc.* 9; *Ep. fest.* 108.).[47] This twofold predication will later be referred to as the *communicatio idiomatum* (communication of idioms), affirmed by Cyril of Alexandria against Nestorius of Antioch. Because the single identity of the person of the Son of God exists as human, properties of either his divine or human nature can be predicated of his divine person because his person is the subject of predication.

Thus, Athanasius most consistently talks about the atonement as the incarnation, crucifixion, and resurrection of the incarnate Word reversing the process of corruption and death and restoring fallen humanity to the image of God. However, he also uses other themes and metaphors.

Athanasius understands the incarnation as taking place "for us" and uses images and language of representation, vicariousness, and perhaps even substitution. Thus, he speaks of Christ giving his body to death in place of or "in the stead" of all (*Inc.* 8). He says that Christ came to accomplish not his own death but the death of all (22), that he "suffered for our sakes" to "bear the curse" laid upon us (25).

Athanasius also speaks of Jesus's death as the paying of a debt and a ransom (*Inc.* 9, 20, 25). To whom was the debt or ransom paid? Athanasius does not specify, but the context indicates that he does not understand this to be a personal debt paid either to God or to Satan. Rather, the expression seems to be metaphorical.

Athanasius occasionally uses liturgical language of offering and sacrifice. It was "in order to [offer] sacrifice for bodies such as His own that the Word Himself also assumed a body. . . . For by the sacrifice of His own body, He both put an end to the law which was against us, and made a new beginning of life for us" (*Inc.* 10). Athanasius refers to Jesus's "sacrifice on behalf of all" and his "offering his body to death and raising it again" (16). The reader might wish that Athanasius had said more about how Christ's death functioned as a sacrifice, but he does not provide any detailed explanation.[48]

Athanasius also uses the language of Christus Victor seen in Irenaeus: the Lord came to "cast down the devil, and clear the air and prepare the way for

47. Weinandy, *Athanasius*, 96.
48. Weinandy, *Athanasius*, 34.

us up into heaven" (*Inc.* 25). Such passages occur rarely and in the context of discussion of New Testament citations that mention Satan. Unlike other church fathers, Athanasius did not write at length about atonement in terms of the overthrow of Satan.

The Holy Spirit and Deification

The Holy Spirit is key to Athanasius's theology because it is the Spirit who unites Christians to the Father and the Son.[49] Against tendencies to identify the Spirit as a creature, Athanasius insists that the Holy Spirit is fully God and uses similar arguments as he had used when discussing the divinity of the Son (*Serap.* 1.2; *C. Ar.* 1.18; 3.24, 25).[50]

The anointing of Jesus with the Holy Spirit at his baptism plays a crucial role in the economy of salvation. At Jesus's baptism, the Holy Spirit anoints the incarnate Son, not for his sake but for ours, that we might share in his anointing. After his resurrection, Jesus sanctifies his disciples by baptizing them in the Holy Spirit (*C. Ar.* 1.47–48; 2.61; 3.24).[51]

Athanasius uses the word *theopoiēsis*, or "deification" (*theōsis*), for this process of sanctification that takes place through the outpouring of the Holy Spirit (*C. Ar.* 1.38). Deification is not a matter of blurring the distinction between Creator and creature, or the difference between being the Son of God by nature and sharing in divine adoption through grace.[52] Rather, deification is concerned above all with incorporation or union. Because Christians share in Jesus's death and resurrection, they also share in his exaltation. Through being united to Christ's risen body, we become one body with him and are thus united to the Father as well (1.38, 43, 44, 45; 3.22).

Communion with the risen Christ takes place through the Holy Spirit, whom Christ pours out on his church (*C. Ar.* 2.14, 18). As the Son is Son by nature, so Christians, being united to the Son through the grace of the Holy Spirit, become children of God through participation (3.24). As was the case with Irenaeus, sacraments are crucial to Athanasius's theology of deification. In Jesus's baptism he was sanctified with the Holy Spirit, and we have been baptized in him (1.48). In our own baptism, we are baptized into the entire Trinity. Whoever the Father baptizes, the Son also baptizes, and the Son consecrates those who are baptized in the Holy Spirit (2.41).[53]

49. Weinandy, *Athanasius*, 107.
50. Leithart, *Athanasius*, 79; Weinandy, *Athanasius* 105, 108.
51. Leithart, *Athanasius*, 158–59; Weinandy, *Athanasius*, 99, 106.
52. Leithart, *Athanasius*, 159.
53. Leithart, *Athanasius*, 160–64; Weinandy, *Athanasius*, 99–100.

Deification means, then, that human beings have been brought into the communion of the Father, the Son, and the Holy Spirit by the incarnation of the Son through the gift of the Holy Spirit. Through union with Christ's risen humanity, Christians are transformed into his likeness as he restores the image of God, and we come to share in the divine life of the Trinity. The Holy Spirit is the bond who unites Christians to Christ's risen humanity.

Concluding Reflections on Athanasius

Athanasius's theology of atonement is very much in the same tradition as Irenaeus's. Atonement is so closely integrated with his theology of the Trinity, creation and fall, and the incarnation and grace that it is only possible to discuss it in the context of the whole. Atonement is restoration of a fallen creation and union with the incarnate Word through whom humanity was created in his image. Athanasius's theology of atonement is Christocentric. On the one hand, the deity of Jesus Christ is central to salvation because only God can save. On the other hand, the incarnate Word is human because sinful human beings are the ones who need to be saved. Atonement is thus a divine act in which the single subject of the Word assumed a human nature in order that, by undergoing death himself and overcoming it in bodily resurrection, he might overcome the death and corruption introduced by sin. Salvation means being united to the humanity of the incarnate Word Jesus Christ in his death and resurrection, reversing the process of corruption and death, and sharing in the eternal communion of the Trinity, which results in incorruption and life.

In contrast to Irenaeus, Athanasius focuses specifically on the cross and resurrection as the center of atonement. The purpose of the incarnation was so that Jesus Christ could die "for us." Athanasius describes Christ as acting vicariously in our place and thus comes closer than Irenaeus to the language of substitution. However, as with Irenaeus, there is no hint that Jesus was punished in our place on the cross or that the atonement satisfied divine justice or wrath. Athanasius speaks of atonement not in terms of the law court but in terms of rescue and re-creation.

At the same time, Athanasius's focus on the cross and resurrection raises the question of whether he had anything like Irenaeus's historically oriented understanding of "recapitulation." For Athanasius, the primary purpose for the incarnation was that Jesus might die on the cross, but it seems that the purpose of his preceding earthly life was mainly noetic—to reveal God through his teaching and deeds.

Nonetheless, what Athanasius says about Jesus's anointing with the Holy Spirit at his baptism indicates that he did understand Jesus's entire human

experience to be of soteriological significance. It was because Jesus was himself sanctified with the Spirit that he is able to sanctify others. This communication of life and holiness (deification) is crucial to Athanasius's soteriology.
Because the Word who is the image of God has become flesh, he is able to
restore the image of God to fallen human beings, to overcome their corruption and death by his own death and resurrection, and, by baptizing with the
Spirit those who have faith in him, to unite them to his own risen humanity
and bring them into communion with the triune God. If Athanasius does
not speak at length about recapitulation, what he says about the significance
of Jesus's anointing with the Holy Spirit strongly implies something like it.

Looking Forward

The atonement theologies of Irenaeus and Athanasius introduce a number
of significant themes that set the stage for later discussions and provide criteria
by which later theologies can be measured.

1. Economic-immanent correlation: While the immanent Trinity has an
   ontological priority over the economic Trinity, the economic Trinity—
   God revealed in history as Father, Son, and Holy Spirit—is a true revelation of God's inner being. Accordingly, atonement is grounded in the
   nature of the triune God.
2. Person-work correlation: It is because Jesus Christ is the Second Person
   of the Trinity, fully God, that he is able to save humanity. Yet it is also
   because Jesus Christ is fully human that he is able to save humanity. The
   saving work of Jesus Christ in the history of salvation is thus closely
   related to his personal ontology. The Chalcedonian formula that Jesus
   Christ is a single divine person, with two complete natures—one divine
   and one human—provides the ontological presupposition of atonement
   theology.
3. Life-death correlation: Although atonement theology has the suffering
   and death of Jesus at its center—"Jesus died for our sins"—his atoning
   work includes and must be related to his entire earthly mission: incarnation, ministry (teaching, healing, and miracles), crucifixion, resurrection, ascension, and second coming (when he will reign as Lord).
4. Exemplarism (ontological and teleological): Jesus Christ is the exemplar
   of humanity, but not merely in the sense that he is the primary moral
   example of how human beings should live. He is the archetypal human
   being who is the primary model for the entire human race, the "second
   Adam" in whose image other human beings are created and through

whom other human beings come to share in the purpose and teleological goal of what it means to be human.

5. New Israel: Jesus is the fulfillment of God's covenant with Israel as God's true Son and the anointed Messiah. Through participation in his atoning life and work, the church becomes the New Israel, the covenant community of salvation. At the same time, the church's mission, like that of Jesus Christ, points beyond its own election to embrace the entire world.

6. The vicarious humanity of Christ: In his life, death, and resurrection, Jesus Christ has acted both "in our place" and "on our behalf." He has done for us what we could not do for ourselves. In his incarnate mission, Jesus has accomplished salvation, not only "for us" but in some sense also "on behalf of" or "instead of" us.

7. A forensic or legal dimension: Atonement includes pardon and the forgiveness of sins.

8. Victory over sin, evil, and death: In his earthly mission, crucifixion, and resurrection, Jesus Christ not only took upon himself the full consequences of human evil, sin, and death but also overcame them in his resurrection from the dead and will fully vanquish them in his glorious return and eternal reign.

9. Cosmological dimension: Atonement is about not only pardon and forgiveness of sins but also the re-creation and restoration of fallen humanity and a world corrupted by evil.

10. Union and participation: The exemplarity and vicarious humanity of Jesus Christ mean not only that Jesus Christ is the prototype for a humanity and acted on our behalf for our humanity but also—through the presence of the Holy Spirit after his resurrection and ascension—that reconciled human beings are united to and share in the triune life through union with Jesus Christ in his death and resurrection.

11. Offering/sacrifice: Atonement is directed toward not only human beings—forgiving and destroying sin, evil, and death and bringing reconciliation, restoration, and life to humanity—but also God. The language of "sacrifice" indicates that Jesus Christ's life, death, and resurrection are the perfect worship and obedience of his perfect humanity—the "offering"—presented to God the Father as humanity's proper response to God's creative covenantal love and providence.

2

• • •

Atonement as Christus Victor

Church Fathers and Gustaf Aulén

Models of atonement that have developed through church history are built around images or metaphors mostly derived from Scripture that describe the saving work of Jesus Christ. The vocabulary of atonement uses words—such as "cross," "sacrifice," "priesthood," "judgment," "ransom," "deliverance," "redemption," "punishment," and "forgiveness"—that are based on images such as the crucifixion of Jesus, temple sacrifices, the Old Testament priestly office, law courts, financial transactions, ransoming slaves or captives, and battle imagery, among others. These images that refer to the person and work of Jesus are usually understood to be metaphors, though some models interpret their preferred metaphors more literally than others.

The model of atonement presented in this chapter is commonly referred to as Christus Victor and focuses on images of conflict and victory and of ransom from slavery. This model views atonement in the context of a dramatic moral dualism, as a divine conflict and victory over evil. In his life, death, and resurrection, Jesus Christ fought against and overcame the hostile powers of sin, death, and the devil. By achieving victory over these powers, Jesus redeemed or ransomed fallen and sinful humanity.[1]

---

1. Aulén, *Christus Victor*, 4–5.

The military language is both metaphorical and paradoxical. Jesus of Nazareth was not a soldier, and the military imagery in the model is turned on its head. It is the crucified Jesus who conquers sin and death by undergoing death rather than by using force against his enemies. The ransom imagery of the model is also metaphorical. There is no financial transaction involved, and it is unclear to whom the ransom is paid. The Christus Victor model thus raises an important question about the relationship between atonement models and theological language: How do theologians make use of the symbolic imagery and metaphors on which a particular model of atonement is based in their development of that model?

The metaphorical nature of the imagery associated with the Christus Victor model has led some to question whether it should even be considered as a model of atonement. The counterargument to this view is that—while not a "rational theory" like the satisfaction model—Christus Victor does have an internal logic. It consistently combines key themes and metaphors in a way that earns it the right to be discussed as a distinct model of atonement. Moreover, it was so predominant in the patristic era of the church that Aulén identifies it as "the classic idea of the atonement."[2]

What follows assumes that the Christus Victor model unites consistent themes or metaphors and has a sufficiently internal logical structure such that it can indeed be considered a model of atonement. However, prior to the modern period, Christus Victor was not discussed at length by any single author, but its various metaphors and themes appeared sporadically in the writings of numerous authors. Consequently, this chapter will not focus at length on the writings of one or two representative figures. Instead, it will examine representative authors and views from different eras in the first part, and the work of modern Lutheran theologian Gustaf Aulén in the second part.

The Patristic Era

As noted in the previous chapter, Irenaeus of Lyons was the first theologian to deal at length with the subject of the atonement. Irenaeus's primary understanding of the atonement is the incarnational model; however, his discussion also includes numerous themes from the Christus Victor model. It might seem paradoxical to join the incarnational model's focus on unity with Christus Victor's moral dualism, but the models are in fact complementary.

2. Aulén refers to Christus Victor as "the classic idea of the atonement" throughout *Christus Victor*.

The incarnational model's theme of restoration to unity presupposes a disruption caused by sin, which creates the need for restoration by Jesus Christ. Through recapitulation, the incarnate Jesus Christ undoes sinful humanity's disobedience by his faithful obedience, thereby not only restoring humanity to union with God but also freeing humanity from—and ultimately defeating—the evil powers of sin, death, and the devil. Incarnation and Christus Victor are thus complementary aspects of Irenaeus's "recapitulation" Christology. The following themes are crucial for Irenaeus.

First, as elsewhere in his theology, Irenaeus draws a close connection between creation and salvation. As Adam (and humanity with him) lost life through sin and was enslaved to death and Satan, so Christ as the second Adam delivered fallen humanity from the slavery of sin and defeated death and Satan: "Now Adam had been conquered, all life having been taken away from him: wherefore, when the foe was conquered in his turn, Adam received new life; and the last enemy, death, is destroyed, which at the first had taken possession of man. . . . For his salvation is death's destruction. When therefore the Lord vivifies man, that is, Adam, death is at the same time destroyed."[3]

Second, there is a close connection between the incarnation and the atonement. The Word became human for the purpose of redeeming sinful humanity: "For it behooved Him who was to destroy sin, and redeem man under the power of death, that He should Himself be made that very same thing which he was, that is, man; who had been drawn by sin into bondage, but was held by death, so that sin should be destroyed by man, and man should go forth from death" (*Haer.* 3.18.7).

Third, Irenaeus repeatedly uses the imagery of conflict, captivity, and victory. As the incarnate Word of God, Jesus Christ was "waging war against our enemy, and crushing him who had at the beginning led us away captives in Adam, and trampled upon his head" (*Haer.* 5.21.1). As Satan had conquered humanity, so also Satan had to be conquered to prevent God from being conquered through the enslavement and death of his creation. As the devil had conquered the first human being, so now God become human has conquered the devil and restored humanity to life. Irenaeus echoes Jesus's imagery of "binding the strong man" (Mark 3:27): "When Satan is bound, man is set free" (*Haer.* 5.21.3; cf. 3.18.6–7; 3.23.1).

Fourth, as mentioned above, Irenaeus's imagery of the conquest and defeat of sin, death, and the devil is closely related to recapitulation. In becoming incarnate, the Word savingly "regathers" or "sums up" the human situation, and in so doing defeats the enemy. As Satan used the woman Eve to enslave

3. Irenaeus, *Haer.* 3.23.7 (*ANF* 1:457).

humanity, so the Word was born from the woman Mary in order to defeat Satan (*Haer.* 5.21.1). As noted previously, recapitulation is especially evident in Irenaeus's discussion of the temptation of Jesus. In resisting Satan's temptations after his baptism, Jesus recapitulated humanity's antagonism against the serpent. By quoting the law, Jesus undid Adam's infringement of the divine commandment. Unlike Adam, he refused to transgress the commandment, thus conquering Satan's pride with his own humility (5.21.1–3).

Irenaeus uses similar language regarding Christ's redemption of sinful humanity on the cross. Though human beings were by nature property of the omnipotent God, we had been tyrannized by the evil powers unjustly. Through the incarnation and the cross, Jesus rescued fallen humanity from this tyranny:

> The Word of God, powerful in all things, and not defective with regard to His own justice, did righteously turn against that apostasy, and redeem from it His own property, not by violent means, as the [apostasy] had obtained dominion over us at the beginning, when it insatiably snatched away what was not its own, but by means of persuasion, as became a God of counsel, who does not use violent means to obtain what He desires; so that neither should justice be infringed upon, nor the ancient handiwork of God go to destruction. (*Haer.* 5.1.1)

While Irenaeus uses images of conflict and conquest in his discussion of Jesus's temptations and the cross, his focus on recapitulation indicates that his main concern is re-creation. In Christ's conflict with Satan, the image and likeness of God are restored and creation is made new again as fallen human beings are united to Christ in his death and resurrection and joined to the body of Christ, the church.[4] Irenaeus concludes his discussion by emphasizing how Jesus redeemed humanity through persuasion rather than violence (*Haer.* 5.1.1). It is through "union and communion" between God and humanity that redemption "destroys" the power of Satan, sin, and death.

Themes associated with the Christus Victor model appear in later patristic writers as well. Origen writes that Jesus's death was "not only an example of death endured for the sake of piety, but also the first blow in the conflict which is to overthrow the power of that evil spirit the devil, who had obtained dominion over the whole world," and that "He submitted to death, purchasing us back by His own blood from him who had got us into his power, sold under sin."[5] Eusebius of Caesarea states that Christ died "to ransom the whole human race, buying them with His precious Blood from their former slavery

---

4. Wingren, *Man and the Incarnation*, 131–32.
5. Origen, *Cels.* 7.17 (ANF 4:618); Origen, *Comm. Jo.* 6.35 (ANF 9:377).

to their invisible tyrants, the unclean demons, and the rulers and spirits of evil."[6] According to Gregory of Nyssa, "He who was shut up in darkness longed for the presence of the light. The captive sought for a ransomer, the fettered prisoner for some one to take his part, and for a deliverer he who was held in the bondage of slavery."[7]

As with Irenaeus's account of recapitulation, the other fathers saw Jesus's entire life and mission, not simply his crucifixion, as a conflict with the demonic powers.[8]

Birth

Origen uniquely interprets the story of the magi's visit to the infant Jesus to illustrate that, even in his birth, Jesus triumphed over evil spirits. Origen suggests that the magi were magicians who had commerce with evil spirits. After the birth of Jesus, they discovered that their spells no longer worked.[9]

The Temptations

Like Irenaeus, Augustine says of Jesus that "He offered Himself to be tempted, in order that He might be also a mediator to overcome his temptations, not only by succor, but also by example." When the devil failed in his efforts—"having finished all his alluring temptation in the wilderness after the baptism"—he decided to renew the battle by destroying Jesus through death.[10]

Death

The fathers regularly refer to Jesus's death using battle and victory imagery. Origen states that "when Christ was crucified, the principalities . . . were made a show of and triumphed over before the believing world" (*Comm. Matt.* 12.18). In the same passage in which Augustine referred to Jesus's temptations in the wilderness, he returns to the theme of Satan's failure to win the battle against Jesus. "There in every respect [the devil] was conquered; and wherein he received outwardly the power of slaying the Lord in the flesh, therein his inward power, by which he held ourselves, was slain" (*Trin.* 4.13.17).

6. Eusebius of Caesarea, *Dem. ev.* 10.8 (2:221).
7. Gregory of Nyssa, *Or. Catech.*, chap. 15 (NPNF[2] 5:485). See also Methodius, *Three Fragments* (ANF 6:399).
8. Turner, *Patristic Doctrine of Redemption*, 49–52.
9. Origen, *Cels.* 1.60 (ANF 4:422).
10. Augustine, *Trin.* 4.13.17 (NPNF[1] 3:78).

Descent into Hades

Jesus's triumph in the realm of death itself is especially celebrated in the realms of liturgy and iconography. The Orthodox Liturgy for Holy Saturday contains these words:

> Going down to death,
> O Life immortal,
> Thou hast slain hell
> with the dazzling light of Thy divinity.
> And when Thou hast raised up the dead
> from their dwelling place beneath the earth,
> all the powers of heaven cried aloud:
> "Giver of Life, O Christ our God,
> glory to Thee."[11]

The "harrowing of Hades" is a notion referring to the time between Jesus's death and resurrection in which he descended to the realm of the dead (Hades), bringing salvation to those faithful who had died since the time of the fall. The notion is based on two biblical passages: 1 Peter 3:19–20, which says that after Jesus's death, "he went and proclaimed to the spirits in prison"; and Ephesians 4:7–10, which says that Jesus, having "descended to the lowest parts of the earth . . . when he ascended on high he led a host of captives." Also influential was the apocryphal *Gospel of Nicodemus*, which describes Jesus's descent into Hades and records the demons' response: "We have been conquered: woe to us!"[12]

The Resurrection

The fathers do not separate Jesus's death and resurrection. Just as Jesus's death defeated the demonic powers, so also did his resurrection. Thus, Origen writes, "But on the third day He rose from the dead, in order that having delivered them from the wicked one, . . . He might gain for those who had been delivered the right to be baptized in spirit and soul and body."[13]

The association of words such as "triumph" and "victory" with the crucifixion of a Jewish rabbi by the Roman Empire is paradoxical to say the least. The church fathers were as aware as any modern of the scandalous nature of the claim that God's power is shown in the weakness of the cross.

11. Nes, *Mystical Language of Icons*, 83.
12. *Gos. Nic.* 2.6.22 (ANF 8:437).
13. Origen, *Comm. Matt.* 12.20 (ANF 9:462).

Methodius of Olympus introduced this theme in his discussion of Christ's triumph over the demonic powers. God could have overcome the demons by his divine omnipotence. By becoming a human being, however, Christ overcame the demonic powers as a man, as someone weaker than the powers that he conquered: "Therefore it was that by a man He procured the safety of the race; in order that men, after that very Life and Truth had entered into them in bodily form, might be able to return to the form and light of the Word, overcoming the power of the enticements of sin; and that the demons, being conquered by one weaker than they, and thus brought into contempt, might desist from their over-bold confidence, their hellish wrath being repressed."[14]

Tensions in the Christus Victor Tradition

The paradoxical nature of Christ's victory over sin and death is strongly emphasized in several early church writers: Jesus conquered not through the use of violence but through the nonviolent tactic of persuasion.[15] Concerns about justice also appear in the discussion of two issues raised by the Christus Victor model of atonement. The first has to do with the interpretation of the metaphor of "ransom" or "redemption," which frequently appears in biblical and patristic descriptions of atonement. Is there an actual transaction? If so, to whom was the ransom paid? Gregory of Nyssa suggests that perhaps the ransom was paid to Satan. Those who have sold themselves into slavery cannot justly be restored to freedom except through the payment of a ransom to the new master.[16] Similarly, Origen suggests that Jesus purchased us from Satan through his blood, while Eusebius of Caesarea writes that Christ bought with his blood those who were in slavery to demons and evil spirits.[17]

This notion of the payment of a ransom to Satan (or God) is associated with another troubling theme—that of the deception of Satan. Gregory of Nyssa writes that "it was by means of a certain amount of deceit that God carried out this scheme on our behalf."[18] Gregory suggests that Satan, in perceiving the weakness of Christ's humanity, failed to discern Jesus's hidden divinity and over-reached. In a famous analogy, Gregory compares Jesus's deity to the baited hook hidden beneath his humanity: "Therefore, in order to secure that the ransom in our behalf might be easily accepted by him who

14. Methodius, *Three Fragments* (ANF 6:399).
15. E.g., Gregory of Nyssa, *Or. Catech.* 20 (NPNF² 5:489).
16. Gregory of Nyssa, *Or. Catech.* 22 (NPNF² 5:490–91).
17. Origen, *Comm. Jo.* 6.35 (ANF 9:377); Eusebius of Caesarea, *Dem. ev.* 10.8 (2:221).
18. Gregory of Nyssa, *Or. Catech.* 26 (NPNF² 5:493).

required it, the Deity was hidden under the veil of our nature, that so, as with ravenous fish, the hook of the Deity might be gulped down along with the bait of flesh, and thus, life being introduced into the house of death, and light shining in darkness, that which is diametrically opposed to light and life might vanish."[19]

Gregory goes on to argue that this deception was not unjust. Since Satan had originally practiced deception in luring humanity into sin, he was himself deceived in the same manner in which he originally deceived. However, Satan deceived with the intent of ruining human nature, whereas God, who is just and wise, deceived for the purpose of bringing salvation to those who had originally been deceived.[20] This theme of divine deception of Satan appears elsewhere in the church fathers, including Augustine of Hippo, who uses the imagery of a mousetrap.[21]

Some modern commentators have found this notion of Jesus's death as a payment of ransom to Satan, along with the accompanying imagery of divine deception, to be particularly abhorrent.[22] But many fail to notice that the patristic writers themselves questioned to what extent this imagery should be literally applied. While Origen did not hesitate to talk about God's deception of the demonic powers, he seems to have been the first to question the literal use of "ransom" language.[23] And despite the great friendship between Gregory of Nyssa and Gregory of Nazianzus, the latter did not share the idea of a ransom paid to Satan or of divine deception. Indeed, Gregory of Nazianzus rejected the notion that the ransom was paid either to Satan or to God:

> Now, since a ransom belongs only to him who holds in bondage, I ask to whom was this offered, and for what cause? If to the Evil One, fie upon the outrage! If the robber receives ransom, not only from God, but a ransom which consists of God Himself, and has such an illustrious payment for his tyranny, a payment for whose sake it would have been right for him to have left us alone altogether. But if to the Father, I ask first, how? For it was not by Him that we were being oppressed; and next, On what principle did the Blood of His Only begotten Son delight the Father, Who would not receive even Isaac, when he was being offered by his Father, but changed the sacrifice, putting a ram in the place of the human victim?[24]

19. Gregory of Nyssa, Or. Catech. 24 (NPNF[2] 5:492).
20. Gregory of Nyssa, Or. Catech. 26 (NPNF[2] 5:493).
21. Augustine, "On the Fortieth Day," 7:220.
22. Rashdall, Idea of Atonement. Rashdall describes the "ransom" theory as "hideous" (245).
23. Origen, Comm. Matt. 16.8 (cited in Rashdall, Idea of Atonement, 259; Turner, Patristic Doctrine of Redemption, 55).
24. Gregory of Nazianzus, Or. Bas. 45.22 (NPNF[2] 7:431).

Similarly, if we look back to Irenaeus's discussion of recapitulation, no-where does he suggest that Satan had "rights" over humanity or that any ransom was paid either to divine justice or to Satan. Rather, Irenaeus refers to Satan as the "apostate angel" who, because he disobeyed the divine com-mand, is destroyed by the law's "voice," "being exposed in his true colours, and vanquished by the Son of man keeping the commandment of God." Because Satan bound humanity unjustly, he is justly punished (*Haer.* 5.21.3). Irenaeus's "ransom" metaphors are the language of victory won through conflict and death, not the juridical terms of the payment of a fee. Satan ac-complishes his ends by tactics of violence; Jesus accomplished "redemption" through nonviolent persuasion: death on a cross.[25]

Anselm's Critique of Christus Victor

Anselm of Canterbury (1033/34–1109) was the first explicitly to reject the Christus Victor model. In his *Cur Deus Homo* (*Why God Became Man*), Anselm acknowledges a certain "fittingness" to the devil being overcome by one who suffered on a tree, since Satan had conquered humanity through the fruit that came from a tree. However, argues Anselm, "fittingness" is not the same thing as necessity.[26] Following dissenting patristic voices like that of Gregory of Nazianzus, Anselm rejected the notion that the devil had any rightful ownership over humanity that God was obligated to recognize. God owes the devil nothing but punishment. Since Satan was unjustly holding humanity captive, God is guilty of no injustice in rescuing humanity from the devil's clutches. Moreover, the "written decree" of which Paul speaks that is "erased" by being nailed to Christ's cross (Col. 2:14) was not a contract between God and Satan. Rather, it was the judgment of God that those who sinned would not avoid sin or its punishment unless someone were to deliver them. There was therefore no reason that God should not rescue humanity and disregard any "rights" of Satan.[27] Furthermore, argues Anselm, in redeeming humanity from sin, God had no need to "conquer" the devil:

> It is . . . not the case that God needed to come down from heaven to conquer the devil, or to take action against him in order to set mankind free. Rather, God demanded it of man that he should defeat the devil and should pay rec-ompense by means of righteousness, having previously offended God through

25. Wingren, *Man and the Incarnation*, 129.
26. Anselm, *Why God Became Man* 1.3–4.
27. Anselm, *Why God Became Man* 1.7.

sin. Certainly God did not owe the devil anything but punishment, nor did man owe him anything but retribution—to defeat in return him by whom he had been defeated. But, whatever was demanded from man, his debt was to God, not to the devil.[28]

To be clear, Anselm's criticism is relevant only to certain early versions of the Christus Victor model. As seen above, not all early advocates used language suggesting that the devil had rights over humanity, or that justice required God to pay a ransom to Satan. Several of the fathers rejected any notion of a ransom being paid either to God or to Satan, and Irenaeus, the earliest advocate of the model, avoided such imagery altogether.

Christus Victor after Anselm

Following Anselm, the "satisfaction" model and variants such as the "penal substitution" model dominated Western discussions of atonement theology. Nonetheless, the Christus Victor model was so embedded in patristic theology and liturgy that it did not vanish. Motifs of Christus Victor continued to appear in Western discussions of atonement, sometimes alongside discussions of other models such as the satisfaction model.

Thomas Aquinas

As we will see in subsequent chapters, Thomas Aquinas largely follows Anselm in his view of the atonement as satisfaction. However, Thomas's discussion also contains motifs of the Christus Victor model,[29] and not simply because he finds them in the church fathers. Thomas's soteriology includes themes of both satisfaction and deliverance from sin and its bondage.[30]

Thomas argues that we are held captive by sin not only because of guilt but also because we are in bondage to the devil, having been deceived by him. Through his passion, Jesus delivered us from the devil's power by reconciling us to God. The "ransom" paid by Christ for humanity's deliverance from guilt and bondage to sin was his own blood (his life). However, the ransom was paid not to Satan but to God. Neither God nor humanity owe anything to the devil, who exceeded the limitations of the power God assigned to him by tempting humanity and by slaying Christ.[31] Thus Thomas includes themes

28. Anselm, *Why God Became Man* 2.19.
29. Morgan, "*Christus Victor* Motifs," 409–21.
30. Morgan, "*Christus Victor* Motifs," 418.
31. Aquinas, *ST* III.48.4–5; III.49.2.

of both satisfaction and deliverance. In making satisfaction for sin, Christ makes possible forgiveness of sin, reconciliation with God, and deliverance from bondage to the power of the devil.[32] Thomas also utilizes themes of the "deception of the devil": Christ overcomes the devil by "showing him a weak nature so that he might be caught by Him as if by a hook."[33]

Thomas's soteriology also includes the Christus Victor motif of the "harrowing of hell." Christ descended into hell to deliver humanity not only from the punishment of hell but also from death itself.[34] In descending into hell, Christ also delivered the "pre-Christian saints" who were imprisoned in Hades before Christ's passion. In his resurrection, Jesus "delivered the captives" and thus triumphed over Satan.[35]

Martin Luther

In his book *Christus Victor*, Gustaf Aulén asserts that "Luther's teaching can only be rightly understood as a revival of the old classic theme of the atonement as taught by the Fathers, but with a greater depth of treatment."[36] Aulén contrasts Luther both with medieval scholasticism (whose position, for Aulén, largely followed Anselm's satisfaction theory) and with later Protestant scholasticism (beginning with Philip Melanchthon) and Protestant orthodoxy, which largely reverted to a variation on Anselm's satisfaction position.[37]

Luther's writings repeatedly echo motifs of the Christus Victor model. Luther wrote of salvation in terms of a conflict between good and evil, and of the defeat of sin, death, and the devil through the crucifixion and resurrection of Jesus Christ. In addition to the foes of sin, death, and the devil, Luther added the additional enemies of the law and the wrath of God. In his *Commentary on Galatians*, Luther writes that Christ's resurrection "is a victory over the Law, sin, our flesh, the world, the devil, death, hell and all evils." Luther describes the enemies defeated by Christ as "strong and powerful ones, who battle against us continually, namely, our own flesh, all the dangers of the world, the Law, sin, death, the wrath and judgment of God, and the devil himself." This is redemption understood as deliverance from all that threatens human well-being.[38]

32. Morgan, "*Christus Victor* Motifs," 418.
33. Aquinas, *Literal Exposition on Job*, 453; cited in Morgan, "*Christus Victor* Motifs," 417.
34. Aquinas, *ST* III.52.1.
35. Aquinas, *ST* III.52.5; Morgan, "*Christus Victor* Motifs," 419.
36. Aulén, *Christus Victor*, 102.
37. Aulén, *Christus Victor*, 123–33.
38. Luther, *Lectures on Galatians*, 1:1; 1:11–12.

Like the patristic writers, Luther closely connects the incarnation and Christ's defeat of the powers. Salvation is not the work of any creature because only God could defeat these powers.[39] In both his Small and Large Catechism, Luther insists that it is Jesus's identity as Lord (God incarnate) that makes it possible for him to redeem fallen humanity from captivity to sin, death, and the devil.

> If anyone asks, "What do you believe in the second article about Jesus Christ?" answer as briefly as possible, "I believe that Jesus Christ, true Son of God, has become my Lord." What is it "to become a lord"? It means that he has redeemed and released me from sin, from the devil, from death, and from all misfortune. Before this I had no lord or king, but was captive under the power of the devil. I was condemned to death and entangled in sin and blindness.[40]

Accordingly, writes Aulén, "there should, then, be no doubt that in Luther we meet again the classic idea of the Atonement."[41]

Luther scholars generally agree with Aulén that Christus Victor is a key motif in Luther's understanding of the atonement. However, critics express concern that Aulén's reading is one-sided.[42] As Ted Peters points out: "Aulén has supplied us with an accurate presentation of the Christus Victor motif in Luther's christology. But he goes astray when he attempts to make a case for holding that this theory is the only one Luther propounded."[43] While Aulén's discovery of the Christus Victor model in Luther is a helpful rediscovery of a neglected theme, Luther spoke about the atonement in other ways as well.

Christus Victor in a Lutheran Mode: Gustaf Aulén

While the Christus Victor atonement model continued to appear in Western theology following Anselm, it was generally eclipsed by Anselm's satisfaction model. However, this neglect was reversed in the twentieth century with the publication of Gustaf Aulén's *Christus Victor*. Since the publication of Aulén's book in 1930, the Christus Victor model has enjoyed a resurgence in the twentieth and early twenty-first century.[44]

39. Luther, *Lectures on Galatians*, 3:13.
40. Luther, "Large Catechism," 434.
41. Aulén, *Christus Victor*, 108.
42. Peters, "Atonement in Anselm and Luther," 308–10; Leinhard, *Luther*, 281–82.
43. Peters, "Atonement in Anselm and Luther," 309.
44. For two accounts of Christus Victor's continuing contemporary influence, see Harper, "*Christus Victor*"; Pugh, "'Kicking the Daylights Out of the Devil.'"

Gustaf Aulén (1879–1977) was professor of theology at the Lund University and bishop of Strängnäs in the (Lutheran) Church of Sweden.[45] Aulén's book compares three types of atonement: the "classic idea" (Christus Victor), the "Latin theory" (Anselm's satisfaction model), and the "subjective type" (appearing first in Peter Abelard and revived particularly in the liberal Protestant theology associated with Schleiermacher and his theological heirs).

For Aulén, atonement theology had been hampered by a false dichotomy between the so-called objective model of the atonement (associated with Anselm's satisfaction theory) and the subjective model (following Abelard). Aulén's key assertions are (1) that the Christus Victor model provides a genuine third alternative to Anselm and Abelard; (2) that Christus Victor is not merely a "doctrine of salvation" but "atonement in the full sense of the word"[46]; and (3) that one must choose between the three models because they are inherently incompatible—they present mutually exclusive understandings of atonement. Though not explicitly stated, he implies throughout that Christus Victor is the preferred model of atonement.

Aulén's book has been alternately admired and deplored. Some appreciate his recovery of key themes in the atonement theologies of the patristic church and of Luther. Others complain that Aulén misrepresents or misunderstands Anselm's satisfaction theory. Some Luther scholars criticize his reading of Luther as selective and one-sided. Other scholars criticize his Christology as deficient.[47]

Recent authors tend to echo these earlier criticisms. Yet many miss that Aulén noted the criticisms and later either adjusted his language or insisted that the critiques had missed their target. At the same time, he insisted that his fundamental disagreement with the satisfaction model had not changed. His complaint was with the "very theological structure" of the model, which he insisted had "fatal results for the image of God."[48] Because Aulén's mature views are found in two later works—*The Faith of the Christian Church* and *The Drama and the Symbols*—we will draw on these more than *Christus Victor* for the following summary of his views.[49]

---

45. Ovey, "Appropriating Aulén?"
46. Aulén, *Christus Victor*, 4.
47. Jaroslav Pelikan provides a summary of the reception of the book in a later edition (foreword to *Christus Victor*, xx–xix); Peters (cited above) complains that Aulén misreads both Anselm and Luther. See also Fairweather, "Incarnation and Atonement"; Ovey, "Appropriating Aulén?," 321–22.
48. Aulén, *Christus Victor*, ix–x; Aulén, *Drama and the Symbols*, ix–x, 170.
49. In what follows, references will abbreviate *Christus Victor* as CV, *Faith of the Christian Church* as FCC, and *Drama and the Symbols* as DS.

Christus Victor in Aulén's Theology

The title of Aulén's book *The Drama and the Symbols* points to a key theme in his theology. As Creator, God is neither part of the created world nor an object among other objects in the world in which we live. Consequently, faith cannot speak of God in himself.[50] This does not mean that human beings cannot know or speak anything truthfully about God. However, it does mean that all language about God originates in divine revelation, and therefore that the biblical message concerning God in Christ is definitive for our knowledge of God.[51]

Since, however, any language we use to refer to God is necessarily drawn from the world in which we live, such language is necessarily inadequate. All biblical language referring to God is ultimately taken from the realms of nature and human personal relationships, and such language is necessarily symbolic.[52] A necessary corollary of these positive symbols is the fundamental axiom of the difference between God and creation.[53] To attempt to replace symbolic language about God with adequate definitions would be to make God an object among other objects in the world. Christian faith does make definite statements about God, but such statements are necessarily symbolic.[54]

Another important corollary to the symbolic character of theological statements is that symbols derive their meaning from their contexts and internal relations. One of the implications of this principle is what Aulén calls "derationalization." Theology is not irrational, but to do theology rationally means to do justice to the nature of the material of faith. This is a principal reason behind Aulén's objection to what he calls "scholasticism." In scholastic theology, one or two of the symbols of the Bible—particularly the notions of merit and satisfaction—were removed from their symbolic context within Scripture and set within a rationalistic context that was alien to the internal logic of what Aulén calls the "radical gospel." Instead of a love that "surpasses all understanding," scholasticism assumed that God's love was something that could be "rationally calculated, motivated, and explained."[55] The more we come to understand the nature of divine love, the more unreasonable it would be to look for a rationalistic explanation for it.[56]

50. *FCC*, 80; *DS*, 90.
51. *FCC*, 77–78.
52. *DS*, 89, 90, 100–110.
53. *FCC*, 81.
54. *DS*, 97.
55. *DS*, x, 130–43.
56. *DS*, 140.

If symbols provide the primary motifs for theology, then "drama" provides the plot. Aulén repeatedly uses the word "drama" to describe the subject matter of Scripture, insisting that Christus Victor is the central plotline.[57] Aulén describes the Christus Victor model as a "dramatic perspective," "marked by the dominant role played by the motif of battle and victory."[58] The invisible God is the principal character of the drama, but because God is invisible, the only adequate way to describe God is through the use of symbols. Within the universal drama, there is the more limited drama of God's election of the covenant people Israel. This is brought to its head in the "drama of Christ," which is the "turning point" and provides the "meaning of the drama, the aim of the battle." The incarnate Christ has the "key role" of throwing light on what has gone before and what will come after, and the image of God is determined through what happens in Christ. God's ultimate aim has been revealed in this drama of Christ, and no image of God can be considered Christian other than that which is seen in Christ at the drama's climax. This revelation of the divine image does not mean, however, that God has ceased to be invisible. Even after the incarnation, knowledge of God remains "more or less adequate," and we still depend on symbolic language. The Christus Victor model is thus a symbolic reading of Scripture as a drama.[59]

While Aulén insists that we cannot define God and that language about God is clothed in symbols, this does not mean that the Christian notion of God is vague or unspecified. Christian faith speaks definitively about God insofar as God's character has been made known by Christ and his work. Specifically, God in Christ seeks out sinful humanity and enters into communion with human beings. The definitive content of the Christian message, then, is that God is love: "Consequently, every affirmation about God becomes an affirmation about his love. Nothing can be said about God, his power, his opposition to evil, or anything else, which is not in the last analysis a statement about his love. . . . Nothing more decisive can be stated about the Christian conception of God than the affirmation: 'God is love.'"[60]

No divine activity can be separated from God's love, and every act of God is, in the final analysis, a realization of God's love—even those acts that at first might seem otherwise.[61] The cross, where God's love is known most fully, reveals that the love of God is a "suffering love." This should not be misconstrued, however, to mean that the primary significance of the cross is

57. FCC, 38.
58. DS, ix.
59. DS, 64; CV, 4, 5; DS, vii, 116, 144, 169.
60. FCC, 112, 106–16.
61. FCC, 139.

that Jesus was a martyr, as is often emphasized in modern theology. On the contrary, Aulén asserts that the "cross is a victory" and "God's suffering love is a victorious love."[62]

Closely aligned with Aulén's emphasis on God's love and directly related to his Christus Victor emphasis is the theme of "moral dualism." Aulén distinguishes between metaphysical dualism and what might be called "moral dualism" or "dramatic dualism"—a "dualism" of God's triumph over evil. Christian faith opposes metaphysical dualism. God is not a divine power in competition with other relatively strong powers; he is the Creator on whom all existence is completely dependent. Evil is a corruption of God's creation, and God is utterly sovereign over evil, whether in grace or in judgment. At the same time, God's loving will struggles or battles against everything that opposes it. Aulén uses the word "dualism" to describe this conflict. The conflict is not chronic, however, since the victory has been won in the crucifixion and resurrection of Jesus Christ.[63]

This theme of opposition between God and the contending power of evil necessarily means that God's will is not always fulfilled. Aulén rejects any understanding of divine sovereignty that suggests divine determinism or omnicausality. To say that everything that happens takes place according to God's will not only obscures the seriousness of God's opposition to evil but also negates the biblical affirmation that God is the God of love. While the sovereign God of love does not will the evil that happens, he is able to use evil to realize his loving purposes in opposition to the powers arrayed against him. Accordingly, for Christian faith, the problem of evil is not to find an explanation for its existence but to overcome it.[64]

Moral dualism also grounds Christus Victor's description of atonement as a conflict with sin, death, and the devil. Aulén suggests that the key motif is of evil as a "demonic spiritual power" that enslaves human beings to sin, that exceeds the wrongdoing of particular individuals, and that shows its power in "the most cruel oppression of human life." Although he distinguishes between the symbolic motif of the demonic and its expression, Aulén was concerned that modern theology will more likely fail to take the conflict motif seriously than to overly literalize the language of ransom and defeat of Satanic powers.[65]

For Aulén, a major strength of the Christus Victor model is that it connects the doctrine of atonement to all of theology rather than focusing

62. DS, 177.
63. CV, 4; FCC, 38, 175, 178.
64. FCC, 126, 169, 171, 175; DS, 73.
65. FCC, 63, 244; DS, 155–56.

on the death of Christ alone. Christus Victor understands atonement as a "drama" with a series of key plot moments rather than a single incident. Aulén especially emphasizes creation and sin, the death of Jesus as well as the life and mission of Jesus and his resurrection, the ongoing life of the church, and eschatology.

Creation

Creation is not simply an event in the past; it is ongoing and has a goal. Creation is connected from the beginning with Christ because all things were created in Christ. The God of creation is the same God as the God of redemption, and redemption itself is an act of continuous creation, a "new creation." The new creation happens through the victory of Christ. In the realm of history, divine love gives meaning to existence in the continuing struggle of the divine will against opposing forces. In the light of Christian faith, every moment is a decision for or against the divine loving will.[66]

Aulén's understanding of sin accords with his understanding of God and creation. He endorses the Reformers' definition of sin as "unbelief" but clarifies that unbelief is not to be interpreted cognitively as the lack of intellectual acceptance of particular beliefs about God. Rather, since "belief" as "faith" entails "trust and confidence in God"—more specifically, "fellowship with God," the dominion of the human being by God's love[67]—sin (or unbelief) is "egotism," opposition to God's will by seeking one's own will rather than allowing oneself to be defined by God's love.[68]

Christology

Just as Aulén connects creation and redemption, so he links the incarnation and the atonement. The incarnation is necessary because only God can accomplish redemption, and Jesus Christ is the personal presence of the love of God in the world.[69] At the same time, the incarnation cannot be separated from the atonement nor the atonement from the incarnation. In Aulén's words, "The incarnation is perfected on the cross. Here divine love appears in unfathomableness and inexhaustible power."[70]

66. FCC, 157, 161; DS, 52, 59, 77.
67. FCC, 234.
68. FCC, 233–38.
69. FCC, 194.
70. FCC, 195.

Aulén insists that the atonement was a divine-human work in which both the deity and humanity of Christ were equally involved. Jesus Christ's work cannot be split into two parts, one divine and one human.[71] In the New Testament, the work of Christ is viewed from two perspectives: On the one hand, Jesus is a human being like other human beings. He battles temptation, prays, and suffers. At the same time, Jesus is acknowledged as Christ "the Lord" and is given the same titles that the Old Testament gives to God. He is Lord, but "this Kyrios is none other than the crucified Jesus of Nazareth." Because the work of Christ is simultaneously "a human work through and through" and "a divine work through and through," the acts of Jesus in his humanity are simultaneously the acts of God.[72]

In addition to the unity both of Christ's person and work and of Christ's identity as fully human and fully divine, Aulén also insists on joining the atonement and Jesus's human life and earthly mission. Aulén refuses to restrict the atonement to Jesus's death on the cross but interprets Jesus's entire life in terms of Christus Victor motifs. The motifs of struggle and victory are present throughout Jesus's ministry.[73] Jesus's way of obedience to his Father conflicts with the way of the demonic powers. He links the coming of the kingdom of God with his own person and associates his battle against evil with the presence of the kingdom (Luke 11:20). His life of constant prayer is itself part of this battle (Matt. 26:38). Jesus's conflict is also with the religious leaders of his day. Like the prophets of the Old Testament, Jesus sometimes preaches with anger and severity. His is not a gentle or mild message, and opposition to his message leads to his crucifixion.[74]

Just as the Christus Victor model integrates Christ's deity with his humanity, his person with his work, and his life and mission with the cross, so Aulén insists on connecting the crucifixion and resurrection. They are intrinsically related: "The cross is as essential for the resurrection as the resurrection is for the cross. The living Lord bears the marks of the cross. But without the resurrection the cross would be simply the cross of martyrdom. In the light of the resurrection it is the sign of victory. For Christians, therefore, *theologia crucis* is at the same time *theologia gloriae Christi*."[75]

The resurrection reveals that Jesus's death was a victory—not only Jesus's victory but also God's victory in Christ, a victory over all the enemies of God. This essential connection between the cross and the resurrection was

71. *CV*, ix; *DS*, 198.
72. *DS*, 202.
73. *FCC*, 199.
74. *DS* 111–15, 153–67.
75. *FCC*, 217.

robustly preserved in the early church. However, in much of later Western theology, the focus of atonement was placed on Jesus's suffering and death on the cross while the resurrection was overlooked. Aulén is especially critical of the satisfaction doctrine of the atonement for this separation.[76]

The Atonement Logic of Christus Victor

At several points in his book *Christus Victor*, Aulén summarizes his understanding of the logic of the Christus Victor model of atonement, distinguishing it from the satisfaction model: "The most marked difference between the 'dramatic' type and the so-called 'objective' type lies in the fact that the dramatic type represents the work of Atonement or reconciliation as from first to last a work of God himself, a *continuous* Divine work; while according to the objective type, the act of Atonement has indeed its origin in God's will, but is, in its carrying out, an offering made by Christ as man and on man's behalf, and may therefore be called a *discontinuous* Divine work."[77]

It is on the basis of such passages that some of Aulén's critics interpret his theology as "monophysite." Aulén's contrast between the *continuity* of divine action and his critique of Anselm's notion that "Christ as man makes atonement on man's behalf" has been taken to demonstrate that Aulén misses the significance of Jesus's humanity for the doctrine of the atonement.[78] Recognizing the force of these criticisms, Aulén emphasizes in later writings that the atonement is simultaneously a divine and a human work. The work of Christ is completed on the cross, but the cross must be seen in connection with the whole life of Christ. The conflict to which Jesus's life was dedicated is epitomized in the struggle and victory of the cross—it is the consummation of the incarnation.[79]

What, then, is the internal logic behind Aulén's assertion that atonement is a "single movement" from God to humanity? The following points seem to be central to his argument: First, divine love is always prior to human action and is "spontaneous." Divine love is not a response to a condition in human beings.[80]

Second, and closely related, God's forgiveness is a free gift of love that cannot be earned or conditioned. Aulén rejects the "dilemma" between divine love

76. *DS*, 168–70.
77. *CV*, 5.
78. E.g., Fairweather, "Incarnation and Atonement," 173.
79. *FCC*, 197.
80. *FCC*, 113–15.

and divine justice posed by Anselm and his followers. Justice does not need to be satisfied in order for God to forgive. God's justice is simply divine love in opposition to evil. Divine love's ultimate response to evil is reconciliation, not judgment.[81] Moreover, divine judgment is not punitive. In the presence of divine love, one either is restored and reconciled to God or, if one rejects divine love, is separated from divine love. This is not a "punishment" but the inevitable consequence of rejecting divine love.[82]

Third, and related to the preceding two points, Aulén affirms that God does not forgive because Jesus has satisfied divine justice. Rather, in his love God forgives freely. Jesus's satisfaction of divine justice in his life, death, and resurrection is the consequence and expression of that love. Jesus has not been punished instead of us. Rather, in Jesus Christ, God has willingly taken upon himself the full consequences of our sin (opposition to divine love) and has conquered evil and death through divine love and resurrection life. In the atoning life, death, and resurrection of Jesus Christ, divine love reestablishes fellowship through an unconditional act of forgiveness that creates faith.[83]

Aulén's essential critique of the satisfaction model is that it is an unbiblical rationalization. The satisfaction model presumes that divine love must be conditioned by divine justice, rather than divine love being free and uncoerced, and divine forgiveness unconditioned. The satisfaction model interprets the judicial metaphors of Scripture in terms of alien, extrinsic legal categories rather than using the intrinsic logic of the symbols that occur in the Bible. Reformation scholasticism continued to understand justification according to the Latin medieval categories of atonement—that God's righteousness must obtain satisfaction *before* God can forgive. Scholasticism thus exchanged the unconditional love of the God of the Bible for a love conditioned by an abstract notion of justice.[84]

Evaluation

Since Aulén, numerous theologians have appropriated Christus Victor motifs either in whole or in part. In recent decades, such motifs have been embraced by paleo-orthodox evangelicals like the late Robert Webber and by Anabaptist theologians such as Gregory Boyd, Thomas Finger, and J. Denny Weaver.[85]

81. *FCC*, 120, 147.
82. *FCC*, 148–51.
83. *FCC*, 141, 182, 183, 259–60; *DS*, 163.
84. *CV*, 156; *FCC*, 149, 210–11; *DS*, 131–32.
85. See Harper, "*Christus Victor*"; Pugh, "'Kicking the Daylights Out of the Devil'"; Weaver, *Nonviolent Atonement*; Finger, "Christus Victor and the Creeds"; Webber, *Ancient Future Faith*, 49–58; Boyd, *God at War*.

What are the advantages of the Christus Victor model of atonement? First, Christus Victor takes seriously the pervasive theme of moral dualism in Scripture. Scripture portrays the work of Christ as a struggle with and victory over the powers of sin, death, and Satan, and it depicts demonic forces as cosmic and corporate powers that enslave human beings and pervert God's good creation. Of the various atonement models, Christus Victor is most in accord with the modern rediscovery of the significance of "principalities and powers" in Scripture.[86]

Second, the Christus Victor model of atonement extends beyond the cross. Christus Victor views atonement in terms of the complete work of God in Christ, encompassing creation, God's covenant with Israel, the incarnation and earthly life of Jesus, the crucifixion and resurrection of Jesus, the ongoing struggle with sin and evil "between the times" of Christ's resurrection and second coming, and ultimately God's complete victory over evil in the "new creation" of the eschaton.

Third, of all the models of atonement, Christus Victor takes most seriously the symbolic or metaphorical nature of atonement language. Even a cursory reading of atonement in terms of conflict and victory reveals that Jesus's struggle with the powers of evil defies any straightforward notion of military conquest. Jesus's victory is won through nonviolence rather than coercion, and it is through Jesus's death and suffering that God accomplishes his purposes. That paradox was one of the delights of the church fathers. It also delighted Martin Luther, who contrasted a theology of the cross (*theologia crucis*)—God's power hidden in the weakness of the cross—with a theology of glory (*theologia gloriae*).

Finally, the Christus Victor model of atonement speaks of atonement in such a way that it truly is good news. Christus Victor describes atonement as a struggle with and victory over evil and all that is opposed to God, and it emphasizes that insofar as all human beings are sinful, we are enslaved to evil and on the wrong side of this struggle. Yet God in Christ opposes and destroys evil through his incarnation, self-emptying of the cross, and victorious resurrection. In Jesus, God conquered and destroyed our sinfulness by willingly taking the consequences of our sin on himself, thus granting us unconditional forgiveness. To be justified by faith means to be delivered from our self-centered egotism as we are embraced by divine love.

Despite these vital positive dimensions, Christus Victor cannot stand alone as a complete model of the atonement, especially as formulated by Aulén.

86. Dawn, "Powers and Principalities." See also Walter Wink's several works on this theme, e.g., *Naming the Powers*.

Although Aulén consistently refers to the Christus Victor model as the "classic view," his insistence that theology can say nothing about God in himself but only in relation to creation is at odds with patristic theology. As seen in the previous chapter, patristic theology highlighted the unity between God's trinitarian being and the economy of salvation, the unity of the deity and humanity of Jesus Christ in the single divine person of the Logos as the Second Person of the Trinity, and the union of sinful and redeemed humanity with the human nature of Christ in salvation and deification. The incarnational theology of Irenaeus and Athanasius makes no sense if we are unable to say anything about God in himself.

A related problem is Aulén's insistence that we can *only* speak of God in symbolic language. This leads to an almost exclusive emphasis on the metaphors or symbols of conflict and victory as well as the theme of redemption as reconciliation. The resulting doctrine omits a significant theme in atonement theology that was the focus of the previous chapter: unity. As noted above, this focus on union was the key to Irenaeus's discussion of "recapitulation." Numerous church fathers go beyond metaphorical language to speak of atonement in the ontological terms of union and transformation. By contrast, union with Christ is more or less absent from Aulén's doctrine of the atonement.[87]

Aulén's rejection of the satisfaction model also leads him to reject any notion of sacrifice as an "offering to God." Aulén is willing to speak of Christ's death on the cross as a "sacrifice of divine love," but he insists that Christ's sacrifice abolishes any interpretation of sacrifice as a way to "influence the divine power." The sacrifice of Christ is not a "compensation."[88] However, there are other ways to speak of Christ's "sacrifice" as an "offering" that imply neither "compensation" nor an attempt to "influence the divine power." Yet Aulén does not acknowledge these.

What ultimately seems absent from Aulén's version of Christus Victor is the significance of the "vicarious humanity" of Jesus Christ. In the atonement theologies of Irenaeus and Athanasius, Jesus's humanity is not only significant in that the incarnate God opposed and conquered the powers of evil. It is equally significant that, as the "second Adam," Jesus lived a perfect human life and represented us before God. Moreover, fallen and redeemed human beings now "participate" in God through union with the perfected humanity of the crucified and risen Jesus Christ. This notion of Christ's "vicarious humanity" is thus central to Irenaeus's theology of "recapitulation," to Athanasius's theology of "participation," and to patristic notions

87. *FCC*, 143.
88. *FCC*, 207.

of "sacrifice" and "offering." It is a major presupposition of later theology as well—for example, in Martin Luther's notion of the "joyous exchange."[89] And, of course, Jesus Christ's "vicarious humanity" is a key presupposition of later theologies of "satisfaction" and "substitution."

An instability results with the Christus Victor model. On the one hand, it emphasizes key themes that are often overlooked by other atonement models. On the other hand, it seems necessary to say more about the work of Jesus Christ than that Jesus opposed and conquered the powers of evil, or even that Jesus reconciled sinners to God. The question of *how* Jesus does this remains unclear. The missing element of the "vicarious humanity" of Jesus Christ leaves Christus Victor incomplete and pushes us in the direction of either (or both) the "incarnational" or "satisfaction/substitution" model of atonement.

89. Leinhard, *Luther*, 131–35.

3

. . .

Atonement as Satisfaction

Anselm of Canterbury

Anselm of Canterbury (1033/34–1109) marks a major transition in the history of the doctrine of the atonement. Historically, he is credited with the first systematic reflection on the doctrine in his work *Cur Deus Homo (Why God Became Man)*. This work not only definitively rejects earlier patristic models, which focus on atonement as a ransom paid to Satan or as a victory over or deception of the devil; it also introduces a new paradigm of atonement as *satisfaction*.[1] Anselm's theological method is one of the first examples of scholasticism, a form of theology that incorporated philosophical categories combined with tight logical reasoning. Scholasticism dominated medieval theology. It continued into the Reformation period and beyond, as can be seen in the post-Reformation scholasticism of both Roman Catholic theology and Lutheran and Reformed theology. Anselm's concept of satisfaction shifts the focus of atonement from Christus Victor metaphors of victory over sin, death, and the devil to legal metaphors of punishment, retribution, and restoration of honor—a shift that led to a significant change of focus in Western atonement theologies.

Anselm's satisfaction model was not immediately popular and met resistance in the theology of Peter Abelard (see next chapter). Nonetheless, owing in large part to the influence Peter Lombard's *Sentences* had on theology,

1. Harnack, *History of Dogma*, 6:56.

satisfaction became a common theme in the theologies of numerous medieval theologians.[2] Though differing at particular points, Anselm's basic concern about divine justice and human punishment reappears in the later penal substitution models of Reformers such as John Calvin. For these reasons, Anselm is widely acknowledged as the most significant figure for Western understandings of the doctrine of the atonement.

Despite Anselm's influence and historical significance, objections similar to those raised by Peter Abelard have appeared in the history of atonement theology. The late nineteenth century in particular witnessed an onrush of objections to Anselm's approach. Church historian Adolf von Harnack wrote that "there are so many defects that this theory is entirely untenable." Among other things, Harnack criticized Anselm's satisfaction theory as rationalistic, full of contradictions, and Nestorian in Christology. Harnack characterized "the mythological conception of God as the mighty private man, who is incensed at the injury done to His honour and does not forego his wrath till He has received an at least adequately great alternative," as the "worst thing" in Anselm's theory.[3]

As discussed in the previous chapter, Gustaf Aulén characterized Anselm's satisfaction theory as the "objective" or "Latin" model in contrast to both the "subjective" model (following Abelard) and what he called the "classic" or Christus Victor model of the church fathers. Aulén criticized Anselm for rationalistically forcing atonement into a "juridical scheme," for making divine mercy conditional on justice, for making atonement a "divided work" between the humanity and divinity of Christ (Christ's human nature pays satisfaction to his divine nature) rather than a single continuous divine work of salvation, and for omitting the intrinsic connection between the crucifixion and resurrection of Jesus.[4]

In more recent decades, feminist theologians have objected that Anselm's satisfaction theory is "abusive," sadistic, a form of "cosmic child abuse."[5] Mennonite theologian J. Denny Weaver has also argued for a nonviolent Christus Victor atonement model in contrast to what he characterizes as the inherently violent models of Anselm and his theological descendants.[6]

In response to these negative evaluations of Anselm's atonement theology, a number of more appreciative studies have appeared in recent decades. These

2. Burns, "Concept of Satisfaction." Lombard's *Sentences* was the standard textbook equivalent in theology throughout the medieval period.
3. Harnack, *History of Dogma*, 6:70–78.
4. Aulén, *Christus Victor*, 81–92.
5. Keshgegian, "Scandal of the Cross."
6. Weaver, *Nonviolent Atonement*.

have followed two basic approaches. The first approach, while acknowledging areas of concern, has argued that these critics have read Anselm carelessly, or at least have misunderstood his argument. The second approach has gone further, suggesting not only that Anselm has been misread but that the controverted passages must be understood in light of other key passages in Anselm, which demonstrate that Anselm's thought is in harmony with earlier patristic atonement theology.

There are thus three basic readings of Anselm's satisfaction model of atonement in recent theology: antagonistic, critically appreciative, and harmonistic. In what follows, we hope to provide a charitable reading of Anselm's atonement theology. At the same time, we seek to take account of the reasons he can be interpreted in such different ways. In the end, no single reading will satisfy all readers of Anselm.

Historical Background

We begin by taking note of some of the concerns raised by Anselm's historical context, which will help to shed light on his argument. Four concerns stand out.

First, Anselm faced a number of theological opponents throughout his career, and his later works in particular were often presented against the views of hostile enemies. The "unbelievers" to whom Anselm refers in *Cur Deus Homo* almost certainly included Northern European Jews. They objected to Christianity, first, because of Christian allegorical interpretation of the Old Testament and, second, out of concern for the honor of the dignity of God. They thought God's honor was threatened by the Christian doctrine of the incarnation, by which God had been dishonored in the crucifixion of Jesus.[7]

Second, Anselm was the Benedictine abbot at Bec and was exposed to scholastic influences through his students who had come from the new "secular" schools connected with cathedrals rather than the monasteries. Anselm's student Boso, who is his dialogue partner throughout *Cur Deus Homo*, accurately summarizes the kinds of arguments used in the *Sententia* of the cathedral school of another Anselm, Anselm of Laon. In engaging with the arguments of the cathedral schools and employing their scholastic method of theology, Anselm was doing something new.[8]

7. Southern, *Saint Anselm*, 200. Cf. Anselm, *Why God Became Man* 1.3.
8. Southern, *Saint Anselm*, 202–5.

Third, some claim that the historical background to Anselm's notion of satisfaction can be found in feudal notions of honor that vassals owed to their liege lords. Anselm understood the relationship between God and humanity as analogous to that between a lord and his vassals. An argument can be made that Anselm's theological position can be distinguished from its feudal imagery, but it is still the case that Anselm's theology reflected his social setting.[9]

Finally, Anselm was a monk, and obedience was the foundation of medieval monastic life, as expressed in the Benedictine Rule. The notion of monastic obedience colors Anselm's understanding of the relationship between God and humanity. He understands the nature of sin to lie in disobedience of human beings as subordinates to God, the One to whom allegiance is due. The background to Anselm's understanding of atonement is thus both feudal and monastic, and his arguments include feudal and monastic imagery. While his theological arguments cannot simply be reduced to these medieval notions of honor and obedience, they do provide key categories for his understanding of God, God's honor, sin, and salvation.[10]

Methodology: Faith Seeking Understanding

Anselm's atonement model is regularly criticized for being rationalistic. As noted above, one of the major influences on Anselm's theology was the cathedral schools and their scholastic methodology. However, it is not quite accurate to describe Anselm's methodology in *Cur Deus Homo* as rationalistic. There are three key tools in his theological toolkit.

First, beginning with his *Proslogion* and continuing with "On the Incarnation of the Word" (*Epistola de Incarnatione Verbi*), Anselm introduces the principle of "faith seeking understanding" (*fides quaerens intellectum*)—or otherwise stated, "I believe in order to understand" (*credo ut intelligam*).[11] *Cur Deus Homo* repeats this principle. In his commendation to Pope Urban II, Anselm makes note of this principle, and he again repeats it by placing it in the mouth of his dialogue partner, Boso.[12]

John McIntyre has provided a helpful discussion of how this works in Anselm's texts. Anselm is not a rationalist in the sense of engaging in "natural theology." In each of Anselm's works, the starting point is the faith that

9. Southern, *Saint Anselm*, 214–15, 221–27.
10. Southern, *Saint Anselm*, 216–21.
11. Anselm, *Proslogion* 1.
12. Anselm, *Why God Became Man*, "Commendation of the Work to Pope Urban II."

has been revealed in the Holy Scriptures and summarized in the creeds. At the same time, in each of Anselm's works, the believer is engaged in an act of understanding. There is an article of faith that is to be investigated and understood in more depth, an unknown "X" that a hostile inquirer has brought into question. Anselm's methodology is to begin with other articles of faith, or with other beliefs that both the believer and the challenger hold in common: A B C D. He then argues that A B C D logically imply "X." Thus, if the challenger accepts A B C D and is consistent, he or she must also accept "X." While the inquiry proceeds from the standpoint of faith, the "X" to be probed is not provided by the standpoint of faith but is raised by the challenger, who contests a particular affirmation of Scripture or the creed.[13] In *Cur Deus Homo*, the "X" is supplied by a question: "By what logic or necessity did God become man, and by his death as we believe and profess, restore life to the world, when he could have done this through the agency of some other person, angelic or human, or simply by willing it?"[14]

Second, crucial to understanding Anselm's discussion in *Cur Deus Homo* is the distinction between "necessity" (*necessitas*) and "fittingness" (*convenientias*). In the crucial question noted above, Anselm asks, "By what *logic or necessity* (*qua scilicet ratione vel necessitate*) did God become man?" In a key passage, Anselm distinguishes between arguments that are "fitting" and those that are "necessary." Describing the economy of salvation, he states, "For it was appropriate [*oportebat*] that, just as death entered the human race through a man's disobedience, so life should be restored through a man's obedience. . . . Also that the devil, who defeated the man whom he beguiled through the taste of a tree, should himself similarly be defeated by a man through tree-induced suffering which he, the devil, inflicted."[15] Anselm is echoing here the kind of typological imagery associated with Irenaeus's discussion of recapitulation. Boso, Anselm's conversation partner, finds this language unhelpful. Such notions, he says, are "beautiful," but they are really no more than pictorial imagery and are unconvincing to unbelievers. On the contrary, "What has to be demonstrated, therefore, is the logical soundness of the truth, that is: a cogent reason which proves [*veritatis soliditas rationabilis, id est necessitas quae probet*] that God ought to have, or could have, humbled himself for the purposes which we proclaim. Then, in order that the physical reality of the truth, so to speak, may shine forth all the more, these

13. McIntyre, *Anselm and His Critics*, 28–40. McIntyre is building on the argument of Barth, *Anselm*.
14. Anselm, *Why God Became Man* 1.1.
15. Anselm, *Why God Became Man* 1.3.

appropriatenesses [*convenientiae*] may be set out as pictorial representations of this physical reality."[16]

The preceding makes clear that Anselm distinguishes between, on the one hand, "fitting" metaphors and types of the atonement (such as the defeat of Satan) and, on the other hand, arguments based on *rational necessity*. As noted in the previous chapter, Anselm rejected the notion of a ransom paid to Satan as morally untenable—as God's enemy, Satan has no rights, and God owes him nothing![17] However, the preceding also makes clear that, while Anselm finds typological and metaphorical accounts of the atonement helpful, and therefore "fitting" supplements to a rational account, any convincing account of the atonement must be rationally demonstrable and necessary. Anselm thus understands his account of atonement as "satisfaction" to be a rational and literal explanation of the necessity of the incarnation, not merely a fitting metaphor or image.

By what rational criteria does Anselm distinguish between fittingness and necessity? The crucial difference seems to lie in another distinction—that of "unfittingness"—and has to do with the nature of God. Fittingness has to do with the kinds of things that God might appropriately do, from which no certain conclusion follows. Accordingly, Anselm never argues from fittingness to necessity. He does, however, regularly argue from unfittingness—what God *cannot* do—to necessity. Anselm consistently argues from the standpoint of God's will, which *must* be fulfilled in a manner consistent with God's good and righteous character. For example, because God is infinitely wise, he cannot do evil but always acts righteously. Anselm presents such arguments in the negative language of unfittingness. Thus, "It was *not fitting* that what God had planned for mankind should be utterly nullified, and the plan in question could not be brought into effect unless the human race were set free by its Creator in person."[18]

By this logic—given that God's nature is necessarily good, wise, and all-powerful—if an outcome is unfitting, God will necessarily prevent it. If the only way to avoid an outcome that would be unfitting is that God perform a certain action, God will necessarily perform it. As we will see in what follows, Anselm argues that it would be unfitting for creation to perish given God's original intention for creation. Accordingly, salvation follows from what could be called a *conditional necessity*.[19] (This is not Anselm's terminology, but it is what he means.) A conditional necessity is a necessity that is contingent in itself but becomes necessary given some other irresistible cause. Having

16. Anselm, *Why God Became Man* 1.4.
17. Anselm, *Why God Became Man* 1.7; 2.19.
18. Anselm, *Why God Became Man* 1.4 (emphasis added); cf. 1.10.
19. Root, "Necessity and Unfittingness."

eliminated all other possibilities, "the one possibility of salvation implied by a process of elimination is now described positively."[20]

Third, among Anselm's more controversial methodological tools is his notion of "apart from Christ" (*remoto Christo*). In the preface to *Cur Deus Homo*, Anselm states that the first book "proves, by unavoidable logical steps, that, *supposing Christ were left out of the case, as if there had never existed anything to do with him*, it is impossible that, without him, any member of the human race could be saved."[21] While puzzling at first glance, the principle is in accord with Anselm's *credo ut intelligam*. Anselm presupposes that his opponent assumes much of the Christian faith—the A B C D—but specifically denies X—the need for an incarnation. As a believer, Anselm does not suspend his own belief in the incarnation. However, in order to enter into the perspective of the unbeliever and thus avoid begging the debated question, he refrains from introducing any argument from Jesus's life or passion. He assumes that the unbeliever will grant the other points of the Christian faith—the A B C D. Arguing from these granted premises, Anselm has confidence that the unbeliever will reach the same conclusion concerning the incarnation that the believer already holds by faith.

Finally, Anselm's atonement theology involves what might be called "losing the devil from the ransom equation." As noted in the previous chapter, the Christus Victor model raised the question, To whom was the "ransom" paid: God or the devil? Anselm finds a payment by God to the devil unconscionable. However, he continues to use the language of "debt" and "payment," which provides a central theme in his notion of satisfaction. Given that the payment cannot possibly be given to Satan, Anselm assumes it must be made to God. Consequently, Anselm's atonement theology abandons a threefold scheme of redemption—God/humanity/Satan—for a straightforward scheme of a conflict between God and humanity. How can humanity—the debtor—pay a debt that must be paid yet is beyond our ability to pay?[22]

The Argument in Summary

Anselm's discussion in *Cur Deus Homo* takes the form of a lengthy dialogue between Anselm and Boso. The argument proceeds as an interchange in which one proposes a position that the other finds inadequate, in response to which a correction is offered by a new proposal, finally arriving at what is perceived by both parties as a satisfactory solution, before then moving on to a new proposal.

20. Root, "Necessity and Unfittingness," 226.
21. Anselm, preface to *Why God Became Man* (emphasis added).
22. Southern, *Saint Anselm*, 207–12.

The book is divided into two parts. Book 1 sets the scene of the human dilemma: humanity has fallen into sin and needs salvation, yet we are unable to save ourselves. Book 2 deals with the topic of how Jesus Christ, the "God-man" (the *Deus-homo* in *Cur Deus Homo*), is the solution to humanity's problem—the means of salvation that satisfies God's honor.

Book 1 can be outlined as follows:

1. God is the Greatest Good (*summum bonum*), and God created human beings righteous in order that, by rejoicing in God, they might be happy. As rational beings, humans have the capacity to distinguish between right and wrong and to prefer the greater over the lesser good. God's intention in creation was that human beings would love and choose the highest good, which is only possible if they are righteous. Human beings ought to (or "owe the debt" to) subject their wills to the will of God. One who does not pay this debt is taking away from God that which belongs to him, and to refuse to honor God by obeying his will is the very definition of sin. Anyone who sins is under obligation to pay back to God that which they owe him. This "paying back" is the "satisfaction" that every sinner owes to God.[23]

   While Anselm speaks of sin as disobedience and failure to pay a debt, he also speaks of sin in terms of the disruption of order in the universe. When human beings submit to God's will, they maintain their proper place within the order of the universe, thus maintaining the beauty of the universe. Disobedience does not harm God, since nothing can add to or subtract from God's honor; but when a sinner refuses to obey God, they disrupt the order and beauty of the universe. It is in this sense that sin "dishonors" God by marring his creation.[24]

2. All human beings have sinned, which leads to a dilemma. On the one hand, sin introduces a disharmony into the creation by dishonoring God. As long as the sinner does not repay the lost honor, they remain in a state of guilt. Mere repentance is not sufficient, because every sinner is obligated not only to repay that which has been lost through dishonoring God but also to provide an additional compensation to God that goes above and beyond that which was lost. It would not be fitting for God simply to forgive such a dishonor, for this would allow the disorder of the universe to continue. Accordingly, it necessarily follows that either "satisfaction" (voluntary compensation) or punishment follows from every sin. The

23. Anselm, *Why God Became Man* 2.1; 1.11.
24. Anselm, *Why God Became Man* 1.15.

distinction between "satisfaction" and punishment is crucial in Anselm's account. Punishment and satisfaction are alternatives (*aut poena aut satisfactio*), not equivalents. Those who do not provide voluntary satisfaction to compensate for an offense will receive punishment instead. Thus, importantly, Anselm does not endorse a *penal* understanding of atonement. Christ's death is a "satisfaction," *not* a punishment, because it is voluntary. By contrast, if a sinner does not willingly give to God the honor that is due to him, then honor must be given unwillingly through punishment. Since humanity was created for the happiness that comes through obeying God's will, the unwilling deprivation of happiness is the "paying back" or "satisfaction" for the sin of disobeying God's will.[25] Anselm also states (almost in passing) that death is a penalty for sin: "If [the human being] had never sinned, he would never die."[26]

3. On the other hand, the introduction of sin and death leads to the problem that God's purpose for the universe might be frustrated. Humanity is incapable of "paying back" the satisfaction required to restore God's honor, but to leave humanity in a state of punishment would leave God's original intention for the universe unfulfilled, which would be "unfitting." It is therefore (conditionally) "necessary" for God to supply some means of atonement in order to satisfy his honor and to restore the universe to its original order. This restoration requires an act of obedience that would provide not only the original honor due to God but also the additional recompense of "satisfaction" for the dishonor introduced by sin. Sinful human beings cannot provide this recompense because, as sinners, they have already failed to pay the original debt of honor and even the slightest sin against the infinite worth of God's honor incurs an infinite debt. Sinners are unable to undo the dishonor introduced by sin, let alone provide the additional required satisfaction. Thus, the fundamental dilemma is that human beings owe to God something that they are incapable of paying back, and yet they cannot be saved unless they repay it.[27]

Book 2 provides the solution to this dilemma:

4. It is necessary that redemption be brought about by someone who is both God and human. On the one hand, only God can provide payment to God as recompense for the infinite debt owed to God's honor—a

25. Anselm, *Why God Became Man* 1.12–15, 22.
26. Anselm, *Why God Became Man* 2.2; cf. 1.9; 2.10.
27. Anselm, *Why God Became Man* 1.20–25; 2.4.

payment greater than everything except God himself. On the other hand, a human being ought to give to God the honor that is due to him for two reasons: first, because the debt to be paid is owed by human beings; and second, because God originally created humanity in Adam, it follows that humanity should be redeemed through one of Adam's race.[28]

5. Submission to God's will alone would not be sufficient repayment of humanity's debt to God, since this is already expected of any rational being. However, because the God-man would not be a sinner, he would be under no obligation to die (death is the penalty for sin), and because he is also omnipotent, he could not be forced to die. Moreover, because this man is God, to take his life would be an infinitely greater sin than all other sins. Accordingly, the God-man's voluntary giving of his life is an incomparably greater good than the evil of all other sins combined and is infinitely capable of paying the debt of honor to God.[29]

6. Because Jesus Christ the God-man never sinned, his death—which is offered by his humanity to his deity—was not an obligation. And because his life was given freely and without obligation, it is necessary for God the Father to return some compensation to Christ for his death. However, the Father could give nothing to Christ, since everything that belonged to the Father (as the First Person of the triune God) already belonged to Christ (as the Son who is the Second Person of the triune God). Because the compensation cannot be given to Christ, it necessarily must be given to someone else, and it is most appropriate that the reward be given to humanity, for the sake of whose salvation God became human.[30]

Having offered this summary of Anselm's basic argument, we now turn to a closer examination of its controverted issues.

The Nature of God

Perhaps the most egregious misreading of Anselm is the critique raised by theologians like Harnack—that Anselm's idea of satisfaction is concerned with personal injury to a wrathful God—or its caricature by some theologians as a form of divine child abuse. To the contrary, the foundations of

28. Anselm, *Why God Became Man* 2.6, 8, 18.
29. Anselm, *Why God Became Man* 2.10–11, 14.
30. Anselm, *Why God Became Man* 2.19.

Anselm's theory are an Augustinian notion of God as the highest good (*summum bonum*) correlated to a eudaemonistic (happiness-directed) anthropology and a morally ordered doctrine of creation. Augustine's eudaemonism is summed up succinctly in the opening prayer of *Confessions*: "You [God] have created us for Yourself, and our hearts are restless until they rest in You" (1.1). The prayer contains the basic tenets of eudaemonism: (1) a teleological goal—namely, that human beings have been created for union with God as the *summum bonum*; (2) human happiness or well-being resulting from this teleological end as human beings "rest" in God as their *summum bonum*; and (3) an orientation toward the goal as well as a path that leads from the present state toward the teleological goal of rest in God.

The key concern in Anselm's doctrine of God has to do with the nature of God (as well as Jesus Christ), not with God's wrath or personal offense over human sin. Early in his argument, Anselm insists—contrary to the unbeliever's objection that the incarnation and cross inflict injury on God's honor—that the crucifixion of the incarnate God proclaims the "ineffable profundity of his mercy." Divine atonement for sin finds its origin in divine love for humanity: "For God has shown the magnitude of his love and devotion towards us by the magnitude of his act in most wonderfully and unexpectedly saving us from the evils, so great and so deserved, by which we used to be beset, and returning us to the enjoyment of the good things, so great and so undeserved, which we had lost."[31]

Anselm identifies God with the "highest good"[32] and insists that God's will is never irrational.[33] He is clear that God cannot be humiliated or dishonored. The incarnation is thus not a lowering of God's dignity but an exaltation of human nature.[34] Anselm also rejects any notion of divine voluntarism, that right or wrong would be identified simply with "whatever God wills." Although Anselm insists that "God is so free that he is subject to no law and no judgment," he qualifies this to make clear that divine freedom always acts in accord with divine justice and benevolence, which are inherent to the divine nature. Accordingly, God cannot do anything that is "unfitting."[35] For example, God cannot tell a lie. Anselm makes a similar point when discussing divine "necessity." God is bound by no necessity, and in terms of God's omnipotent power, it is incorrect to say that God "cannot do something," since all necessity is bound to his will. Moreover, when God wills something,

31. Anselm, *Why God Became Man* 1.3.
32. Anselm, *Why God Became Man* 2.1.
33. Anselm, *Why God Became Man* 1.8.
34. Anselm, *Why God Became Man* 1.8.
35. Anselm, *Why God Became Man* 1.12.

it cannot be undone. Thus, when it is said that God is "incapable" of doing certain things, this does not imply a limitation on God's power or that God is limited by some external force but rather that God always acts consistently with his own character: "For when we say that it is a necessary fact that he never lies, all that is being said is that inherent in him there is such a high degree of constancy with regard to upholding the truth that nothing can make him not speak the truth, or tell lies."[36] Because Jesus Christ is God incarnate, a similar logic applies in Christology. Just as God cannot lie, so Jesus Christ can neither lie nor sin.[37]

Creation and Sin

Anselm coordinates his notion of God as the highest good with his doctrine of creation and a eudaemonistic anthropology. As God is the Greatest Good, so humanity was created righteous for the purpose of enjoying God: "Rational nature was created righteous to the end that it might be made happy by rejoicing in the highest good, that is, in God. Man, being rational by nature, was created righteous to the end that, through rejoicing in God, he might be blessedly happy."[38] Anselm also draws a connection between God, creation, and anthropology in his discussion of sin. As noted above, nothing can add to or subtract from the honor of God in itself, since God's honor is inherently incorruptible and incapable of change. However, the creature gives honor to God by desiring what is right, thus maintaining its proper place in the universe and maintaining the "beauty of the universe." Conversely, a rational creature who does not will to do what is right and disobeys God disturbs the beauty and order of the universe by not subordinating themselves to God's governing order. While not bringing any dishonor to God in himself, which is impossible, the disobedience of the creature "dishonors" God by disrupting the divinely established harmony of the created universe.[39] This notion that the orderly universe reflects divine honor is a key theme in Anselm's theology, so much so that some interpreters claim it as the central theme in light of which Anselm's other themes of atonement are to be understood.[40]

Up to this point, Anselm's outline echoes many of the themes in earlier patristic discussions of atonement. For example, Anselm's discussions of God,

36. Anselm, *Why God Became Man* 2.17.
37. Anselm, *Why God Became Man* 2.10.
38. Anselm, *Why God Became Man* 2.1.
39. Anselm, *Why God Became Man* 1.15.
40. See esp. Hogg, *Anselm of Canterbury*, 157–88.

creation, a teleological anthropology, and sin as the disruption of creation echo themes found earlier in Irenaeus and Athanasius. However, in Anselm's subsequent discussion he appears to shift metaphors. From a eudaemonistic anthropology that focuses on humanity's orientation to God as the highest good of human happiness and on sin as disruption of the order of the universe, Anselm shifts to transactional and juridical metaphors of sin as debt, of divine justice as demanding either punishment or satisfaction, and of salvation in terms of the satisfaction and restoration of divine honor. Are these metaphors to be understood in light of Anselm's teleological anthropology and doctrine of creation as the harmony of the universe, or do they represent a shift to a different set of metaphors that are at odds with the earlier teleological and creational imagery? Crucial to any interpretation of Anselm is the question of how to correlate these seemingly divergent patristic and medieval ways of speaking.

Harmonistic Reading

As noted above (setting aside the antagonistic approach), there are two basic schools of interpretation of Anselm: harmonistic and critically appreciative. The harmonistic approach reads Anselm's discussion of sin and satisfaction in light of his earlier discussion of creation and anthropology. Thus, some harmonists assert that Anselm follows patristic logic: "The divine action follows the same course as in the 'classic' model. . . . This is surely a variant of a *Christus victor* soteriology. . . . Anselm's is not a new narrative of salvation."[41]

Because divine honor is correlated with the order of the universe and not with a personal affront against God, such harmonizers of Anselm insist that sin as disobedience is primarily concerned with the disordering of the created world. For God to take sin seriously means both that divine honor is understood as a defense of a just world in which human beings can flourish, and that divine justice is understood as a reflection of God's nature as love. It is our nature to reflect God's goodness and to rejoice in God, and God's justice is concerned with the restoration of this harmony of love and goodness.[42] Accordingly, harmonists claim that, for Anselm, love and justice are not played off against each other but are rather two sides of the same coin: "God's justice and mercy are shown to be one thing, one action, life, and being. . . . The righteousness that condemns is also the love that restores."[43]

41. Hart, "Gift Exceeding Every Debt," 342.
42. Sumner, "Why Anselm Still Matters," 29; Schmiechen, *Saving Power*, 197–98.
43. Hart, "Gift Exceeding Every Debt," 344. See Schmiechen, *Saving Power*, 205, 220.

The close connection between God's righteousness, the created order, and human flourishing means that human disobedience inevitably leads to death insofar as separation from God is also separation from life. For Anselm, "God's honor is inseparable from his goodness, which imparts life and harmony to creation, the rejection of which is necessarily death."[44] Because happiness for humanity consists in an unceasing union with God as the Greatest Good, the death resulting from sin is necessarily a loss of eternal happiness.

As sin and dishonor of God are viewed by harmonists in terms of the disorder of creation, so Anselm's notion of "satisfaction" is interpreted as a restoration of creation to its original order and beauty, not as punishment.[45] Accordingly, it is not Jesus's death alone but his life and death together that effect satisfaction for sin.[46] Some go so far as to suggest that Anselm's Christology follows the lines of Irenaeus's recapitulation model.[47]

Consequently, harmonists repudiate the frequently raised objection that Anselm's soteriology is Nestorian.[48] The atonement is a divine-human act performed by the *Deus-homo*: "The burden of St. Anselm's work . . . is that man *cannot* make the satisfaction required by God. It is the Divine nature of the *Deus-homo* which achieves sufficient merit for that purpose. . . . God's decision to redeem men, to become incarnate in the *Deus-homo*, to suffer and to die, forms for St. Anselm a continuous line, and Aulén's case is not complete."[49]

However, harmonists are not agreed on every aspect of Anselm's atonement theology. While all non-antagonistic readers agree that his theology is not an example of penal substitution, harmonists disagree to what extent he offers a variation on substitution models. For some, Anselm's narrative "is explicitly not a story about a substitutionary sacrifice . . . but concerns rather the triumph over death, the devil and sin accomplished in Christ's voluntary self-donation to the Father."[50] Others disagree: "Anselm did not use penal language—he used satisfaction language, which is its cousin. So long as the element of 'in our stead,' of substitution is there, the kind of language you use is a matter of both/and, of complementary metaphors."[51]

44. Hart, "Gift Exceeding Every Debt," 346; see also Sumner, "Why Anselm Still Matters," 30; Burns, "Concept of Satisfaction," 287.

45. Sumner, "Why Anselm Still Matters," 31; Schmiechen, *Saving Power*, 206.

46. Burns, "Concept of Satisfaction," 288.

47. Hart, "Gift Exceeding Every Debt," 348.

48. Hart, "Gift Exceeding Every Debt," 343; see also Sumner, "Why Anselm Still Matters," 30; Schmiechen, *Saving Power*, 212.

49. McIntyre, *Anselm and His Critics*, 19 (emphasis original).

50. Hart, "Gift Exceeding Every Debt," 343.

51. Sumner, "Why Anselm Still Matters," 34; see McIntyre, *Anselm and His Critics*, 172.

There is similar disagreement among harmonists about such matters as the significance of other doctrines, such as the resurrection or the Trinity. Some see a "close connection between atoning death and resurrection"[52] while others lament that Anselm "says so little about the Resurrection."[53] Conversely, some admit that Anselm does not speak of the Trinity[54] while others observe "how trinitarian the structure of Anselm's story is."[55] However, even when harmonists acknowledge that Anselm does not mention crucial themes in his account of atonement, such as the resurrection or re-creation, this is not considered a problem because (it is argued) Anselm presupposed these themes—he did not need to mention them because his audience was already aware of them. "As for the absence of a clear ontological dimension in Anselm's account of the atonement, of any talk of the change wrought in human nature by salvation that might balance out its 'forensic' and 'fiduciary' grammar, it might be observed that Anselm already writes from within the precincts of the church's pneumatological life."[56] Another harmonist argues that the Eucharist is "central to Anselm's argument."[57] However, given that Anselm never mentions the Eucharist in *Cur Deus Homo*, is it tenable to argue this?

Critically Appreciative Reading

In sharp contrast to such harmonistic readings is what we have referred to as the critically appreciative readings. While acknowledging that Anselm ties his doctrine of atonement to his doctrine of God as the *summum bonum*, that Anselm's discussion of divine honor has to do with the order and disorder of creation rather than a personal affront against an offended divine dignity, and that Anselm's notion of "satisfaction" is not that of penal substitution, the critical reading strongly disagrees with the harmonist reading regarding Anselm's use of forensic/juridical language.

On the one hand, critically appreciative readers acknowledge that Anselm's basic ontology is an Augustinian eudaemonism. However, in discussing sin, salvation, and satisfaction, they argue that Anselm shifts from the language of creation and re-creation/restoration to a new forensic/honor/debt-payment language without acknowledging a change of metaphor. Consequently, the

---

52. Sumner, "Why Anselm Still Matters," 31.
53. Hart, "Gift Exceeding Every Debt," 344.
54. Sumner, "Why Anselm Still Matters," 35.
55. Hart, "Gift Exceeding Every Debt," 343.
56. Hart, "Gift Exceeding Every Debt," 345.
57. Schmiechen, *Saving Power*, 216.

Augustinian ontology of Anselm's doctrine of God and creation stands in strong contrast to the "consummately juridical" language of Anselm's soteriology. An attempt to read this juridical language "on an ontological basis by relating God's honor to the maintenance of the very structure and hierarchy" would encounter great difficulties, and "any such attempt would necessarily end up as *eisegesis*."[58]

Anselm's parables of the dirtied pearl and the dishonored king illustrate this problem. In the parable of the pearl, Anselm provides the example of a merchant who dropped a pearl in the mud and then picked it up again. He asks whether the merchant would not first clean the pearl before displaying it in its beautiful container. Given that humanity has fallen into sin, would it not be suitable for God to cleanse and restore humankind from sin? The metaphor here is that of cleansing and restoration, and one expects that Anselm would use the language of new creation and cleansing from sin as the counterpart to this analogy. Instead, he uses the language of satisfaction. Without repayment of a debt, God cannot let sin go unpunished.[59] Similarly, in Anselm's parable of the king, he gives the example of an entire people who had rebelled against their king with the exception of one man. This man performs such a great service to the king that he is willing to pardon any who request forgiveness for their past offense based on the great work of this one man.[60] In both examples, Anselm's language is juridical and punitive rather than restorative and re-creative.

Is the source of this juridical language medieval feudalism? Some claim that Anselm's case can be made without the feudal imagery and that the indebtedness language is not "economic."[61] Others counter, however, that such medieval imagery cannot be dispensed with:

> The *Cur Deus Homo* was the product of a feudal and monastic world on the eve of a great transformation. With all its originality and personal intensity of vision, it bears the marks of this rigorous and—if the word can be used without blame—repressive regime. . . . We may regret that God should appear in the guise of a lord castigating disobedient serfs, but this was the only appropriate image available to him. . . . The attempted violation of God's honour constitutes the essential sin of disobedience. . . . Due honour is equated with the well-known secular *servitum debitum*: It is capable of being paid, withdrawn, restored. Satisfaction is required from Man as payment for the honour

58. Rodger, "Soteriology of Anselm," 28.
59. Anselm, *Why God Became Man* 1.19.
60. Anselm, *Why God Became Man* 1.19; 2.16.
61. McIntyre, *Anselm and His Critics*, 67, 73.

withheld from God, with an additional payment. . . . Supreme justice requires the preservation of God's honour. Christ offers his life *ad honorem Dei*; and God uses the punishment of the sinner *ad honorem suam*. The language could scarcely be more feudal, and the thought it expresses is only intelligible if the language is understood in a strictly contemporary sense. . . . This background . . . which sets Anselm as far apart from Patristic [including Augustine] as from modern, or even later medieval thought [including Thomas Aquinas], is the complex of feudal relationships.[62]

This presses a key question: Does Anselm view the relationships between sin, death, punishment, and satisfaction as intrinsic and ontological or extrinsic and juridical? Patristic theology understood these relationships to be intrinsic: death is the inevitable and inescapable consequence of sin and separation from God. As noted above, harmonists view Anselm's account in this way. However, a literal reading of Anselm's text suggests an extrinsic relationship. Anselm's discussion of the relationship between sin and death is the shortest in the book and seems to describe death as a punishment that God might or might not have imposed on sinners.[63] Similarly, Anselm concludes that God ought not to have imposed death on Christ because he never sinned. The connection between sin and death certainly appears to be extrinsic and juridical rather than intrinsic and ontological.[64]

A further indication that Anselm views the connection between sin and punishment as juridical and extrinsic is his notion of debt and punishment as proportionate to sin. Sin is *quantifiable* as a debt, and payment is *proportionate* to the amount of sin. Since human sin dishonors God, who is infinite, the compensation must be infinite in extent. Since Christ is the God-man, to crucify Christ would be an infinite sin and Christ's voluntary death is of infinite value. Therefore, it is necessary that those crucifying Christ not know that it is God they are crucifying; otherwise, their debt would exceed the possible amount of repayment. Because to crucify Christ would create an infinite debt, the additional debt of knowingly doing so would exceed the possible recompense or satisfaction: even Christ's voluntary death could not compensate for the sins of those who *knowingly* crucified the incarnate God.[65]

As with his account of sin and death, critically appreciative readers assert that Anselm's notion of satisfaction also appears to be juridical and extrinsic rather than ontological and intrinsic. Satisfaction is presented as payment of

62. Southern, *Saint Anselm*, 222, 225.
63. Anselm, *Why God Became Man* 2.2; Rodger, "Soteriology of Anselm," 30.
64. Anselm, *Why God Became Man* 1.9, 10; Rodger, "Soteriology of Anselm," 30.
65. Anselm, *Why God Became Man* 1.20; 2.14, 15; Wiendt, "What is Anselm Singing?"

a debt, yet there does not seem to be any intrinsic relationship between Jesus's death and the conquest of death, the reversal of sin and death, nor the source of new life through union with Christ. Rather, satisfaction is repayment of the debt along with "something extra." Because Jesus did not deserve to die, his death produces a surplus of merit, which can then be transferred to another. In God's response to Christ's death, he bestows a "reward" that is then (extrinsically) transferred to another. Thus, "In order to establish the value of the Death of Christ . . . [Anselm] has to employ the notion of *supererogation*. The idea upon which the whole argument turns is that Christ in dying does something extra which God's Will does not enjoin."[66]

Another point at which Anselm seems to depart from the patristic vision is his contrast between justice and mercy. As noted in previous chapters, patristic thinkers such as Irenaeus and Athanasius understood God's justice simply to be the way that God's love expresses itself in opposition to sin. Because God's nature is inherently good, he necessarily opposes anything that opposes his love. But God's love and forgiveness are not conditional; God's forgiveness is always available to all human beings. Harmonists claim that Anselm does not play off one divine attribute against another. But a plain reading of Anselm indicates that he understands divine love to be conditioned by justice, insofar as satisfaction necessarily precedes forgiveness. In other words, God cannot simply forgive without satisfaction—to do so would be a failure to take sin seriously—and satisfaction is interpreted as repayment of debt to divine honor. For Anselm, satisfaction must precede forgiveness. God's justice must be satisfied before his love can be manifested, and God cannot forgive until his honor is restored. Thus, "The whole process of satisfaction, initiated within the Godhead and continued in the Incarnation of the Eternal Son and in the Death of Jesus Christ, is regarded by St. Anselm as that which forms the *ground* of God's forgiveness and through which it takes place. That is what Atonement means, and this is how forgiveness works."[67] In the patristic view, by contrast, God restores by forgiving and re-creating. God's justice is God's love made manifest in the destruction of sin.

A further difficulty in Anselm's account is that he appears to fail in his intended goal. He claims to reject metaphorical imagery of atonement and to provide instead a literal and logically necessary account of how atonement takes place. Yet he does not seem to realize that his honor/debt-payment model is, in fact, a medieval feudal metaphor that he has substituted for the patristic ransom metaphor: "Anselm is still arguing with an analogy. In place of the

66. McIntyre, *Anselm and His Critics*, 171.
67. McIntyre, *Anselm and His Critics*, 200 (emphasis added).

aesthetic imagery that relies on such principles as balance or appropriateness or the image of ransom, . . . he introduces the image of honour. The image relies heavily on the world of feudal relationships."[68]

Anselm's account contains problems that even harmonists admit. Jesus's earthly life and resurrection are essentially afterthoughts in *Cur Deus Homo*. Several harmonist interpreters want to include Jesus's earthly life as part of his atoning work; however, for Anselm, Jesus's earthly life is not saving because it is the minimum that is owed to God. He can only speak of it as a moral example.[69] It is Jesus's death that provides "satisfaction" because it was not "owed" by one who is not a sinner and therefore "goes beyond" the required minimum. Jesus's death is the "something extra" that is then "credited" to human beings. Consequently, "Anselm is vulnerable to the charge of making the death an end in itself, or a transaction between God and Christ for the sake of appeasing God. . . . Is Jesus offering his life of obedience, in spite of the threat of death? Or have we departed from the basic structure of the argument in such a way that the death per se is of value and required to honor God?"[70]

Relatedly, despite complaints that critiques of Anselm's Christology as Nestorian are unfair, even Anselm's defenders acknowledge a certain imbalance in his account: "We cannot escape the conclusion that [Anselm] has virtually thought of the *homo* in the *Deus-homo* as offering to God the satisfaction which He requires for man's sin. . . . A perfect man could have done all that St. Anselm requires of the person making satisfaction."[71]

Finally, certain key themes from the first two chapters are simply missing in Anselm's account: resurrection, union with Christ, deification/sanctification, re-creation. He offers no essential connection between the atonement and Jesus's resurrection—a theme that is central to the accounts of Irenaeus and Athanasius. Just as troubling, Anselm omits any mention of the Holy Spirit. Despite claims that his account is "trinitarian in structure," it is essentially a story of the death of the Son for the satisfaction of the Father. As noted above, harmonists suggest either that Anselm did not need to mention these themes because his readers would have presupposed them or that, given the opportunity, he would have provided a more complete account. But, granting either concession, this is a crucial admission that important parts of the package are missing in Anselm's account of atonement as satisfaction.

68. Schmiechen, *Saving Power*, 210.
69. Anselm, *Why God Became Man* 2.11.
70. Anselm, *Why God Became Man* 2.11; Schmiechen, *Saving Power*, 214.
71. McIntyre, *Anselm and His Critics*, 170.

Conclusion

In final assessment, Anselm's contribution to atonement theology is ambiguous at best. Anselm does introduce a new metaphor into atonement theology. While the church fathers had focused on imagery of recapitulation and participation (atonement as incarnation) as well as defeat of evil (Christus Victor), Anselm shifts the discussion to the forensic imagery of honor and guilt, judgment and satisfaction, which will afterward become important themes in atonement theologies. Discussions of sin sometimes distinguish between the problem of *sin* and the problem of *sins*. The problem of *sin* is that of habitual sinful behavior, and language of participation and recapitulation speaks to the need for moral transformation. Christus Victor portrays sin as the enemy to be conquered and defeated—that is, salvation is deliverance from the oppression and power of sin. Forensic language addresses judgment for the moral *offense* caused by and *guilt* for actual "sins" committed. Its primary concerns are accountability and forgiveness. Anselm thus introduced new concerns that will be echoed in later theologies—for example, Thomas Aquinas's distinction between image formation and image restoration, and Reformation distinctions between justification and sanctification.

Despite Harnack's claim that Anselm is the first to provide a systematic account of atonement and Aulén's claim that Anselm introduces a single definitive model, Anselm's theology might best be understood as transitional to other theologies of atonement in that subsequent theologies do not simply repeat Anselm. Peter Abelard will reject satisfaction altogether and introduce more "subjective" interpretations of the atonement. Later medieval theologians such as Aquinas will incorporate aspects of "satisfaction," but with significant modifications, and balance satisfaction with other themes. Reformers like John Calvin will modify Anselm in the direction of penal substitution. More recent theologians, such as Karl Barth and Thomas F. Torrance, will include forensic themes but also challenge Anselm.

Although Anselm's theology is not entirely rationalist in that he defines theology as "faith seeking understanding," his methodology of eliminating Jesus Christ from the discussion (*remoto Christo*) necessarily introduces an *a priori* rationalist element in that he imposes notions of justice drawn from outside the biblical text rather than engaging in a careful reading of what the Gospels actually say. Whether Anselm's notion of justice derives from "medieval feudalism" or "Benedectine monasticism" is not so important as that it is not christologically formed—and that was deliberate. Both Aquinas and Barth will do better here. In addition, although Anselm claimed to be abandoning metaphor for literal, rational explanation, forensic metaphors are just that—metaphors. Later theologians (for example, Charles Hodge) will pursue both rationalism and literalism even further.

Finally, Anselm's focus on Christ's death alone as a satisfaction for sin also leads to ambiguities. That even sympathetic readers look elsewhere for the missing theological ingredients—either in Anselm's broader theology or in patristic or medieval theologies—makes clear that, as it stands, Anselm's atonement theology is incomplete. The danger of reducing the doctrine of the atonement to Jesus's death on the cross will be a constant temptation going forward, but theologians following Anselm will also make clear that any adequate atonement theology must take into account the entire person and work of Jesus Christ.

4

. . .

Atonement as Divine Love

Peter Abelard and the Wesleys

Among the medieval detractors of Anselm of Canterbury's understanding of atonement as *satisfaction*, perhaps none is better known than Peter Abelard (1079–1142). In contrast to the older Anselm—and to the consternation of Abelard's contemporary and opponent, Bernard of Clairvaux (1090–1153)[1]—Abelard argued for a way of understanding atonement that emphasized the love of God operant in the life and death of Jesus Christ. Abelard's approach is often referred to as the "moral influence" model of atonement. It has been associated with—and sometimes equated with—*moral exemplarism*: the belief that the purpose of Christ's life and death was to serve as a preeminent example of human love for God and obedience to God's will, an example that inspires in the observer a response of similar love and obedience to God. Whether such a portrayal is justified will be considered in this chapter. What is clear is that Abelard's emphasis upon the work of Christ as the *reconciling love of God* has become an integral feature in the landscape of atonement theology. And we see that feature reappearing in the theology of other historic figures, such as John and Charles Wesley.

1. See Lane, *Bernard of Clairvaux*.

Abelard and Atonement

Peter Abelard was arguably the most talented and controversial European thinker of the twelfth century. A brilliant and prolific logician, musician, and poet, Abelard lived a life marked by great achievement and great tragedy. He was trained in classical literature and philosophy, and he shared with Anselm of Canterbury a commitment both to the role of reason in theology and to the use of dialectic. This method of disputation (*quaestio disputata*) inherited from classical philosophy employed *pro* and *contra* arguments to resolve theological questions—and Abelard employed it masterfully. The use of dialectic would reach its apex in the theology of Thomas Aquinas but was not widely employed in Abelard's time. Abelard's lasting contribution thereto was his highly influential theology sourcebook, *Yes and No (Sic et non)*, in which he presents 158 theological questions that feature positive and negative responses from the church fathers.

Unfortunately, Abelard's brilliance was matched by his arrogance and ambition, and he made enemies while vying for popularity as a magister of theology with the schools of the day. Pride led to his downfall. At the peak of his astounding popularity in Paris, Abelard instigated an affair with a young noblewoman in his tutelage, Heloise. The result was disastrous, and Abelard's fall from favor was but one of a series of "calamities"[2] that plagued him the remainder of his life. His use of dialectic led him to views deemed unacceptable by more traditional theologians, especially Bernard of Clairvaux. This resulted in the condemnation and burning of his work on the Trinity in 1121 and a papal censure in 1141. Abelard died the following year.

One of the main accusations brought by Abelard's opponents was that he rejected the objective necessity of Jesus's death as atonement for sin. We must acknowledge from the outset that this is not true, despite both medieval and modern claims to the contrary. What is true is that Abelard emphasized the subjective dimension of Christ's reconciling work and did so in critique of the atonement theologies of his day. It was this emphasis that earned the suspicion of Abelard's contemporaries and the misdirected praise of many moderns.

As we saw in the previous chapter, Anselm of Canterbury had repudiated the still popular notion that the death of Jesus was a ransom paid by God to the devil in exchange for the liberation of captive humanity. Anselm insisted that the devil had deceived human beings and therefore had no right to hold them captive. Yes, Jesus's death and resurrection had defeated Satan and liberated humanity, but only God is the proper object of Christ's reconciling work.

2. See Abelard, *Historia calamitatum*.

If a ransom is to be paid, it is paid to God alone. This being the case, how is the reconciliation of humanity to God accomplished by the incarnation and death of Jesus Christ? Anselm's answer was *to satisfy God's honor*. In *Cur Deus Homo*, Anselm argued that the Son of God had to become human and die in order on behalf of fallen humanity to pay the infinite debt of honor incurred by our rebellion against the infinite God—a debt we could never pay ourselves. For Anselm, only the death of the God-man could satisfy the justice of God.

Abelard found neither the ransom nor satisfaction theologies of atonement acceptable. Unfortunately, a work in which he appears to have developed a full treatment of his atonement theology, *The Tropologies*, has been either lost or destroyed. What remains are several brief but evocative arguments that appear in his *Commentary on the Epistle to the Romans*, particularly in the disputation following his comments on Romans 3:26.[3] That disputation will be the main focus of this chapter.

Disputing Anselm

In the question (*quaestio*) section of this disputation, Abelard agrees with Anselm that no ransom was paid by God to the devil in Jesus's death. However, Abelard goes on to question the claim that Jesus *had* to die to satisfy God's justice: If the Son of God could declare sins forgiven during his earthly life (e.g., to the paralytic in Matt. 9:1–4), why was his death *necessary*? Could not the compassionate Son simply forgive sinful humanity? Anselm had argued that for God to do so would be "unfitting" to God's justice. In pointed response, Abelard asks in what sense it was just that the crime of Adam and Eve's disobedience should be forgiven through the murder of the innocent Son of God? Is not the latter a far greater injustice and offense against God than the former? Does not humanity then owe God an even greater debt to be paid? Furthermore, presses Abelard, "How very cruel and unjust it seems that someone should require the blood of an innocent person as a ransom, or that in any way it might please him that an innocent person be slain, still less that God should have so accepted the death of his Son that through it he was reconciled to the whole world."[4] As far as Abelard was concerned, Anselm's question "Why the God-man?" had yet to be answered satisfactorily.

3. See Abelard, *Epistle to the Romans*, 164–68. For a detailed grammatical analysis of the disputation, see Bond, "Another Look," 11–32.

4. Abelard, *Epistle to the Romans*, 167.

It is worth noting at this point that the substance of Abelard's questioning was not itself a problem. The fact that Anselm had already anticipated similar questions in *Cur Deus Homo* shows that Abelard was not alone in raising them. Moreover, the dialectical method employed by both scholars was designed to raise interrogatory questions to test the strength of a view being considered. Still, Abelard's critics were disturbed by the perceived implications of his questions, especially the seeming implication that Christ need not have died in order for the human race to be forgiven. This was the basis of their accusation that Abelard denied the objective necessity of Christ's death. In Abelard's defense, he did not deny that Christ's death objectively achieved reconciliation with God; indeed, as we will see, he openly affirmed it. Rather, as did Thomas Aquinas later, he questioned the *necessity* of Christ's death as the *only* means by which the omnipotent God could have saved humanity. Abelard's emphasis here "is not so much on whether Christ's death was redemptively efficacious, but on whether God had no other means by which he could redeem humanity. . . . God is under no compulsion to choose any particular means of redemption."[5] Nevertheless, Abelard's open questioning of the ransom and satisfaction models fueled the criticism of his opponents.

Abelard next proceeds to the answer (*solutio*) portion of the disputation, where he presents his own positive position in the opening sentence. This sentence serves as an overture to the entire *solutio* and is representative of Abelard's atonement theology as a whole. "Nevertheless it seems to us that in this we are justified in the blood of Christ and reconciled to God, that it was through this matchless grace shown to us that his Son received our nature, and in that nature, teaching us both by word and example, persevered to death and bound us to himself even more through love, so that when we have been kindled by so great a benefit of divine grace, true charity might fear to endure nothing for his sake."[6]

This is a complex sentence, in both English and Latin, and vulnerable to misinterpretation. To Abelard's opponents, the phrases "grace shown [*exhibitam*] to us" and "teaching us both by word and example [*exemplum*]" sounded Pelagian—or at least Pelagian enough to support their case against him. This sentence and others like it led Bernard to accuse Abelard of teaching in a moral exemplarist fashion that Christ came "for no other purpose than that he might teach us how to live by his words and example, and point out by his passion and death to what limits our love should go. Thus he did

5. Cartwright, introduction to Abelard's *Epistle to the Romans*, 47.
6. Abelard, *Epistle to the Romans*, 167–68. Cf. Bond, "Another Look," 18–26.

not communicate righteousness but only revealed to us what it is."[7] Ironically, many modern theologians have agreed with Bernard's assessment but instead celebrate Abelard for having laid to rest the embarrassingly old-fashioned notion of Jesus's death as a substitutionary atonement. Thus, Hastings Rashdall in his 1915 Bampton Lectures claims, "In Abelard not only the ransom theory but any kind of substitutionary or expiatory atonement is explicitly denied. We get rid altogether of the notion of a mysterious guilt which, by an abstract necessity of things, required to be extinguished by death or suffering. . . . The efficacy of Christ's death is now quite definitely and explicitly explained by its subjective influence upon the mind of the sinner."[8]

If Bernard and Rashdall (and modern theologians following Rashdall) are right, then Abelard was indeed both Pelagian and a moral exemplarist. However, the overwhelming consensus of recent scholarship strongly argues that Abelard cannot be interpreted in such a manner,[9] either to condemn him or to press him into the service of modern "religious progress."[10] Alister McGrath sums up this scholarship pointedly: "Abailard did not teach an exemplarist theory of the Atonement."[11] Even a plain reading of Abelard's quotation above resists such an interpretation. And a careful examination of Abelard's *solutio* both reveals key concepts that are congruent with the tradition of atonement theology seen in our previous chapters and offers an alternative—or at least a complement—to Anselm's satisfaction approach.

We must first recall that Abelard's disputation takes place in the exegetical context of Romans 3:21–26, wherein Paul teaches the Roman believers regarding justification by grace through faith in Jesus Christ. Abelard's language in the *solutio*, and especially in this first sentence above, resonates with the language of Paul. Compare Abelard's opening sentence above with Romans 3:23–25: "For all have sinned and fall short of the glory of God, and are justified by his grace as a gift, through the redemption that is in Christ Jesus, whom God put forward as a propitiation by his blood, to be received by faith." Abelard clearly understands the substance of his *solutio* to be an extension of his commentary on the Romans 3 text. He affirms unequivocally in his opening line that "we are justified in the blood of Christ and reconciled to God." While Abelard had questioned the absolute necessity (*a priori*) of Jesus's death in the *quaestio*, he did not question that it was, in fact

7. Bernard of Clairvaux, *Tractatus*, vii, 17 (translation from McGrath, "Moral Theory," 207).

8. Rashdall, *Idea of Atonement*, 358.

9. E.g., Lane, *Bernard of Clairvaux*, 35–40; McGrath, "Moral Theory"; Quinn, "Abelard on Atonement"; Weingart, *Logic of Divine Love*; T. Williams, "Sin, Grace, and Redemption."

10. Rashdall, *Idea of Atonement*, 360.

11. McGrath, "Moral Theory," 206.

(*a posteriori*), an intrinsic aspect of God's chosen means of atonement. It is true that Abelard does not in this sentence explicitly employ the language of propitiation and forgiveness, which contributed to his opponents' accusations of moral exemplarism. However, the context suggests that he assumes them; moreover, he explicitly employs such language at numerous points elsewhere in the Romans commentary.[12] In short, an accurate reading of Abelard's *solutio* requires that we read it in the context of both Scripture and the rest of Abelard's thoughts.

Abelard goes on to specify that our justification and reconciliation in Christ's blood is God's "unique grace [*singularem gratiam*] held out to us [*nobis exhibitam*]." Note that the phrase echoes Romans 3:24–25: "And are justified by his grace as a gift, through the redemption that is in Christ Jesus, whom God put forward as a propitiation by his blood." Abelard's use of *exhibitam* parallels its biblical (Vulgate) counterpart *proposuit* ("put forward") and connotes not a mere display but rather a presentation or offering.[13] Both Abelard's *exhibitam* and the Vulgate's *proposuit* refer to the justification of believers through the propitiation of Christ's blood. Though Abelard's *exhibitam* might by itself be taken to convey a mere showing or exhibition of God's grace, such a reading does not make sense in the context of the Romans 3 passage or the commentary as a whole. A more accurate reading of Abelard is that God's unique grace is objectively proffered to us through the reconciling work of Jesus Christ.

Thus, the question for Abelard is not *whether* the death of Jesus is an objective means of our reconciliation but *in what way* God employs it to achieve our reconciliation. It is from this point on that Abelard's distinctive approach to atonement begins to emerge. First, Abelard specifies that God's grace is proffered to us in the incarnation ("his Son received our nature"), ministry ("teaching us both by word and example"), and death ("persevered to death") of God's Son. Thus, while he affirms the death of Jesus as an atoning event, Abelard includes it within the whole arc of the Son's incarnation and faithful earthly ministry, which together are the means and medium of God's unique grace proffered to us. Jesus's death is the culmination of God's saving work that begins with the incarnation. From the outset, this stands in contrast to any notion of atonement that focuses exclusively upon the death of Christ.

Second, and related, Jesus's "teaching us both by word and example" is clearly an integral aspect of that grace proffered to us through the whole of

12. E.g., see Abelard's comments on Rom. 4:25; 5:19, 21; 6:9; 7:14; 8:3–4, 32.
13. Cartwright's translation of Abelard above reads "matchless grace shown to us," but compare Bond ("Another Look," 19), who argues persuasively for "unique grace held out to us."

the Son's incarnate ministry, which includes his death. This phrase cannot be taken as Pelagian without doing violence to that whole. On the contrary, Abelard's emphasis upon the words and deeds of Jesus indicates that there is *more* to the Son's reconciling ministry in his thinking, not less. The grace revealed in Jesus's faithful teaching by word and example is continuous with his faithfulness unto death and accomplishes our justification and more—*it unites us to God in love*. The remainder of the sentence makes this clear, as we will see below.

Third, Abelard portrays the reconciling work of Christ as a unitive, singular action of the grace of the entire Godhead. In contrast to the ransom and satisfaction approaches, in which Christ's death is accepted by God as sufficient payment for sin, here God is the active, initiating agent who offers his unique grace to fallen humanity through the atoning work of his Son. While at one level Abelard is simply following the Romans text, his emphasis upon the whole economy of Jesus's earthly ministry as a single work of the grace of God demonstrates that this is not incidental. Moreover, Abelard's language of being "bound" to God through "love" is strongly suggestive of the work of the Holy Spirit, who in the Augustinian tradition is understood as the "bond of love" (*vinculum caritatis*) between Father and Son, but also between the Son and believers. Indeed, "love" is one of the principal terms by which Abelard refers to the Holy Spirit. Elsewhere in the Romans commentary he states explicitly, "[Christ's] Spirit is himself the love and the bond by which his members are united to this head. Indeed, concerning this Spirit it is especially said that 'God is charity.'"[14] Read in this light, Abelard's opening sentence depicts the triune action of God, who graciously reconciles humanity to himself through the work of his Son and Spirit.

Abelard goes on to affirm in his *solutio* that, through this gracious work, the Son has "*bound us to himself even more through love*." Here we come to the aspect of Abelard's atonement theology for which he has been mischaracterized and which therefore bears careful consideration. Note first and foremost that the grace of God proffered to us in the incarnate ministry of his Son is objectively effectual, in that both (1) by it we are justified and reconciled to God and (2) through it we are "bound" to Christ in love. The syntax of Abelard's sentence leaves no doubt that God in Christ (with the Holy Spirit) is the agent of these actions, while "we" are their recipients. Thus, for Abelard, the grace of God given to us through the work of Christ includes (1) our justification and reconciliation and (2) our being bound to God in love, the latter of which is an integral aspect of the former. While we

---

14. Abelard, *Epistle to the Romans*, 268. See also Knell, *Immanent Person*, 53–56.

may distinguish between the grace and love of God, they are inseparable. In demonstration of this point Abelard later adds, "He showed us such great grace, than which a greater cannot be found, by his own word: 'No one,' he says, 'has greater love than this: that he lays down his life for his friends.'"[15] And in the conclusion of his *solutio* Abelard adduces Romans 5:8: "But God demonstrates His own love toward us, in that while we were still sinners, Christ died for us" (NASB). What is distinctive about Abelard's atonement theology, far from diminishing the objective work of Christ, is his reframing of it as the gracious working of God's love.

Abelard concludes his sentence by describing the outcome of God's reconciling love: "so that when we have been kindled by so great a benefit of divine grace, true charity might fear to endure nothing for his sake."[16] This metaphor of being "kindled" (*accensi*) by the grace of God is important for Abelard and underscores the objectivity of divine action. It depicts the lighting of a fire and connotes a state of being inflamed or aroused by an external agent. Abelard uses this verb multiple times throughout the *solutio* to refer to persons being aroused to the love of God by the grace of God. He adduces scriptural support for this language in Jesus's words from Luke 12:49: "I came to bring fire to the earth, and how I wish it were already kindled!" And he explicitly connects this kindling to the work of the Holy Spirit by citing Romans 5:5: "God's love has been poured into our hearts through the Holy Spirit that has been given to us."

Thus, we see in Abelard two reconciling works actively effected by God's love/Holy Spirit through the life and death of Jesus Christ: being bound to God and being kindled by God. These comport with Abelard's frequent use of the phrase "love of God" in both subjective (our love for God) and objective genitive (God's love for us) constructions, which has precedent in the New Testament, especially in the epistles of John and Paul.[17] On the one hand, we are objectively bound to God by his gracious love through the atoning life and death of his Son. On the other hand, we are subjectively kindled by that love in order to love God in response. Given its subjective character, to be kindled by God's love might be interpreted in an exemplarist or moral influence manner—although the association with the work of the Holy Spirit resists such a reading. However, the former metaphor of being bound by God to himself simply cannot be read as an exemplarist statement. It is an objective work of God in the believing person that is an intrinsic aspect of

15. Abelard, *Epistle to the Romans*, 168.
16. Abelard, *Epistle to the Romans*, 168.
17. Abelard, *Epistle to the Romans*, 75.

God's reconciling grace proffered in the life and death of Jesus Christ. For Abelard, "The action of God in Christ is direct, not indirect; man's responsive act of love is a direct result of Christ's gracious transformation of the sinner's person."[18] Neither "moral influence" nor "moral exemplarism" suffice to describe what Abelard is arguing for.

Finally, in regard to Abelard's opening sentence, note that the outcome of God's gracious love is that "true love [*caritas vera*] might fear to endure nothing for his sake." The "love of God" is not a secondary benefit for Abelard; it is both the source and the goal of God's reconciling grace given to us in Jesus Christ. Throughout the Romans commentary, Abelard insists that when we have gained "true love" through the grace of God, we are freed from fear of God to live in love with God. "Therefore," he says in the latter part of the *solutio*, "*our redemption is that supreme love [summa dilectio] in us through the Passion of Christ*, which not only frees us from slavery to sin, but gains for us the true liberty of the sons of God, so that we may complete all things by his love rather than by fear."[19] For Abelard, the supreme love of God means that we would love God not only because he has forgiven us but also because he alone is the object most worthy of our love. However, such love is born in us only by the grace of God given "through the Passion of Christ," whereby the "love of God" (both objective and subjective) frees us from fear of judgment to love God for his own sake—and to love our neighbor as ourselves.

To sum up, we find in Abelard a theology of atonement as *the effectual working of the love of the triune God through the life and death of Jesus Christ to reconcile and unite believers to God, thereby enabling them to love God as God desires*. Several observations are worth noting here.

First, despite characterizations to the contrary, there is no inherent contradiction between Abelard's atonement theology and any variety of constitutive models of atonement. Indeed, directly contradicting Rashdall, Abelard at numerous points explicitly affirms both substitutionary and expiatory aspects of Jesus's death, including the occasional use of penal language—all the while framing it within the movement of God's reconciling love. His comment on Romans 4:25 is a good example:

> He is said to have died on account of our transgressions in two ways: at one time because we transgressed, on account of which he died, and we committed sin, the penalty of which he bore; at another, that he might take away our sins

18. Weingart, *Logic of Divine Love*, 126.
19. Abelard, *Epistle to the Romans*, 168 (emphasis added). One of Abelard's accusations against Bernard was that Bernard denied that the love of God has power. Abelard, *Apologia Contra Bernardum* 8, cited in Knell, *Immanent Person*, 47n16.

by dying, that is, he swept away the penalty for sins by the price of his death, leading us into paradise, and through the demonstration of so much grace—by which, as he says, "No one has greater love"—he drew back our souls from the will to sin and kindled the highest love of himself.[20]

What is distinctive in Abelard is not a rejection of substitutionary atonement but an emphasis upon Jesus's reconciling work as the means and medium by which God actively unites believers to himself in love.

However, second, the emphasis of Abelard's atonement theology stands in sharp contrast to both the reductively literalist ransom theologies of his day and Anselm's satisfaction approach. "Why the God-man?" asks Anselm. "To unite humanity to God in love," would answer Abelard. For Abelard, the primary purpose of God in the atoning life and death of Jesus Christ is neither to satisfy the justice of God nor to free humanity from Satan's dominion, although these are indeed entailed. Rather, the *primary* purpose is to unite us to God in love, in order that we may love God above all else and our neighbor as ourselves. And this requires not only the past completed action of Jesus's saving works but also the present agency of the Holy Spirit in effectually impressing the reality of Jesus's works upon the minds and wills of believing persons.

Third, and related, this framing of atonement as divine love raises the more basic question of God's fundamental disposition toward fallen humanity: Is God most basically disposed toward sinners in love or in justice? While these are by no means mutually exclusive, both the ransom and the satisfaction approach stress the inability of fallen humanity to pay the ransom or debt owed to a holy and just God because of sin. By contrast, Abelard's approach emphasizes God's loving intention to restore fallen humanity to a union of love with himself through Jesus Christ. Accordingly, says Abelard, "the love of God toward us *is* that disposition of divine grace for our salvation."[21]

This leads to a fourth observation, which we have touched on above but bears repeating: Abelard's approach is theocentric and trinitarian. The emphasis in his atonement theology is upon the unity of divine action that comprises the work of the entire Godhead. The human words and deeds of Jesus are presented as the work of the incarnate Son acting in concert with the Father and the Holy Spirit. Jesus is not portrayed as an essentially human victim whose death is understood as an event separate from the person and agency of the Father. Rather, his death is the culmination of the whole earthly

20. Abelard, *Epistle to the Romans*, 204.
21. Abelard, *Epistle to the Romans*, 349 (emphasis added).

ministry of the incarnate Son, whose work is undertaken in the fellowship of the Father and the Spirit.

We should note that this understanding of atonement as the united activity of the Godhead disposed in love toward the salvation of sinful humanity is very close to that of Augustine of Hippo. Augustine's own commentary on Romans 3 is worth citing here:

> But what is meant by "justified in His blood"? What power is there in this blood, I beseech you, that they who believe should be justified in it? And what is meant by "being reconciled by the death of His Son"? Was it indeed so, that when God the Father was angry with us, He saw the death of His Son for us, and was appeased towards us? Was then His Son already so far appeased towards us, that He even deigned to die for us; while the Father was still so far angry, that except His Son died for us, He would not be appeased? . . . Pray, unless the Father had been already appeased, would He have delivered up His own Son, not sparing Him for us? . . . But I see that the Father loved us also before, not only before the Son died for us, but before He created the world; the apostle himself being witness, who says, "According as He has chosen us in Him before the foundation of the world." Nor was the Son delivered up for us as it were unwillingly, the Father Himself not sparing Him; for it is said also concerning Him, "Who loved me, and delivered up Himself for me." Therefore together both the Father and the Son, and the Spirit of both, work all things equally and harmoniously; yet we are justified in the blood of Christ, and we are reconciled to God by the death of His Son.[22]

While medieval detractors and modern promoters depict Abelard's approach alternatively as heretical or prescient, Abelard clearly understood himself to be in continuity with Scripture and the church fathers, especially Augustine. As mentioned above, an Augustinian understanding of the Holy Spirit as the "bond of love" both within and without the Godhead is squarely in view in Abelard's *solutio*. Moreover, Abelard's emphasis upon loving God without fear is also classically Augustinian,[23] and Abelard cites Augustine (with great deference) far more frequently than he does any other theologian.

Finally, to some contemporary ears Abelard's understanding of the grace of God *as* the love of God may sound "liberal" or "progressive." However, Abelard's argument reminds us that this is a thoroughly biblical idea found throughout Scripture and especially in the writings of Paul and John.[24] Unfortunately, the association of Abelard's motif of the love of God with liberal

22. Augustine, *Trin.* 15 (NPNF[1] 3:175).
23. See esp. *Tract. ep. Jo.*
24. E.g., John 3:16–17; Rom. 5:5–8; 1 John 4:9.

theology reflects both his misappropriation by modern theologians such as Rashdall and the bifurcation of the modern theological landscape whereby God's love and holiness are emphasized to their mutual exclusion. Abelard's work is a reminder that such bifurcation is both canonically and theologically untenable.

Though the history of theology may have chosen Abelard as its champion of divine love, his framing of atonement as the reconciling love of God is by no means unique. As we have seen, it is an essentially biblical idea that can be found in the work of Augustine and other early theologians. In Abelard's day, reflection upon divine and human love was the focus of many works in theology and spirituality. Ironically, Bernard of Clairvaux devoted much of his work to this theme, and others—such as Hugh and Richard of St. Victor—developed it extensively.[25] The theme persisted throughout the medieval period in the writings both of mystics such as Meister Eckhart and Julian of Norwich and of theologians such as Bonaventure and Thomas Aquinas. Both Martin Luther and John Calvin emphasize the love of God in their theologies of atonement.[26] And the centrality of God's love and personal experience thereof were a principal focus of Continental Pietism.[27]

The Wesleys and Atonement

Perhaps most influential in the post-Reformation continuation of the atonement motif of God's love has been the theology of John (1703–91) and Charles (1707–88) Wesley. As we will see, there are strong similarities between the Wesleys' approach to atonement and that of Abelard. However, there are also differences. To begin with, their contexts were very different. The Wesleys were raised in the Church of England by parents influenced by both Puritanism and Pietism.[28] As young men, they dedicated themselves to the service of God and the renewal of the Christian faith in England. Beginning with their "Holy Club" at Oxford, the "Methodist" movement grew throughout the decades of the 1700s, eventually parting ways with the Church of England to become its own tradition. Together with their friend George Whitefield, and in parallel with the work of Jonathan Edwards, the Wesleys' open-air preaching and magnificent hymns catalyzed the evangelical revivals of the Great Awakening in England and America.

25. See, e.g., Feiss, On Love.
26. See R. Peterson, Calvin's Doctrine of the Atonement; Althaus, Theology of Martin Luther.
27. See Erb, Pietists.
28. See Torpy, Prevenient Piety of Samuel Wesley.

Theologically speaking, the Wesleys were reacting to the moral and spiritual stagnation of the Church of England. Their points of theological emphasis were therefore different than Abelard's. Central to the Wesleys' evangelistic preaching was the call to repentance and faith in the atoning death of Jesus Christ for the forgiveness of sins. In common with Whitefield and Edwards, they emphasized Jesus's death as a substitutionary sacrifice for the sin of humanity with a strong emphasis on penal substitution. The Wesleys were great readers of the Eastern fathers of the church; however, in respect to their understanding of the objective features of atonement, we see little emphasis upon recapitulation or Christus Victor. Rather, they were squarely in the Reformation tradition in viewing the objective problem of sin principally as a violation of God's law and viewing Jesus's death as punishment for sin and satisfaction of God's wrath on behalf of sinful humanity.[29]

To be sure, the Wesleys employed a variety of atonement metaphors in their prose and hymnody. These include reference to the "merits" of Christ's death as well as metaphors such as "ransom," "debt," and "redemption." The inclusion of these terms reflects the breadth of the Wesleys' Anglican heritage, which retained the rich complex of atonement metaphors in Scripture and tradition and preserved them in liturgical phrasing, such as the 1662 Prayer of Consecration in Holy Communion: "Almighty God, our heavenly Father, who, of thy tender mercy, didst give thine only Son Jesus Christ to suffer death on the cross for our redemption, who made there . . . a full, perfect and sufficient sacrifice, oblation, and satisfaction, for the sins of the whole world."[30]

Despite this breadth of metaphors, the Wesleys' controlling objective model of atonement is Jesus's death as penal satisfaction of God's wrath. This emphasis subsumed other objective concepts such as God's justice or victory. For the Wesleys, the chief problem of sin is neither our failure to uphold God's justice nor our captivity to sin and death, though both are also in view. Rather, it is our guilt for breaking God's law and our resulting alienation from God that must principally be dealt with. God is holy. God's law revealed at Sinai is not an arbitrary set of rules; it is a revelation of God's holy character. To violate it is to reject God, to turn away from him and rebel against his will, thereby incurring his wrath and condemnation.[31]

The Wesleys rejected any notion of the wrath of God as rage subject to irrational outbursts or a hatred of humanity. However, wrath did include God's righteous anger and opposition to human iniquity, which was grounded both

29. See Collins, *Theology of John Wesley*, 98–110; Lindstrom, *Wesley and Sanctification*; Maddox, *Responsible Grace*, 96–98; Wood, "John Wesley's Use of Atonement."
30. *1662 Book of Common Prayer*, 262.
31. Maddox, *Responsible Grace*, 98–101.

in his justice and in his aggrieved love for humanity. Thus, prior to all other considerations, addressing the guilt that separates sinners from God was the Wesleys' chief concern—both for the human race *en masse* and for individuals. Accordingly, commenting on Colossians 1:14, John Wesley remarks, "The voluntary passion of our Lord appeased the Father's wrath, obtained *pardon* and *acceptance* for our sins, and, *consequently*, dissolved the dominion and power which Satan had over us through our sins."[32]

Why did the Wesleys prioritize the problem of guilt and divine wrath, and its solution of penal satisfaction, over other atonement motifs? Because, like Abelard, their soteriology was fundamentally oriented toward the love of God. Yes, God is holy, but God is also love. Indeed, the Wesleys considered God's essential being and character to be "holy love."[33] The vicarious suffering and death of God's Son was the means by which God's holiness and justice could be upheld and pardon declared for sinners, thereby revealing God's essential character of love, which desires reconciliation with fallen humanity. Nowhere more than on the cross was the holy love of God revealed, and by no greater means than the cross could human beings be restored to that love.

Accordingly, the Wesleys gave scant attention to the atonement theology of the Arminian Hugo Grotius, which might uphold justice but not love. And they minimized the Reformed emphasis upon the active obedience of Jesus as a vicarious fulfillment of God's law, which could lead to antinomianism and "dead religion."[34] By contrast, the substitutionary death of Christ in the place of sinners reveals the depths of God's reconciling love for human beings and enables them to love God and neighbor in return. Says John Wesley:

> And as our faith both in God the Father and the Son, receives an unspeakable increase, if not its very being, from this grand event, as does also our love both of the Father and the Son; so does the love of our neighbour also, our benevolence to all mankind, which cannot but increase in the same proportion with our faith and love of God. For who does not apprehend the force of that inference drawn by the loving Apostle: "Beloved, if God so loved us, we ought also to love one another." If God SO loved us,—observe, the stress of the argument lies on this very point: SO loved us, as to deliver up his only Son to die a cursed death for our salvation. Beloved, what manner of love is this wherewith God hath loved us; so as to give his only Son, in glory equal with the Father, in Majesty co-eternal! What manner of love is this wherewith the only-begotten Son of God hath loved us so as to empty himself, as far as possible, of his eternal Godhead;

32. Wesley, *Explanatory Notes* (emphasis added). See Maddox, *Responsible Grace*, 98; Collins, *Theology of John Wesley*, 103–7.

33. Collins, *Theology of John Wesley*, 20–22.

34. Maddox, *Responsible Grace*, 104–5.

as to divest himself of that glory which he had with the Father before the world began; as to take upon him the form of a servant, being found in fashion as a man; and then, to humble himself still further, "being obedient unto death, even the death of the cross!" If God SO loved us, how ought we to love one another![35]

This quotation is instructive, and several points closely correspond to Peter Abelard's atonement theology. First, the entire scope of Jesus's atoning work is trinitarian. Reconciliation is the will of both the Father and the Son. Likewise, the Son's saving life, suffering, and death reveals the love of the Father and the Son. And the Son's reconciling work results in faith in and love for the Father and the Son. While Wesley does not here mention the agency of the Holy Spirit, it is an axiomatic assumption of his soteriology. Much like Abelard, he identified the Holy Spirit with the "grace" and "love" of God. "Grace for Wesley [was] the pardoning, transforming love of God, present to us in the indwelling Person of the Holy Spirit."[36] Says Wesley: "By 'the grace of God' is sometimes to be understood that free love, that unmerited mercy, by which I, a sinner, through the merits of Christ am now reconciled to God. But in this place it rather means that power of God in the Holy Ghost which 'worketh in us both to will and to do of His good pleasure.'"[37]

Second, both faith and love for God receive "an unspeakable increase, if not [their] very being, from this grand event" of Christ's substitutionary passion and death. The love of God is not simply demonstrated or exhibited in the cross. Rather, through Christ's passion God's gracious love in the person of the Holy Spirit *is effectual in awakening faith and love for God in the believing subject*, thereby reconciling the believer to God. In the context of the evangelical revivals, this message was directed both to those who did not believe and to those who had an intellectual belief but no "lively faith." For both sets of hearers, the message was the same: the goal of God's objective work of love in Jesus Christ is to produce in the believer a faith alive with the love of God.

Third, this revelation of divine love in Christ is not limited to the cross. Rather, paraphrasing Philippians 2, Wesley locates the cross as the culmination of the arc of the Son's self-humiliation for the sake of fallen humanity. As with Abelard, the revelation of God's love on the cross is made all the greater by virtue of its continuity with the incarnation and earthly ministry of Jesus. Jesus is no passive victim; the cross is the very purpose for which he "became flesh."

35. Wesley, "God's Love to Fallen Man."
36. Luby, "Perceptibility of Grace," 120.
37. Wesley, "Witness of Our Own Spirit."

Fourth, the Wesleys understood God's most basic disposition toward humanity to be holy love, not wrath. Indeed, the very purpose of Christ's reconciling work was to heal the breach caused by sin and restore sinners to the love of God. As with Abelard, this restored relation will bear fruit in the love of neighbor. For the Wesleys, such love would take the form of a holy life dedicated both to righteous living in obedience to God's law (love of God) and to the care of the poor, the widow, and the orphan (love of neighbor).

Finally, like Abelard, the Wesleys were convinced that faith alive with the love of God would be free from fear of God's wrath and condemnation. They were especially fond of quoting 1 John 4:18: "There is no fear in love, but perfect love casts out fear." Nowhere is this idea captured more powerfully than in the final stanza of Charles Wesley's great hymn "And Can It Be?":

> No condemnation now I dread,
> Jesus, and all in him, is mine.
> Alive in him, my living head,
> And clothed in righteousness divine,
> Bold I approach th'eternal throne,
> And claim the crown, through Christ my own.
> Amazing love! How can it be,
> That Thou, my God, shouldst die for me?[38]

Evaluation

We see a remarkable degree of similarity in the atonement theologies of Peter Abelard and the Wesleys, though we also see significant differences of emphasis. The Wesleys stress more than Abelard the objective problem of God's wrath and the corresponding necessity of God's pardon. By contrast, Abelard emphasizes the subjective appropriation of God's atoning love. However, this is a difference of degree, not kind. Abelard predicates his apology for divine love upon the substitutionary death of Christ, while the Wesleys emphasize the substitutionary death of Christ as the working of divine love. Wesley scholars have been quick to distance the Wesleys from Abelard; however, this appears to be because they have accepted the common depiction of Abelard as a moral exemplarist.[39] In reality, as Anthony Lane acknowledges, "[Abelard] made the

---

38. Wesley, *Works of John Wesley*, 7:323 (Hymn 193).

39. E.g., Collins, *Theology of John Wesley*, 110; Maddox, *Responsible Grace*, 106–8; Wood, "John Wesley's Use of Atonement," 66.

subjective effects of Christ's work *primary*, but without eliminating the objective effects."[40]

Differences aside, Abelard and the Wesleys together represent a vital motif in the Christian tradition of atonement theology: atonement as the working of divine love. Recalling our division between constitutive and illustrative approaches, this model is constitutive but in a subjective mode. While not objectively constitutive of atonement in respect to what God has accomplished in Christ "once for all" in the past, this model is personally and relationally constitutive of atonement in that it emphasizes the effectual application of the objective work of Christ by the Holy Spirit to the life of the individual believer, thereby reconciling the believer to God. Without this subjective aspect, the atoning work of Christ remains a historical event in the past and effects no reconciliation in the present.

By advancing this subjective aspect of reconciliation, this motif also advances the role of the Holy Spirit in God's economy of atonement. It is the Spirit who makes the objective atoning work of Christ subjectively present to the believer, effectually uniting the believer to God in love and awakening the believer to the "love of God." Here Abelard's metaphors of binding and kindling are helpful. They capture the present, active, irreducibly personal and relational intersection of divine and human agency entailed in reconciliation. The result of the reconciling work of divine love is the human person alive and united to God in Christ through the Holy Spirit. An exclusively moral exemplarist approach, by contrast, emphasizes the past completed action of Christ as a historical datum with no intrinsic relation to the present response (or non-response) of the autonomous individual. Such an approach fits perfectly within a modern, rationalist, and individualist anthropology but effectively denies the present active agency of the Holy Spirit, not to mention the Trinity as a whole.

In highlighting the work of the Holy Spirit in the motif of divine love, we also bring to the fore the united atoning action of the Holy Trinity. As both Abelard and the Wesleys (and Augustine) demonstrate, the love of God in the person of the Holy Spirit *is* the love of the Father and the Son, united in the Godhead's decision to save fallen humanity. This essentially trinitarian character of atonement stands as a controlling principle in relation to paradigms that would tend to isolate the work of Jesus Christ from the conjoined agency of the Father and the Spirit. "Father, forgive them; for they do not know what they are doing," utters Jesus Christ *in extremis* (Luke

40. Lane, *Bernard of Clairvaux*, 40.

23:34), directing us to recognize the atoning love of the Father proffered in the Son's saving work.

A related contribution made by the atonement motif of divine love is its emphasis on the teleology of atonement. Both the Wesleys and Abelard stress the goal of God's atoning work in the restoration of human being to the love of God and neighbor. In this respect, we may speak of "moral influence" as an outcome; however, "influence" does not adequately capture the relational and participatory character of either Abelard's binding and kindling metaphors or the Wesleys' pietism. "Moral transformation" would be more accurate. Whatever our terms, the telos of this approach is the restoration of human beings *by* the love of God in Jesus Christ to their original creaturely vocation *to* love God and neighbor. This is the primary goal of reconciliation. Randy Maddox sums up this aspect accordingly: "One is tempted to describe this as a Penalty Satisfaction *explanation* of the Atonement which has a Moral Influence *purpose*."[41]

Both Abelard and the Wesleys echo patristic approaches surveyed in previous chapters. In Abelard, we find similarities to Athanasius's emphasis upon Christ as the wisdom of God, our divine teacher. Jesus is our moral exemplar because, as the eternal and incarnate Word of God, he is the ontological exemplar of all creation and of humanity made in God's image. And in both Abelard's emphasis upon the love of God as the supreme love (*summa dilectio*) toward which we are called as well as the Wesleys' emphasis upon personal holiness in conformity to Christ, we recognize the patristic emphasis upon personal moral and spiritual transformation (*theōsis*).[42]

Regarding the three interrelated aspects of atonement theology we have been considering—narrative, history, and ontology—the model of atonement as divine love powerfully unites all three. If atonement finds its source in the love of God, the whole narrative arc of Scripture from creation to consummation fits under a unifying hermeneutic as the outworking of God's love. God's reconciliation of humanity in Jesus Christ is entirely congruent with God's creation of all things through Christ and God's ultimate eschatological purposes—all of which are the outflowing of God's love. Regarding the person and work of Jesus, we also find in this model a unifying principle of Christ's incarnate ministry—from his birth to his resurrection and ascension—such that we can affirm that Jesus Christ is the truest revelation of the love of God in human history. Moreover, insofar as the Holy Spirit is identified as the essential agent of God's love, this model offers a course correction regarding the trinitarian character of atonement theology. As we saw in Irenaeus, both

41. Maddox, *Responsible Grace*, 109.
42. See Christensen, "John Wesley."

the Word and Spirit of God work together to accomplish God's creating and reconciling purposes. Abelard and the Wesleys apply this trinitarian logic to the personal and relational dimension of atonement, with emphasis upon the Holy Spirit as the means of our ongoing participation in God's redeeming love.

Finally, having acknowledged the positive dimensions of atonement as divine love, we must also recognize a certain vulnerability inherent in this model. As we will see in the chapter on moral exemplarism, the modern theological inclination to emphasize—à la Hastings Rashdall—this subjective aspect of atonement to the neglect of objective aspects can result in a doctrine of atonement that renders the history and ontology of Jesus of Nazareth relatively unimportant or even unnecessary. While Abelard cannot rightly be accused of doing this, his tendency to emphasize the subjective dimension of God's love while rejecting the objective models of his day established a historical precedent that has persisted.

By contrast, the Wesleys' approach (as well as those of later medieval and Reformation figures) is arguably more balanced. Their emphasis upon the working of divine love through penal substitution demonstrates that the model of atonement as divine love is in principle compatible with any of the other constitutive models of atonement, precisely because it is predicated upon the objective work of God in Jesus Christ. As such, it is an essential, complementary aspect of our reconciliation to God. As we see in our comparison of Abelard and the Wesleys, differing points of emphasis regarding our objective condition of sin and judgment do not preclude agreement that the "love of God" is the primary motive and goal of atonement.

5

. . .

Atonement as Fittingness

Thomas Aquinas

Gustaf Aulén claimed that Thomas Aquinas's theology "involves no change in outlook" from Anselm's satisfaction model of the atonement.[1] While Aquinas incorporates a variation of Anselm's "satisfaction" model in his discussion of the atonement, it is not at all the case that he has no change in outlook. On the contrary, Anselm and Aquinas provide examples of how theologians may employ versions of the same atonement model in very different ways.[2]

First, Aquinas does not focus simply on one model or metaphor for the atonement. Referring to the numerous ways in which the work of Christ brings salvation,[3] he discusses the atonement from several different angles, which include "the standard accounts of Christ's passion prevalent during his time."[4] The basis of this synthetic approach is Aquinas's search for the "fittingness" underlying God's activity. In his summary of the reasons for Christ's passion, he lists the following:

1. Aulén, *Christus Victor*, 93.
2. Aquinas's *Summa Theologiae* will be cited as *ST* followed by part, question, and article. The Prima Secunda and Secunda Secundae will be cited as I-II and II-II respectively, followed by question and article number. Replies to objections will be cited as "ad" followed by number.
3. Davies, *Thought of Thomas Aquinas*, 321.
4. Adam Johnson identifies a modified form of satisfaction, ransom theory, and exemplarism. Johnson, "Fuller Account," 303.

But in this that man was delivered by Christ's passion, many other things besides deliverance from sin concurred for man's salvation. In the first place, man knows thereby how much God loves him, and is thereby stirred to love him in return, and herein lies the perfection of human salvation. . . . Second, because thereby he set us an example of obedience, humility, constancy, justice, and the other virtues displayed in the passion, which are requisite for man's salvation. . . . Third, because Christ by his passion not only delivered man from sin, but also merited justifying grace for him and the glory of bliss. . . . Fourth, because by this man is all the more bound to refrain from sin. . . . Fifth, because it redounded to man's greater dignity, that as man was overcome and deceived by the devil, so also it should be a man that should overthrow the devil; and as man deserved death, so a man by dying should vanquish death. (*ST* III.46.3)

The above passage summarizes at least three standard models of atonement: exemplarist, satisfaction, and defeat of the powers of evil (Christus Victor). In Aquinas's early commentary on Peter Lombard's *Sentences*, he does focus on fulfillment of divine justice as the reason for the incarnation. However, in his later writings, especially the *Summa Theologiae*, his approach is influenced by his biblical commentaries and his reading of John of Damascus's *De Fide Orthodoxa*. In this new outlook, Thomas "allows the divine goodness to control his overall approach to the Incarnation."[5]

Second, Aquinas rejected the position that would later be associated with the Franciscan theologian John Duns Scotus—that the Son of God would have become incarnate even if humans had not sinned. Aquinas admitted that God in theory *could* have become incarnate if humans had not sinned (*ST* III.1.3); however, his reasoning about the atonement is guided by two crucial and correlated themes: the freedom of God and the limitations of human knowledge. Because theology proceeds *a posteriori* (after the fact), we only consider God's intentions on the basis of what God actually has done. Accordingly, Aquinas insists, only through revelation can we know God's intentions with any certainty, and divine revelation (as found in Scripture) consistently indicates that God became incarnate because of human sin (III.1.3).

Third, this insistence on divine freedom leads to another point on which Aquinas disagrees with Anselm. Although we know from Scripture that the Son of God became incarnate to save sinful humanity, Aquinas agrees with Abelard and others that, strictly speaking, the incarnation was not necessary: "For God with his omnipotent power could have restored human nature in many other ways" (*ST* III.1.2). Aquinas distinguishes between something being "absolutely necessary" and something being necessary to achieve an

5. Cessario, "Aquinas on Christian Salvation," 117–18.

intended outcome. Anselm speaks of the incarnation as being "conditionally necessary" because without it the divine order of justice would not be satisfied. According to Aquinas, however, because there is no one higher than God and sin is primarily an offense against God, God could have freely forgiven sin without committing any injustice or harm: "God has no one higher than himself, for he is the sovereign and common good of the whole universe. Consequently, if he forgive sin, which has the formality of fault in that it is committed against himself, he wrongs no one: just as anyone else, overlooking a personal trespass, without satisfaction, acts mercifully and not unjustly" (III.46.2 ad 3).[6]

Fourth, Anselm had found attempts to justify the atonement based on "fittingness" to be unsatisfactory, attempting instead to establish an argument in *Cur Deus Homo* based on necessity. By rejecting the notion that the incarnation was strictly necessary to forgive sin, Aquinas implicitly rejects Anselm's methodology of necessity. God became incarnate not of necessity but because it was the most "fitting" way to bring about salvation. "Fittingness" (*convenire*) refers to the process of "bringing things together" (*con + venire*). That act is most "fitting" (*conveniens*) that "brings about the most effects ordered towards that end." The incarnation "brings together the greatest number of desired effects."[7] Thus, he prefaces the passage cited above listing the many ways in which Christ brings salvation by stating, "Among means to an end that one is the more suitable whereby the various concurring means employed are themselves helpful to such end" (*ST* III.46.3). While Anselm also uses the notion of fittingness, his notion is tied closely to necessity, which contrasts sharply with Aquinas: "Whereas Anselm uses fittingness to narrow down or eliminate possibilities as he explores the necessity of the incarnation, Thomas uses it to give increased breadth to the scope of his account of the effects flowing from Christ's passion." This enthusiasm to explore the "multiple effects" associated with fittingness leads Aquinas to embrace multiple atonement motifs rather than focus on only one. Thus, fittingness is "the central feature of Thomas' understanding of atonement," a "kind of wellspring of Aquinas' entire Christology." Fittingness appears, for example, in his discussions of Christ's incarnation, his passion, and his descent into hell (III.1.1; III.46.3; III.52.1).[8]

Fifth, and perhaps most critically significant, Aquinas's approach stands in striking contrast to Anselm's method of reasoning "apart from Christ"

6. Cessario, "Aquinas on Christian Salvation," 122.
7. Johnson, "Fuller Account," 305.
8. Johnson, "Fuller Account," 304–7; Gondreau, "Humanity of Christ."

(*remoto Christo*). Aquinas works on the assumption that Jesus Christ's incarnation, life, death, and resurrection have occurred, then seeks to understand why God chose this particular means of accomplishing salvation as "more fitting."[9] In doing so, Aquinas embraces an understanding of atonement that considers the entire subject matter of the Christian faith witnessed in Scripture and summarized in the creeds. That understanding touches on every area of theology: the nature of the triune God; creation and fall; God's covenant with Israel, including the Old Testament law; a discussion of the entire life of Jesus, his crucifixion, resurrection and ascension; the unity of the risen Christ with the church as the body of Christ; and, finally, eschatology. Accordingly, Aquinas does not restrict discussion of the atonement to Jesus's death on the cross.[10]

Faith Seeking Understanding: Knowing and Being

Aquinas and his contemporaries did not use the word "theology" in the modern sense. In his *Summa Theologiae*, he uses the term *sacra doctrina* ("holy teaching").[11] *Sacra doctrina* concerns the subject matter of theology and integrates three dimensions of this subject matter: (1) knowledge (or epistemology); (2) being (or ontology)—that is, the different ways in which God and creatures exist and how creatures are related to God; and (3) salvation—that is, the human being as created in the image of God, fallen into sin, reconciled through God's saving work in Jesus Christ, and a pilgrim (*viator*) on the way to union with God in the "beatific vision" (eschatological union with God and immediate "seeing" of God in his presence). *Sacra doctrina* is "faith seeking understanding." However, this faith is not mere intellectual belief but is informed by the love for the triune God who is both Creator and Savior, both the origin and the eschatological goal of the rational creature. Thus, the faith of *sacra doctrina* is faith as "participatory" knowledge.[12]

Knowing: Beginning with Scripture

To speak of the place of knowledge in Aquinas's discussion of *sacra doctrina* is to speak of the necessity of divine revelation and Scripture. Revelation is necessary because, by themselves, human beings are incapable of

9. Davies, *Thought of Thomas Aquinas*, 332; Johnson, "Fuller Account," 305.
10. Cessario, "Aquinas on Christian Salvation," 121.
11. Torrell, *Saint Thomas Aquinas*, 2:1–2; Marshall, "*Quod Scit Una Uetula.*"
12. Torrell, *Saint Thomas Aquinas*, 2:2–3.

knowing what the purpose of life is or how to attain it. Even if humanity had never sinned, we would not be able to know or attain God's purpose for us without revelation. Revelation is thus necessary for human salvation (*ST* I.1.1).[13]

Sacra doctrina is thus the study of divine truth made known by revelation. We know this revelation through Scripture, read primarily in its literal sense. Scripture refers to transcendent realities principally through metaphorical language rooted in physical realities, which are the primary objects of our knowledge. Aquinas acknowledges that much biblical language is therefore properly understood as metaphorical—for example, "The Lord is my shepherd" or "Our Father in heaven" (*ST* I.1.9–10). He recognizes other sources of authority besides Scripture (the church fathers and tradition) but insists that these are merely probable sources of authority (I.1.8).

According to Aquinas, the formal "object of faith" is the "first truth" revealed by God in Scripture. The "material things" to which faith assents include not only God but also those things that are related to God and specifically those things that enable the human being to return to God (*ST* II-II.1.1). The chief objects of faith order us directly to eternal life and form the central "articles of faith"—the articles of the Creed (II-II.1.6). The articles of faith focus on God's nature and purpose and on Christ's incarnation, which brings us to God. They include the trinitarian persons, creation, grace, eschatology, and Christ's incarnation, virgin birth, crucifixion, resurrection, ascension, and coming judgment (II-II.1.8).

The articles of faith are not an "addition" to Scripture. The truth of faith is contained in Scripture but in different "forms of expression" (genres) and "sometimes obscurely." Accordingly, the church has drawn up a "symbol" (creed), which is "a clear summary" of the teachings of Scripture (*ST* II-II.1.9). Despite the systematic organization of the *Summa Theologiae*, Aquinas's theology is first and foremost a biblical theology.[14]

Being (Ontology): Beginning with the Trinity

Aquinas's correlation of knowing and being is evident in the role that the doctrine of the Trinity plays in the *Summa Theologiae*, which provides the overarching structure for his entire theology. The God of whom he speaks is the God of the "articles of faith"—the Holy Trinity. Aquinas opens his discussion with three crucial affirmations concerning the triune God. First, there is no "natural" knowledge of the Trinity (*ST* I.32.1). The Trinity is known

---

13. Marshall, "*Quod Scit Una Uetula*," 3, 5.
14. See esp. Healy, "Introduction," 18–19.

through revelation alone, through what Thomas calls the "divine missions," or what the church fathers called the "economy" of salvation.[15]

Second, there is a close correlation between creation and salvation in the doctrine of the Trinity.[16] Aquinas states: "There are two reasons why the knowledge of the divine persons was necessary for us. It was necessary for the right idea of creation. The fact of saying that God made all things by his Word excludes the error of those who say that God produced things by necessity. . . . In another way, and chiefly, that we may think rightly concerning the salvation of the human race, accomplished by the Incarnate Son, and by the gift of the Holy Spirit" (ST I.32.1 ad 3). The doctrine of the Trinity shows that God creates freely and not of necessity.[17] If God had chosen not to create, he would not have been deprived or lacking in some sense. Rather, God's love is expressed fully and sufficiently within the personal relations of the Trinity. Creation therefore reveals an uncoerced generosity, a free and unnecessary "overflowing" of the trinitarian divine love. At the same time, the processions of the immanent Trinity are reflected in creation itself. That God is triune is reflected in created reality (I.37.2 ad 3).

Third, the heart of Christian faith concerns the missions of the Trinity (the economic Trinity). The Father creates through the agency of the Son and the Spirit; the Son reconciles in the incarnation; and the Spirit enables us to share by grace in the communion of the triune persons (ST II-II.2.8).[18]

Creation and Grace

The third crucial element in Aquinas's articulation of the subject matter of theology—*sacra doctrina*—is his understanding of creation, anthropology, and soteriology. The doctrine of creation corresponds to the priority of the Trinity in his theology of salvation and grace. The doctrine of the triune God, correlated with creation and eschatology, provides the structure for Aquinas's account of human nature.[19] The human being is created in the image of God and oriented toward union with God (ST I.1.1; I.93.1; I-II prologue). The moral life, which comprises knowing and loving God, reflects God's triune nature as the God who knows himself in the Word and loves himself in the Holy Spirit (I.43.3, 5 ad 2). Every human being is made in the image of the triune God—with a created capacity to know and love God in a manner that

---

15. Emery, *Trinitarian Theology*, 13.
16. Emery, *Trinitarian Theology*, 8.
17. Emery, *Trinitarian Theology*, 42.
18. Emery, *Trinitarian Theology*, 8.
19. Merriell, "Trinitarian Anthropology"; Torrell, *Saint Thomas Aquinas*, 2:80–100.

reflects God's self-knowledge and self-love—and is made to worship God (I.93.4, 6–9). This orientation toward union with God as the Greatest Good provides the basis for all human choices—even sinful ones—and is not lost in the fall into sin. Indeed, we cannot even sin without depending on God and his grace.[20]

As mentioned above, the teleological goal of humanity is union with God in the "beatific vision." This is possible only by God's grace (*ST* I-II.3.8); no human being can attain it through self-effort. Aquinas's doctrine of grace is both teleological and eudaemonistic (directed toward happiness) in that grace brings humanity to its teleological goal of "beatitude" (complete well-being or "blessedness") and friendship with God.[21]

Aquinas understands salvation as forgiveness of sin but also as re-creation in Christ and elevation above what the human being could accomplish through natural capacities. In the fallen and restored human being, the renewed image of God consists in being conformed to Christ by grace as we come to know and love God. This is true only of the justified, those who have begun to possess a "habit" (*habitus*) or indwelling disposition of faith, hope, and charity (*ST* I-II.110). The teleological structure of Aquinas's anthropology means that the reconciled human being is a "pilgrim" (*viator*)—created and fallen, but also restored and on the road to salvation (I.113.4; I-II.69.2; II-II.24.4, 7).

The correlation of these three dimensions provides the theological background to Aquinas's account of Christology and atonement: (1) the knowledge of God, human nature, and salvation given through divine revelation, (2) the being of the triune God, who has created and restored creation in the salvation of humanity through the incarnation of the Word and the indwelling of the Holy Spirit, and (3) the teleological and eudaemonistic account of humanity as created in the triune image of God, oriented toward eschatological union with God, fallen into sin, and reconciled and restored through the incarnation of the Son of God and the indwelling of the Holy Spirit.

Beginning with Love

Why did God become human? Aquinas is clear on the basis of Scripture that sin alone did not make the incarnation necessary. While his account of atonement and soteriology includes the forgiveness of sin and restoration of a fallen creation, Thomas includes an additional element that is tied closely to his theological presuppositions above. Beginning with the *Summa contra*

20. On sin in Aquinas, see *ST* I-II.71–89.
21. Kerr, *After Aquinas*, 128–30.

Gentiles, he introduces a "fresh approach," stating that "it was convenient that *God become man to give man the possibility of seeing God*"—the beatific vison.[22] (Note that "seeing" is literal here, not metaphorical.) The humanity of the incarnate Christ is the way that leads us back to the love of God. As Aquinas notes, human beings need a "guiding hand." In the incarnation of the Word, Christ's humanity makes God's love physically manifest as a visible sensible object, thus enabling embodied human beings to love the invisible God, whom we have not seen, through the incarnate Christ, whom we have seen (*ST* II-II.82.3).

Thus, Aquinas's approach begins with divine love. It correlates the triune love of God with the human being's orientation toward, and incompleteness without, God's love: "The Father loves not only the Son, but also Himself and us, by the Holy Spirit" (*ST* I.37.2). In the incarnation, the divine love that is shared between the three divine persons has now been shared with humanity: "It belongs to the essence of the highest good to communicate itself in the highest manner to the creature, and this is brought about chiefly by 'his so joining created nature to himself that one Person is made up of these three—the Word, a soul and flesh,' as Augustine says (*De Trin.* xiii). Hence it is manifest that it was fitting that God should become incarnate" (*ST* III.1.1).[23]

In becoming human, God did not merely provide human beings with an example of his love. By uniting himself to human nature, God provided a way for human beings to achieve beatitude. Moreover, since friendship is only possible between those who share some mutual likeness, it was only by becoming human that God and human beings could truly become friends: "Moreover, friendship is based on a certain equality, and consequently it would seem that those who are very unequal cannot be united in friendship. And so, that friendship between man and God might be more intimate, it was well for man that God should become man—since friendship between man and man is natural—in order that by knowing a God made visible to us, we might be drawn to the love of things invisible."[24]

Why did God become human? Aquinas's answer is that, in the incarnation, God freely shared with human beings the triune love between the Father, Son, and Holy Spirit by becoming one of them, thus enabling friendship between God and human beings. The goal of that friendship is the eschatological union between human beings and God that fulfills the teleological purpose of humanity's creation—and results in beatitude.

22. Torrell, *Saint Thomas Aquinas*, 2:107 (emphasis added).
23. Cessario, "Aquinas on Christian Salvation," 120.
24. Aquinas, *ScG* 4.54.

Models of Atonement

In the twelfth and thirteenth centuries, theologians attempted to overcome the divide between Anselm and Abelard by incorporating Anselm's emphasis on justice with Abelard's focus on love in their accounts of salvation. Albert the Great, Bonaventure, and Thomas Aquinas all include variations on Anselm's satisfaction account, combined with the centrality of Christ's charity, discussions of merit, and the significance of the church as the "mystical body" of Christ. Aquinas also incorporates a new appreciation for the Old Testament that had begun in the eleventh century. He understands Christ to be the fulfillment of both torah (law) and temple through the offices of prophet, priest, and king: Christ came into the world to "publish the truth" (prophet), to "free men from sin" (messianic king), and "that by him we might have access to God" (priest).[25]

A key aspect of Aquinas's understanding of atonement is found in the distinction between "image formation" and "image restoration." Aquinas distinguishes between things that refer to "furtherance in the good" (*ad promotionem hominis in bono*) and those that refer to "deliverance from evil" (*ad remotionem mali*). Image *formation* "points to the realization of image-perfection in the human creature": the incarnate Word speaks the truth, moves us to hope in eternal life, provides an example of the divine love, and through his humanity enables us to share in the divine life. Image *restoration* concerns the evils from which the incarnation delivers humanity: deliverance from Satan's bondage, deliverance from despair, and satisfaction for sin.[26] In addition, image restoration itself has two aspects: satisfaction and liberation from sin. The former corresponds to the demands of divine justice, while the latter focuses on human "merit." Aquinas also distinguishes between "satisfaction" and "meriting grace." Satisfaction is the solution to past sin; insofar as Christ's death "merits grace," it is the solution to the problem of continued future sin. Thus, "Christ's suffering and dying have two principal effects: satisfaction for our past sins and salvation from our sinful nature."[27]

Thus, the saving work of Christ breaks down into two broad divisions for Aquinas: image formation and image restoration, with image restoration dividing into the two subcategories of satisfaction and liberation. These categories correspond to the distinctions between "prophet" (image formation), "king" (image restoration: liberation), and "priest" (image restoration: satisfaction). In what follows, we will refer instead to Aquinas's discussion

25. Levering, *Christ's Fulfillment of Torah*, 6–7, 41–42.
26. Cessario, "Aquinas on Christian Salvation," 119.
27. Cessario, "Aquinas on Christian Salvation," 126; Stump, *Aquinas*, 430.

of Christ's saving work using the terms discussed in previous chapters: exemplarism, satisfaction, and participation.

Christ as Ontological Exemplar

Aquinas emphasizes that Jesus was both a teacher and a moral example, but his revelatory activity in the economy of salvation must be understood in the context of his personal identity as the incarnate Word of God become human. To understand how Jesus is our example, we must first understand who Jesus is. Christ can be our (moral) example only because he is first our (ontological) exemplar.[28]

As the Word of God who is the Second Person of the Trinity, the Word is the "exemplar" (intelligible pattern or model) for the creation of all creatures. The perfection of creatures is traced to its "explanatory principle in the Son," who, being the perfect image of the Father, is the divine pattern and rational principle for the existence of creatures. In their existence and perfection, all creatures "imitate and reproduce something of the divine nature."[29] So Aquinas writes: "Whatever is contained in the Father's knowledge is necessarily and entirely expressed by his only Word and in the very same manner in which all things are contained in His knowledge. . . . Therefore, because the Son is a Word that perfectly expresses the Father, the Son expresses all creatures."[30]

However, the Word is the divine model not only for the creation of all creatures but also for their restoration. While Aquinas believed that any of the three divine persons could have become incarnate, it was "more fitting" that the Word should have done so for two reasons. First, because the Word is the exemplar on the basis of which God the Father knows and creates, there is a special resemblance between creatures and the Word. This is even more the case for rational creatures, since the attribute of wisdom is specifically appropriated to the Son as the Word, the eternal Wisdom from whom all human wisdom derives (ST III.3.8).[31]

Second, Christ's exemplarity is evident in the correlation between the divine Sonship of Jesus and our human sonship. The Son's filial relationship to the Father is unique in that he alone is Son by nature (by eternal generation), whereas we creatures have a filial relation to the Father only through "participation." Aquinas identifies three degrees of sonship: First, unlike creatures, the Son

---

28. Gondreau, "Humanity of Christ," 260. See also Torrell, *Christ and Spirituality*, 87, 91, 120–21.

29. Torrell, *Saint Thomas Aquinas*, 2:59.

30. Aquinas, *De Veritate* 4.4, qq. 1–9.

31. Levering, *Christ's Fulfillment of Torah*, 35.

proceeds "naturally" from the Father as his eternal Word. Second, for creatures, there is a certain likeness between all creatures and the Son, insofar as (like an artisan) God's "concept" (the Word) of what he creates is the intelligible model (exemplar) of whatever he makes. Finally, there is the likeness of adoption that takes place through grace. As the Word shares in a natural union with the Father, those who are adopted through grace share in the love between Father and Son, for this love has been "poured forth in [human] hearts by the Holy Spirit" and they have received "the Spirit of adoption of sons" (*ST* III.23.3).

In the previous two cases, exemplarity applies to Christ as the Second Person of the Trinity either as the Word, who is the exemplar of creation, or as the Son, whose sonship as the Second Person of the Trinity is the model for the adoptive sonship of Christians. A third instance of exemplarity in Aquinas concerns the exemplarity of the incarnate Word as "head of the church" and the source of all mediated grace. Aquinas's notion of Christ as head of the church serves as a summary statement of his Christology as a whole.

Aquinas endorses the historical Chalcedonian position that Christ is a divine person who is both fully God and fully human, and that both are necessary for salvation. While Jesus Christ's personal identity is that of God the Word—Christ is a divine person—the incarnate Jesus Christ is also fully human, having not only a human body but also a human mind, will, and soul (*ST* III.5.1–4).[32] Aquinas goes to great lengths to describe the complete human-ity of Christ.[33] In contrast to theologians who reduce the work of Christ to his passion and death, Aquinas understood the expression "actions and suffer-ing of Christ" (*acta et passa Christi*) to refer to everything that Jesus Christ experienced as a human being, all of which forms part of his saving work.[34]

The fundamental rationale for Aquinas's affirmation of Chalcedonian Chris-tology is soteriological.[35] Only God can save, and it is through the mediation of God who has become a human being that human beings are saved. Aquinas's initial motivation is a theology of deification, that only God can give the rational creature a share in the divine life (*ST* I-II.112.1).[36] However, God does not pro-duce deification directly but through the mediation of the assumed humanity of Christ: "Christ's humanity is an 'organ of his Godhead,' as [John] Damascene says (*De Fide Orth*. iii, 19). . . . Christ's humanity does not cause grace by its own power, but by virtue of the divine nature joined to it, whereby the actions of Christ's humanity are saving actions" (*ST* I-II.112.1 ad 1).

32. Gondreau, "Humanity of Christ," 263.
33. See Gondreau, "Humanity of Christ," 265–69.
34. Torrell, *Saint Thomas Aquinas*, 1:261–66; Cessario, "Aquinas on Christian Salvation," 121.
35. Wawrykow, "Hypostatic Union," 232.
36. Torrell, *Saint Thomas Aquinas*, 2:126; Torrell, *Christ and Spirituality*, 92.

Aquinas here introduces a key notion in his soteriology—that of Christ's humanity as the "instrumental cause" of salvation. The notion of instrumental causality is something unique in Aquinas's time that he appropriates from John of Damascus, and it appears late in Aquinas's theology.[37] To be clear, Christ's humanity is not a separate instrument in the manner that a carpenter might use a saw or a musician play a piano. Rather, Christ's humanity is a *conjoined* instrument—that is, it is not separate from the divine person who wields it. Because the incarnate Jesus Christ truly is God the Son, he is God living and acting *as* a human being. The subject of Christ's humanity is the Word incarnate.[38]

Yet because Jesus Christ's humanity has a human intellect and will, God in Christ acts and lives as a human being. Christ's humanity is not an impersonal instrument (like an ax) but a free and rational instrument. Thus, both Christ's deity and humanity retain their integrity: "Therefore in Christ the human nature has its proper form and power whereby it acts; and so has the divine. . . . The operation of Christ's human nature, as the instrument of the Godhead, is not distinct from the operation of the Godhead; for the salvation wherewith the manhood of Christ saves us and that wherewith his Godhead saves us are not distinct; nevertheless, the human nature in Christ, inasmuch as it is a certain nature, has a proper operation distinct from the divine" (*ST* III.19.1).

Moreover, Christ's humanity is not that of a separate *human* instrument, like a messenger would be. The humanity of Jesus perfectly expresses his deity because his singular personal identity is that of God. Thus, through his incarnate humanity, God the Son is able to produce divine effects. God achieves salvation through the mediation of the humanity of Christ. To give either grace or the presence of the Holy Spirit belongs to Christ as God, but, instrumentally, the giving of grace belongs to Christ as human. "To give grace or the Holy Spirit belongs to Christ as he is God, authoritatively; but instrumentally it belongs also to him as man, inasmuch as his manhood is the instrument of his Godhead. And hence by the power of the Godhead his actions were beneficial, i.e. by causing grace in us, both meritoriously and efficiently" (*ST* III.8.1 ad 1).[39]

This last point is perhaps the most important. Building on the apostle Paul's notion of Christ as head of the church and the church as Christ's body, Aquinas affirms that Christ is the head of the church as his "mystical body" (*ST* III.8.1). It is as mediator between God and humanity and head of the church that the incarnate Christ in his humanity is the instrumental cause by which the Holy Spirit and "habitual grace" are given to the members

37. Gondreau, "Humanity of Christ," 263–64.
38. Wawrykow, "Grace," 213.
39. White, *Incarnate Lord*, 113.

of his body, the church.[40] But Aquinas speaks of Christ as head not only in reference to the giving of habitual grace but also in terms of satisfaction for sin: "The head and members are as one mystic person; and therefore Christ's satisfaction belongs to all the faithful as being His members" (III.48.2 ad 1).[41] As will be seen in the next sections, Thomas's discussion of soteriology has two key aspects: satisfaction and participation. Christ's position as head of the church is the theme that ties both together.[42]

Christ as Moral Exemplar

As mentioned above, ontological and moral exemplarity belong together in Aquinas's theology. Only because the incarnate Word is humanity's ontological exemplar can he also be our moral exemplar and example. Aquinas speaks of several ways in which Christ as exemplar is revealer, moral example, and teacher.

First, the life and teaching of Jesus Christ manifest his divinity. Jesus's words and deeds reveal his personal identity as God the Son become a human being.[43] Aquinas states:

> Our Lord shows his divinity by these two things. Referring to his teaching, he says, The words that I say to you, by the instrument of my human nature, I do not speak of myself, but from him who is in me, that is, the Father: "I declare to the world what I have heard from him," the Father [John 8:26]. The Father, therefore, who speaks in me, is in me. . . . Referring to his works, he says, the Father who dwells in me does the works, because no one could do the works that I do: "The Son cannot do anything of himself" [5:19].[44]

Second, Jesus is both the exemplar and the example of divine love. In the life of Jesus Christ, God's love has been manifested. As noted above, Aquinas lists the manifestation of divine love as the first reason for the atonement. God's love for us in Christ leads us to love him in return and to love our fellow human beings:

> In the first place, man knows thereby how much God loves him, and is thereby stirred to love Him in return, and herein lies the perfection of human salvation;

40. B. Peterson, "Paving the Way?," 272–73; Levering, *Christ's Fulfillment of Torah*, 38–41; Torrell, *Saint Thomas Aquinas*, 2:145, 189; White, *Incarnate Lord*, 87–88.
41. See also *ST* III.49.3.
42. B. Peterson, "Paving the Way?," 271–73.
43. Emery, *Trinitarian Theology*, 9.
44. Aquinas, *Commentary on John* 14 (sec. 1893).

hence the Apostle says (Rom. 5:8): "God commendeth His charity towards us; for when as yet we were sinners . . . Christ died for us." Secondly, because thereby He set us an example of obedience, humility, constancy, justice, and the other virtues displayed in the Passion, which are requisite for man's salvation. Hence it is written (1 Pet. 2:21): "Christ also suffered for us, leaving you an example that you should follow in His steps." (ST III.46.3)[45]

We might be tempted to think that because Jesus Christ is the Son of God, he could not provide a moral example for us. After all, we are not divine but are weak human beings, enslaved by habits of sin. To the contrary, Aquinas argues that it is because Jesus Christ is both fully God and fully human that he is the exemplar for humans and fully discloses human nature. And because he is our divine-human exemplar, only he can provide a true moral example for human living: "Now the example of a mere human being would not be adequate for the entire human race to imitate, both because human reason cannot take everything into account, and it does err in what it does take into account. And so there was given to us the example of the Son of God, which cannot be in error and is adequate for all situations" (*Commentary on John* 13 [sec. 1781]).

Aquinas writes that "in his manner of living our Lord gave an example of perfection as to all those things which of themselves relate to salvation" (*ST* III.40.2 ad 1) and frequently states that "Christ's action is our instruction" (III.40.1 ad 3). He is particularly fond of the expression "An example is more fitting than words" (*plus movent exempla quam verba*).[46] Thus he writes about Jesus's washing of the apostles' feet at the Last Supper: "He said the reason I did this was to give you an example; so you also ought to wash one another's feet, because that was what I intended by this action. For when we are dealing with the conduct of people, example has more influence than words" (*Commentary on John* 13 [sec. 1781]).

In discussing the mysteries of the life of Christ in the *Summa Theologiae*, Aquinas repeatedly refers to each event in Jesus's life as an example for Christian living: fasting, temptation, living among crowds, and so on. In particular, he points to Jesus's crucifixion as the prime example to be emulated. In his listing of the reasons for Christ's passion, Aquinas lists first that we might know of God's love for us but second to provide us an example of godly virtue: "because thereby He set us an example of obedience, humility, constancy, justice, and the other virtues displayed in the Passion, which are requisite for man's salvation" (*ST* III.46.3).

45. Johnson, "Fuller Account," 309; Davies, *Thought of Thomas Aquinas*, 324.
46. Torrell, *Christ and Spirituality*, 88.

Finally, Aquinas writes about Jesus's exemplary role as teacher. He points particularly to the Sermon on the Mount (Matt. 5–7) as "containing the whole process of forming the life of a Christian." In this sermon, Jesus first directs our will by prescribing that we should abstain not only from evil actions but also from evil intentions. Jesus next directs our intentions toward our neighbor by forbidding us to judge unjustly or to entrust sacred things to those who are unworthy of them. Jesus finally teaches us to fulfill the teaching of the gospel by seeking God's help, entering by the narrow way of virtue, being wary of evil influences, and not merely professing faith or hearing Christ's words but practicing his commandments (*ST* I-II.108.3).

Satisfaction

In the previous two sections, we examined Jesus Christ's role as exemplar in Aquinas's theology—what we called image formation. In the next two sections, we look at image restoration, which has two aspects: satisfaction for past sin and deliverance from ongoing and future sin. As noted above, Aquinas joins these two aspects of Christ's saving work under the image of Christ as the head of the church. According to Aquinas, union with Christ as the head of the church accounts for both the satisfaction of divine justice and the restoration of the divine image (*ST* III.48.2 ad 1).

In his discussion of satisfaction, Aquinas uses language that sounds very much like Anselm. Aquinas speaks of the satisfaction of justice rather than honor; however, in a manner similar to Anselm, he states that divine justice would not remit sin without satisfaction. Humanity itself could not provide adequate satisfaction for sin. Insofar as a sin against God creates a kind of infinite offense because of the infinity of the divine majesty, only an infinite effect could satisfy for sin (*ScG* 4.54.9). Aquinas also believed that it was possible for one person to satisfy for another (3.158.7). Accordingly, someone had to satisfy for sin who was both human and divine (*ST* III.1.2). At the same time, what Aquinas says about justice "requiring" satisfaction for sin and the act of satisfaction having "infinite efficiency" must be read in light of what has been said about "fittingness." Divine justice does not require satisfaction in an absolute sense (III.46.2 ad 3) but in accordance with the fittingness of God's chosen means of atonement.[47]

In addition, Christ's passion satisfies not only God's justice but also God's mercy: "That man should be delivered by Christ's passion was in keeping

---

47. See Johnson, "Fuller Account."

with both his mercy and his justice. With his justice, because by his passion Christ made satisfaction for the sin of the human race; and so man was set free by Christ's justice, and with his mercy, since man of himself could not satisfy for the sin of all human nature" (*ST* III.46.1 ad 3).

Moreover, key to Aquinas's understanding of satisfaction was Christ's love that made his passion acceptable as a satisfaction for sin:

> But by suffering out of love and obedience, Christ gave more to God than was required to compensate for the offense of the whole human race. First of all, because of the exceeding charity from which He suffered; secondly, on account of the dignity of his life which He laid down in atonement, for it was the life of one who was God and man; thirdly, on account of the extent of the passion, and the greatness of the grief endured. . . . And therefore Christ's passion was not only a sufficient but a superabundant atonement for the sins of the human race. (*ST* III.48.2)

Importantly, while Aquinas's discussion contains echoes of a Christus Victor model of atonement, he includes these themes within satisfaction. It is through the justice of satisfaction in Christ's passion that humanity is delivered from bondage to the devil (*ST* III.46.3 ad 3).

Scholarly consensus has generally agreed that Aquinas follows Anselm in distinguishing between satisfaction and punishment. Satisfaction is not punishment but an alternative to punishment.[48] Punishment either is medicinal (a corrective of sin) or restores right order by withdrawing some good against the sinner's will. While Anselm emphasizes the latter, Aquinas emphasizes the former. Thus, Aquinas appears to share Anselm's view that satisfaction excludes punishment.[49] As noted above, central to Aquinas's understanding is that Christ's merit comes about through love and obedience.[50] Love, not punishment, is the key, and atonement does not change God's mind: "Christ is not said to have reconciled us with God, as if God had begun anew to love us, since it is written (Jer. 31:3): 'I have loved thee with an everlasting love'; but because the source of hatred was taken away by Christ's Passion, both through sin being washed away and through compensation being made in the shape of a more pleasing offering" (*ST* III.49.4 ad 2).

The immutability of God's love means that "the eternal God does not relent on account of something that Christ accomplishes in history." Christ's

---

48. Erdman, "Sacrifice as Satisfaction," 461–80; Stump, *Aquinas*, 435; Van Nieuwenhove, "'Bearing the Marks,'" 289; White, *Incarnate Lord*, 350.

49. Van Nieuwenhove, "'Bearing the Marks,'" 286, 289.

50. Van Nieuwenhove, "'Bearing the Marks,'" 290.

satisfaction does not mean that God "once again" becomes compassionate; rather, "the human person becomes free to accept God's love."[51] God's justice does not have to be satisfied before God can demonstrate love. Rather, satisfaction is a demonstration of God's unchanging love in a manner that "fittingly" satisfies the requirements of justice in order to transform our situation.

In addition, union with Christ and participation are crucial to Aquinas's understanding of satisfaction.[52] "Satisfaction does not refer to a legalistic transaction. Christ's death . . . atones (*satisfacit*) because of the charity in which he bore it. This 'satisfaction' changes us and our relationship with God, not God as such. . . . Through Christ's satisfaction we begin to participate in God's redeeming work: satisfaction is an inchoative participation in our abiding with God."[53]

However, does this mean that there is no element of punishment in Aquinas's understanding of satisfaction? Passages in which Aquinas speaks of satisfaction do not simply focus on Christ's love but also include Christ's suffering.[54] And in a number of passages Aquinas speaks of Christ's death as a "penalty" (*poena*). For example, he says that Christ's death reveals both the severity and the goodness of God: "God's 'severity' (cf. Rom. 11:22) is thereby shown, for he would not remit sin without penalty [*peccatum sine poena dimittere noluit*]. . . . Likewise his 'goodness' (Rom. 11:22) shines forth, since by no penalty [*poenam*] endured could man pay him enough satisfaction" (*ST* III.47.3 ad 1).

Should Aquinas's notion of punishment be understood as a version of penal substitutionary atonement? Some scholars answer in the affirmative and appeal to his statement, "The cause of the interior pain [of Christ] was, first of all, all the sins of the human race, for which He made satisfaction by suffering" (*ST* III.46.6).[55] However, others point to his distinction between "punishment simply" (*poena simplicitur*) and "satisfactory punishment" (*poena satisfactoria*). The former is "entirely" against the person's will while the latter is a "mitigated punishment," one borne voluntarily but "absolutely speaking" against the will. Aquinas's notion thus appears to be a "hybrid concept," containing both voluntary and involuntary aspects.[56] According to Aquinas, "punishment simply" can only be borne by the actual sinner,

51. Cessario, "Aquinas on Christian Salvation," 128.
52. Van Nieuwenhove, "'Bearing the Marks,'" 290.
53. Van Nieuwenhove, "'Bearing the Marks,'" 291.
54. Johnson, "Fuller Account," 314.
55. Johnson, "Fuller Account," 316–17.
56. B. Peterson, "Paving the Way?," 274; citing Sweeney, "Vice and Sin," 157. The relevant passage is *ST* I-II.87.6.

but "satisfactory punishment" can be borne by another:[57] "A satisfactory punishment is, in a way, voluntary. And since those who differ as to the debt of punishment may be one in will by the union of love, it happens that one who has not sinned bears willingly the punishment for another: thus even in human affairs we see men take the debts of another upon themselves. If, however, we speak of punishment simply, in respect of its being something penal, it has always a relation to a sin in the one punished" (I-II.87.7). Thus, Aquinas concludes, "Christ bore a satisfactory punishment, not for his, but for our sins" (I-II.87.7 ad 3).

This does appear to bring Aquinas closer to a version of penal substitutionary atonement. However, as he develops his views in the third part of the *Summa Theologiae*, he correlates his treatment of Christ's satisfactory punishment in accordance with his overarching emphasis on God's love.[58] He states that Christ's punishment is the "matter" of satisfaction, while the "efficacious principle" is Christ's love by which he willingly suffered on our behalf (*ST* III.14.1 ad 1). Thus, our reconciliation with God occurs because of Christ's love exhibited in the passion, an offering that God loves more than he detested the offense of sin. Christ's satisfactory punishment was the *matter* through which the loving deed took place (III.48.2).[59] Satisfaction for Aquinas thus appears to include a "*kind of* punishment, rather than an *alternative* to it." Moreover, and critically, Christ's "satisfactory punishment" (punishment for another) takes place through the union of love between Christ as head and the church as the members of his body; it is thus not substitution per se but union.[60]

Why did Aquinas modify Anselm to include a "kind of punishment" in his concept of satisfaction? Likely because of his close attention to the language of Scripture, particularly Matthew 26:39, which led him to speak of Christ's satisfactory death as a "kind of (mitigated) punishment." Aquinas's reading of this passage (*ST* III.47.2 ad 2) is more straightforward than that of Anselm, who refused to say that Christ's death was in any way contrary to his will.[61]

Participation

As previously mentioned, scholars have suggested that participation is the key to understanding Aquinas's doctrine of the atonement. Here it is important

57. B. Peterson, "Paving the Way?," 274–75.
58. B. Peterson, "Paving the Way?," 275.
59. B. Peterson, "Paving the Way?," 275.
60. B. Peterson, "Paving the Way?," 276, 277.
61. B. Peterson, "Paving the Way?," 281–82.

to distinguish between two aspects of "image restoration" in Aquinas's soteriology: satisfaction (dealing with past sin) and liberation (dealing with continuing and future sin). "Participation" properly concerns only the latter. While Aquinas's discussion of satisfaction is relatively restricted to a single topic, participation language appears in numerous places in his discussions of the priesthood, resurrection, the new law, and sacraments.

Priesthood

Aquinas's discussion of Christ's priesthood is unique in his time for the simple reason that Peter Lombard did not discuss the topic in his *Sentences*. Aquinas did not discuss the topic until after he had written a commentary on Hebrews—another thing for which he was unique. In the *Summa Theologiae*, his discussion of Christ's priesthood follows his Hebrews commentary fairly closely.[62]

Aquinas does not locate his discussion of Christ's priesthood in the second part of the *tertia pars*, where he discusses the life and work of Christ (qq. 27–59). Instead, he places it in the first part (qq. 2–26), immediately following his discussion of Christ's ontology and prior to his discussion of the "mysteries" of the life of Christ. This is because Aquinas "understands the priesthood as one of the consequences of the hypostatic union with regard to Christ considered in his relation to God the Father."[63] Of particular significance is his notion of mediation. Aquinas states, "The office proper to a priest is to be a mediator between God and the people. . . . Now this is most befitting to Christ. For through him are gifts bestowed on men. . . . Moreover, he reconciled the human race to God, according to Col. 1:19,20: 'In him' (i.e., Christ) 'it hath well pleased [the Father] that all fulness should dwell, and through Him to reconcile all things unto Himself.' Therefore it is most fitting that Christ should be a priest" (*ST* III.22.1).

In the above description, Aquinas affirms two directions of Christ's mediation. On the one hand, he offers prayers to God and makes satisfaction for humanity's sins; on the other hand, he gives divine gifts to human beings. Within this twofold function, Aquinas mentions five ways in which Christ acts as mediator: (1) he teaches the law (speaks *for* God); (2) he offers the people's prayers to God (speaks *to* God); (3) he makes satisfaction for sin; (4) he enables deification ("partakers of the divine nature"); and (5) he brings

---

62. Torrell, *Christ and Spirituality*, 127–28. On Aquinas's discussion of Christ's priesthood, also see Levering, *Christ's Fulfillment of Torah*, 76–79; O'Collins and Jones, *Jesus Our Priest*, 110–21.

63. Torrell, *Christ and Spirituality*, 130.

about reconciliation. Importantly, mediation is not an aspect of priesthood; rather, priesthood is a constituent of mediation. It is because Jesus Christ is a mediator that he is a priest.[64]

Aquinas thus locates Christ's status as mediator in his ontological identity as the incarnate Word—the Second Person of the Trinity become a human being—who brings about reconciliation through his work on the cross (*ST* III.26.1). At the same time, as we have seen above, Aquinas insists that Christ acts as mediator between God and humanity precisely insofar as he is human. As human, he is distinct from God by nature and is able to communicate God's gifts to humanity, while offering satisfaction and prayers to God on behalf of humanity: "We may consider two things in a mediator: first, that he is a mean; secondly, that he unites others. . . . Now neither of these can be applied to Christ as God, but only as man. For, as God, he does not differ from the Father and the Holy Spirit in nature and power of dominion. . . . But both can be applied to him as man. Because, as man, he is distant both from God, by nature, and from man by dignity of both grace and glory" (III.26.2).

Following Hebrews, Aquinas understands Christ to be both priest and sacrifice (*ST* III.22.3 ad 1), and his discussion of sacrifice also includes themes of both satisfaction and participation. According to Aquinas, Christ's death met the condition of three categories of Old Testament sacrifice: sin offering—through Christ's death sins are blotted out; peace offering—through Christ's death we receive grace; and holocaust (i.e., burnt offering)—through Christ's death we have access to glory: "Now these effects were conferred on us by the humanity of Christ. For, in the first place, our sins were blotted out. . . . Second, through him we received the grace of salvation. . . . Thirdly, through him we have acquired the perfection of glory. . . . Therefore Christ himself, as man, was not only priest, but also a perfect victim, being at the same time victim for sin, victim for a peace-offering, and a holocaust" (III.22.2). Thus, Aquinas ascribes three effects to Christ's sacrifice in which human beings participate: remission of sin, preservation in a state of grace, and union with God. All of these were "conferred on us by the humanity of Christ."

Resurrection

Discussion of Christ's sacrifice might give the impression that Aquinas understood Jesus's death alone to suffice for human salvation. However, Aquinas insists that it was necessary that Jesus also rise again from the dead for a number of reasons: (1) for the commendation of divine justice, since God

---

64. Torrell, *Christ and Spirituality*, 131–34.

vindicates those who humble themselves for God's glory; (2) for our instruction, since our belief in Christ's deity is confirmed by his rising from the dead; (3) to raise our hopes, because seeing that Christ our head has risen, we can have confidence that we will rise; (4) "to set in order the lives of the faithful" (especially significant in our discussion of participation); and (5) to finish the work of salvation: "Just as for this reason did he endure evil things in dying that he might deliver us from evil, so was he glorified in rising again in order to advance us towards good things" (ST III.53.1).

Thus, for Aquinas, atonement necessitates not only Christ's passion but also his resurrection. Salvation includes not only deliverance from guilt and punishment but also vindication of the oppressed, instruction in the faith, the promise of hope, and most significantly "to set in order the lives of the faithful" and to "complete the work of salvation" (ST III.53.1). As Aquinas states in his conclusion of this discussion, "Christ's passion wrought our salvation, properly speaking, by removing evils; but the Resurrection did so as the beginning and exemplar of all good things" (III.53.1 ad 3). Accordingly, Christ's resurrection is the exemplary cause of our own (III.56.1 ad 3).[65]

The New Law

As we have seen, Aquinas speaks of Christ's work in terms of exemplarity. As the exemplar of grace, Christ is the source of grace in others. As head of the church, Christ both possesses the perfection of all grace and gives grace to others as prophet, priest, and king (ST III.22.1 ad 3). Christ has in himself the fullness of grace insofar as "the [human] soul of Christ, which is more closely united to God than all other rational creatures, receives the greatest outpouring of His grace." At the same time, Christ received this grace in order that he might pour it out on others. The risen Christ gives grace (or the Holy Spirit) not simply in virtue of his deity but specifically as he is human, in that his humanity is the instrument of his deity (III.8.1 ad 1).

At the heart of Aquinas's discussion of grace is his teaching on the "new law" and friendship with Christ. In language that foreshadows Reformation discussions, Aquinas distinguishes between law and gospel. The old law consisted in written commandments, which were obeyed from fear of punishment and were a "pedagogue" to lead people to Christ. But the "old law . . . kills" insofar as it "prescribes what is good, without furnishing the aid of grace for its fulfillment." By contrast, what he calls the new law is the "law of the New Testament . . . instilled in our hearts." The new law derives

65. See Levering, *Christ's Fulfillment of Torah*, 106.

its power from the grace of the Holy Spirit in human hearts: "The New Law consists chiefly in the grace of the Holy Spirit, which is shown forth by faith that works through love. Now men become receivers of this grace through God's Son made man, whose humanity grace filled first, and thence flowed forth to us." Likewise foreshadowing Reformation teaching, Aquinas (following Paul) contrasts "faith" and "works" and identifies the new law with a law written in our hearts by the presence of the Holy Spirit (*ST* I-II.106.1).

Aquinas brings together his teaching on law, Aristotle's understanding of friendship, Jesus's teaching on friendship in John's Gospel, and the Augustinian understanding of the Holy Spirit as the procession of love within the Trinity, in order to speak of grace as friendship with God and the indwelling of all three trinitarian persons in Christians.[66] As the purpose of human law is to create friendship between human beings, the purpose of divine law is to establish friendship between humankind and God (*ST* I-II.99.2). Significantly, Aquinas identified friendship with charity (or love)[67] and interprets John 15:15 to mean that charity is friendship of human beings with God (II-II.23.1). As Aquinas identified God's begetting of the Word with divine wisdom, so the Holy Spirit is the coming forth in God of love (*ScG* 4.20).[68] As Christ is the head of the church, so the Spirit is its heart (*ST* III.8.1 ad 3). Charity among human beings is the love that has been poured into our hearts through the Holy Spirit. The members of the church are united by faith and charity insofar as they are indwelt and loved by all three members of the Trinity and believe in and love the triune God: "Seeing, then, that by the Holy Spirit we are made lovers of God, and that every beloved object is in its lover as such, it follows that by the Holy Spirit, the Father and the Son also dwell in us. . . . Consequently, the effect of the Holy Spirit is that not only is God in us, but also that we are in God" (*ScG* 4.21).

Sacraments

Aquinas's discussion of the sacraments is part of his discussion of Christology and the culmination of everything he has written in *Summa Theologiae*. For him, the sacraments are not isolated means of sanctification but "a bonding of believers with Christ in the unity of the Mystical Body."[69] Aquinas's theology of the sacraments extends his Christology and theology of the atonement in the following ways.

---

66. See esp. Torrell, *Christ and Spirituality*, 45–64.
67. Torrell, *Christ and Spirituality*, 45.
68. Torrell, *Saint Thomas Aquinas*, 2:162–63.
69. Walsh, "Sacraments," 328, 332.

First, the sacraments are a "kind of sign" of Christ. They are visible symbols in both Old and New Testaments, but in the latter they are also effective signs of Christ. Importantly, Aquinas does not say that sacraments are simply signs but rather that they are a "kind of sign" (*in genere signi*) (*ST* III.60.1).[70] Nor are sacraments "mere symbols"; rather, a sacrament is a specific kind of sign, the sign of a sacred reality that sanctifies human beings (III.60.2). That reality signified in the sacraments is Christ himself—with past, present, and future dimensions: "A sacrament is a sign that is both a reminder of the past, i.e. the passion of Christ; and an indication of that which is effected in us by Christ's passion, i.e. grace; and a prognostic, that is, a foretelling of future glory" (III.60.3).[71] Because human beings are sinful, "sacraments are needed because Christ is needed."[72] Indeed, "Sacraments are necessary for man's salvation, in so far as they are sensible signs of invisible things whereby man is made holy" (III.61.3).

Second, the sacraments communicate Christ's presence as instrumental causes of grace. The sacraments "cause grace" in the sense that through them, Christians are incorporated into Christ (*ST* III.62.1). Aquinas appeals to the apostle Paul on baptism: "As many of you as have been baptized in Christ have put on Christ" (Gal. 3:27 Vulgate). Using his earlier notion of instrumental causality, Aquinas suggests that as Christ's humanity is the conjoined instrument of his deity to bring about salvation, so the sacrament is an external instrumental cause of grace (*ST* III.62.5).[73] A sacrament is thus both a sign and a cause that effects what it signifies (III.62.1 ad 1), and "the instrumentality of sacraments is a prolongation of the instrumentality of Christ's humanity."[74]

Finally, Aquinas develops the notion of "sacramental character" to affirm that sacraments are a real participation in the priesthood of Christ. Sacramental character is fundamentally oriented toward worship. The sacrament includes both a downward movement of God and a corresponding upward movement of grace-inspired worship. Building on Hebrews, Aquinas holds that this sacramental character is Christ himself: "The eternal Character is Christ Himself . . . 'who being the brightness of His glory and the figure, or character, of His substance' (Heb. 1:3)" (*ST* III.63.3). Thus, sacramental character is a participation in Christ's priesthood shared by all Christians: "Consequently, it is clear that the sacramental character is specially the character of Christ, to whose character the faithful are likened by reason of the

70. Walsh, "Sacraments," 333.
71. Walsh, "Sacraments," 334–35.
72. Walsh, "Sacraments," 343.
73. Walsh, "Sacraments," 345.
74. Walsh, "Sacraments," 347.

sacramental characters, which are nothing else than certain participations of Christ's priesthood, flowing from Christ himself" (III.63.3).

Conclusion

In the preceding chapters, we examined the notion of atonement as satisfaction introduced by Anselm of Canterbury. Satisfaction is usually considered to be both the definitive medieval understanding of atonement and the first theological attempt to discuss atonement systematically. Whereas the typical discussion of satisfaction would focus primarily (or even exclusively) on Anselm, we have deliberately brought Aquinas into the conversation, devoting more space to Aquinas's discussion of atonement than to Anselm's. Our goal has been to demonstrate the manner in which the same theological idea ("satisfaction") can be treated quite differently by two theologians.

While retaining Anselm's "satisfaction" language, Aquinas departs from him at almost every step of the way. Where Anselm's intention is to establish an argument for the necessity of the atonement—in order to forgive, God's justice must first be satisfied—Aquinas insists that the life, death, and resurrection of Jesus Christ are the "most fitting" way for God to save humanity but not necessary to human salvation. In God's divine freedom, he could have saved humanity some other way.

The most striking contrast between Aquinas and Anselm concerning atonement is between Anselm's "apart from Christ" apologetic in which he attempts to argue *a priori* for the necessity of the incarnation and atonement, and Aquinas's *a posteriori* approach. In Aquinas we find a discussion of the atoning work of Christ that thoroughly integrates his entire account of the Trinity, the incarnation of the Word, and Jesus's entire earthly life and mission, his death, and also his resurrection, continuing mediation of grace to the church, and his second coming.

Consequently, Aquinas's Christology is holistic in contrast to Anselm's exclusive focus on the death of the God-man as a satisfaction of divine honor. As a corollary of this more holistic approach, Aquinas does indeed use the language of satisfaction, including an aspect of punishment, but he also incorporates other traditional atonement imagery—Christus Victor, ontological union, and exemplarism. His fuller account of the life and mission of Jesus combined with an emphasis on participation also has affinities with Irenaeus's recapitulation motif.

Aquinas brings together elements of theology that others often isolate: symbolism, ontology, the immanent and economic Trinity, the person and work of Jesus Christ, the sacraments, ecclesiology, and eschatology. He correlates various anthropological realities and needs: what it means to be human—to be created in the image of God and oriented toward union with God—and how this is retained within discussions of human sin and salvation. He connects Christology and soteriology: Jesus Christ as the Word of God is the exemplar of all creation, the incarnate Word who is fully human and fully divine, who became human to save and re-create sinful humanity. In all of it, we see a theology of atonement that is connected to every aspect of God's economy of creation and salvation.

6

. . .

Atonement as Penal Substitution

John Calvin and Charles Hodge

In preceding chapters, we saw that Anselm's "satisfaction" model of atonement is not properly "penal substitution" because Anselm understood satisfaction and punishment to be exclusive alternatives. Although Aquinas uses "penalty" language, we saw that he understands atonement not as a matter of God punishing Jesus but rather as God in Jesus voluntary assuming the penalty of sin on behalf of sinful humanity.

Thus, while penal substitution is a version of the satisfaction model, it is distinguished by the following characteristics: First, this account of atonement is, strictly speaking, substitutionary. In his saving work, Jesus Christ acts not so much *on behalf of* sinful humanity as *instead of* individual sinners. Jesus takes the place of each sinful human being in the sense that he receives the punishment that person deserves *instead of* him or her receiving it.[1]

Second, in this model, atonement is not simply a satisfaction of justice but is specifically punishment. Penal substitution presupposes a model of retributive justice. God cannot forgive sin unless justice is satisfied, and satisfaction of justice demands punishment.

---

1. This discussion does not address the question of limited versus universal atonement. Penal substitution may be employed by proponents of either view.

Third, while penal substitutionary atonement includes the satisfaction of divine justice, that satisfaction is specifically of God's "wrath." God's justice is expressed in "anger," "wrath," or "fury" against sin. Rather than pour out this wrath on sinners, God pours it out on Jesus Christ.

Fourth, retributive justice is neither corrective nor restorative but traditionally presupposes (a) that those who commit wrong acts deserve a proportional punishment; (b) that it is intrinsically good to give wrongdoers the punishment they deserve—irrespective of other benefits that might arise; and (c) that it is immoral to punish the innocent or to inflict disproportionate punishment on wrongdoers. However, while both satisfaction and penal substitution presuppose a model of retributive justice, penal substitution modifies the traditional understanding of retributive justice by altering the third principle of retributive justice—that it is immoral to punish the innocent. Instead, atonement consists precisely in the substitutionary punishment of an innocent Jesus Christ in the place of deserving sinners.

Finally, penal substitutionary atonement raises the question of the relationship between God's love and God's justice. Traditional atonement theologies claim that atonement is grounded in God's free gracious love. One of the questions raised by penal substitution models is whether God's love is conditional upon God's retributive justice having been fulfilled.

Many Reformation theologians endorsed some variation of the penal substitution model, but John Calvin is the one most closely associated with penal substitution. While Calvin endorsed this view, his atonement theology is not monolithic but a rich tapestry of themes. Because Calvin so closely ties his theology to the Old and New Testaments, "he is able to develop a rich and multifaceted perspective on Christ's life unto death" that avoids a reductive version of penal substitution. Rather, Christ's death is "the central act in the continuing drama of God's life with us and our life with God."[2] Calvin's account of the work of Christ includes not only penal substitution but also Christ's threefold office of prophet, king, and priest; Christ as obedient second Adam; Christ the Victor; Christ our legal substitute; Christ our sacrifice; Christ our merit; and Christ our example.[3]

Knowledge of God and Self

Calvin's *Institutes of the Christian Religion* begins, "Nearly all the wisdom we possess, that is to say, true and sound wisdom, consists of two parts: the

2. Jones, "Fury of Love," 214.
3. From R. Peterson, *Calvin's Doctrine of the Atonement*, table of contents.

knowledge of God and of ourselves" (*Inst.* 1.1.1). While Calvin centers his
theology in God's revelation and salvation in the reconciling work of God
incarnate as Jesus Christ, he grounds that theology in God's disclosure in the
created world. God is known through his "powers" or "perfections" made
evident in his works. The universe is the "living image of God, the theater
of God's glory."[4]

Thus, the natural order of the universe is the "school" in which we should
learn piety, leading to eternal life and perfect happiness (*Inst.* 1.6.1). Calvin
claims that the human mind has a natural awareness of God (*sensus divini-
tatis*). God has implanted in all human beings a "certain understanding of
his divine majesty" (1.3.1). Although God's essence is incomprehensible and
escapes human perception, God's created works contain "unmistakable marks
of his glory." The order of the universe is a "sort of mirror" in which we can
contemplate the otherwise invisible God (1.5.1).

Awareness of God as Creator is not sufficient, however; we must also recognize God's goodness—that he is the "fountain of every good." God regulates
the universe by wisdom, preserves it through his goodness, rules humanity
through righteousness, and watches over and protects his creation. All wisdom, righteousness, power, and genuine truth flow from God as their cause
(*Inst.* 1.2.1). Because God is the "fountainhead and source of every good"
and the "Author of every good," because God is "good and merciful," we can
have "perfect trust" in his "loving-kindness" (1.2.2).

At the same time, what human beings come to know about ourselves from
creation is the reality of our sinfulness: "Since, therefore, men one and all
perceive that there is a God and that he is their Maker, they are condemned
by their own testimony because they have failed to honor him and to conse-
crate their lives to his will" (*Inst.* 1.3.1). Calvin thus begins his theology of
reconciliation with the problem of human sin. He presents the problem of
sin first, with Christology as a subsequent solution to the problem:[5] "The
natural knowledge of God has therefore only a negative value in the first place:
it deprives men of all excuse before God; legitimizes their condemnation."[6]
This approach is markedly different from that of theologians like Irenaeus and
Aquinas, who begin their discussions with a positive account of the doctrine
of the triune God, of the creation of the human being in the image of God,
and of the teleological orientation of the human being to union with God
through participation in the beatific vision—a teleological orientation that
is not lost, even in the fall. This does not mean that sin is not a significant

4. Zachman, "Christology of John Calvin," 284, 285.
5. Van Buren, *Christ in Our Place*, 3, 4.
6. Wendel, *Calvin*, 162.

theme in the atonement theologies of Irenaeus or Aquinas, but it does mean that, comparatively, human sinfulness plays a distinctive role in Calvin's atonement theology.

Calvin pulls no punches when describing the effects of human sin. While the image of God was not destroyed by the fall, "it was so corrupted that whatever remains is frightful deformity." It is "almost blotted out," and whatever remains is "confused, mutilated, and disease-ridden" (*Inst.* 1.15.4). Original sin is a "hereditary depravity and corruption of our nature," which both makes us liable to God's wrath and brings forth evil works. Human beings are "vitiated and corrupted in every part of our nature" and stand "justly condemned" before God (2.1.8). While agreeing with Augustine that pride was the beginning of sin, Calvin locates the essence of sin in disobedience and unfaithfulness rather than in "self-love" (2.1.4).[7]

Calvin partly agrees with those who identify original sin with "concupiscence": "Whatever is in man, from the understanding to the will, from the soul even to the flesh, has been defiled and crammed with this concupiscence" (*Inst.* 2.1.8). Calvin also affirms "total depravity"—that no aspect of human nature has been left uncorrupted by sin (2.1.9). However, he goes beyond these to describe the human being as a constant source of sin: "This perversity never ceases in us, but continually bears new fruits . . . just as a burning furnace gives forth flame and sparks, or water ceaselessly bubbling up from a spring" (2.1.8).

In addition to a moral distance between God and humanity due to sin, Calvin also affirms God's ontological transcendence. Calvin is concerned always to respect the infinite distance separating God from creatures. One of the benefits of the incarnation for Calvin is that it overcomes the distance that separates God and sinners, enabling God to draw near to his people in love and mercy. At the same time, his concern for divine transcendence leads Calvin to reject any notion of an "infusion" of grace, any notion of "deification" or *theōsis*.[8]

Christ as Mediator

This dramatic separation between God and humanity resulting from sin and the infinite distance between God and creation provide the rationale for Calvin's theology of revelation and Scripture. Because the whole human race had

7. Wendel, *Calvin*, 187; Van Buren, *Christ in Our Place*, 4.
8. Wendel, *Calvin*, 151; Jones, "Fury of Love," 218, 219.

perished in Adam, the knowledge of God revealed in creation would have no value apart from Christ: "The whole knowledge of God the Creator . . . would be useless unless faith also followed, setting forth for us God our Father in Christ" (*Inst.* 2.6.1). Knowledge of God is thus twofold: the knowledge of God as Creator that, in light of the fall, confirms humanity in its sinfulness; and the knowledge of God as Redeemer in Christ, who functions as a mediator between God and humanity (1.6.1).

In fashioning the universe, God is known as Creator; in Jesus Christ, God is known as the Redeemer. Both follow the same trajectory: "Just as the powers of God are portrayed in the works of God in the universe, so are the powers of God represented in the person and work of Christ." Christ's divine nature is as equally unknown to us as that of God the Father, yet knowledge of God becomes possible through the works of his humanity. Christ not only makes the invisible God visible but also makes the infinite God finite in a manner that we can know him.[9] In Calvin's words: "Irenaeus writes that the Father, himself infinite, becomes finite in the Son, for he has accommodated himself to our little measure lest our minds be overwhelmed by the immensity of his glory. . . . God is comprehended in Christ alone" (*Inst.* 2.6.4).

The incarnation of God in Christ also bridges the infinite gap between God and sinners. The divine "condescension" overcomes the chasm separating God and sinners, enabling God to dwell with his people in a new way, yet always maintaining the distinction between God and creatures.[10] Calvin writes, "The situation would surely have been hopeless had the very majesty of God not descended to us, since it was not in our power to ascend to him" (*Inst.* 2.12.1).

Thus, Calvin typically refers to the incarnation and work of Christ by the designation of Christ as "Mediator." After the fall of humanity, there is no saving knowledge of God apart from the Mediator (*Inst.* 2.6.1). God did not show favor or the hope of grace to his people Israel apart from the Mediator. Following Paul (Gal. 3:15–18), Christ is the promised salvation of Abraham's seed (*Inst.* 2.6.2). Even apart from the fall, the infinite gap between God and creation would require a mediator, because humanity would be incapable of reaching God on our own. How much more was a mediator required after we had fallen into sin (2.12.1)!

For Christ to mediate between God and creation, it was necessary that he be fully God and fully human (*Inst.* 2.12.1). Like earlier theologians, Calvin writes that only God could save sinful humanity: "For the same reason it was

9. Zachman, "Christology of John Calvin," 285–86. See *Inst.* 1.2.1.
10. Jones, "Fury of Love," 218–19.

also imperative that he who was to become our Redeemer be true God and true man. It was his task to swallow up death. Who but the Life could do this? It was his task to conquer sin. Who but very Righteousness could do this? It was his task to rout the powers of the world and air. Who but a power higher than world and air could do this?" (2.12.2). Calvin is equally emphatic that the Mediator had to be human in order to save sinful human beings: "Clothed with our flesh, he fulfilled the office of Mediator" (2.13.1). Calvin's christological concerns are thus primarily with the economy of salvation—Jesus Christ must be fully God and fully human in order to save sinful humanity.

The Three Offices: Prophet, King, Priest

The threefold office (*triplex munus*) of Christ as prophet, king, and priest was not systematically developed in Calvin's first edition of the *Institutes*. However, in the 1559 edition, it appears as a key insertion between his discussion of the incarnation and of Christ's work of salvation.[11] In addition to serving as a transition from Christ's person to his work, Calvin's discussion of Christ's offices serves also to connect Jesus to Israel.[12]

Calvin summarizes the threefold distinction by placing all three offices within the larger office of "Messiah"/"Christ," which means "anointed" (*Inst.* 2.15.1). Jesus is called "anointed" because the "spirit of wisdom and understanding and might" (Isa. 11:2) rests on him. Jesus's anointing was shown in his baptism when the Spirit hovered over him: "The Spirit has chosen Christ as his seat, that from him might abundantly flow the heavenly riches of which we are in such need" (*Inst.* 2.15.5). In the Old Testament period, prophets, priests, and kings were anointed with holy oil. The title "Messiah" is bestowed upon the Mediator, who is called Messiah primarily with respect to kingship but who is also anointed as prophet and priest (2.15.2).

Calvin says relatively little about the office of prophet. God left an "unbroken line of prophets" in order to provide "useful doctrine sufficient for salvation," yet the full light of understanding would come with the Messiah. The task of the prophets was to "hold the church in expectation and at the same time to support it at the Mediator's coming" (*Inst.* 2.15.1). Christ was "anointed by the Spirit to be herald and witness of the Father's grace." When Paul writes that Christ is our wisdom (1 Cor. 1:30), he means that "the prophetic dignity in Christ leads us to know that in the sum of doctrine as he has given it to us all parts of perfect wisdom are contained" (*Inst.* 2.15.2).

11. Wendel, *Calvin*, 225.
12. Zachman, "Christology of Calvin," 289.

The title "Messiah" is most associated with Jesus as king. As king, Christ bestows the good things we lack. From heaven, he gives the Holy Spirit to his church to enrich, defend, and ultimately lead them to their heavenly goal.[13] In contrast to Old Testament kings, Christ's kingly office is "spiritual in nature." Through his Son, who has survived death, God promises to protect and defend his church (*Inst.* 2.15.3). Additionally, that Jesus is king means that the Father has given him all power that he might govern through him: "That he sits at the right hand of the Father is equivalent to calling him God's deputy, who has in his possession the whole power of God's dominion." Christ thus fulfills the duties of king and pastor for all those who willingly submit to him. Finally, Christ's kingship will be shown in his judgment of the ungodly (2.15.5).

Although it appears last in the *Institutes*, the office of priest is the "foundation" of Calvin's understanding of Christ's role as Mediator. It is "through his priestly work [that] Christ opens the way for his work as prophet and king."[14] Calvin's discussion of Christ's role as priest provides an introduction and transition to his doctrine of atonement as penal substitution. The following concise statement includes many of the themes of Calvin's atonement theology: "As a pure and stainless Mediator [Christ] is by his holiness to reconcile us to God. But God's righteous curse bars our access to him, and God in his capacity as judge is angry toward us. Hence an expiation must intervene in order that Christ as priest may obtain God's favor for us and appease his wrath. Thus Christ to perform this office had to come forward with a sacrifice" (*Inst.* 2.15.6).

Christ's work as priest has two functions: he operates as both "priest" and "sacrifice." No other satisfaction was adequate to provide the sacrifice for our sins apart from the work of the Mediator. At the same time, Christ continues his priestly work as our intercessor before God. Our prayers have no access to God unless our high priest has washed away our sins, sanctified us, and given us grace: "[Christ is thus] an everlasting intercessor. . . . Christ plays the priestly role, not only to render the Father favorable and propitious toward us by an eternal law of reconciliation, but also to receive us as his companions in this great office" (*Inst.* 2.15.6).

Calvin's treatment of the threefold office provides a transition from the person of Christ to the work of Christ, and his summary of Christ's priestly office is the culminating point of this transition. It concisely lays out the major themes that Calvin will pursue in his discussion of atonement.

13. Zachman, "Christology of Calvin," 289.
14. Edmondson, *Calvin's Christology*, 89.

Atonement and Penal Substitution

Like Aquinas, Calvin rejected the notion that the Son of God might have become incarnate if human beings had not sinned because it is without foundation in Scripture. Christ came to save fallen humanity, and Scripture, not abstract speculations, must supply our knowledge of God's salvation: "We well know why Christ was promised from the beginning: to restore the fallen world and to succor lost men" (*Inst*. 2.12.4).

An overarching theme of Calvin's theology of atonement is the principle of exchange. As Mediator, the incarnate Christ has taken on what is ours in order that he might give to us what is his: "Who could have done this had not the self-same Son of God become the Son of man, and had not so taken what was ours as to impart what was his to us, and to make what was his by nature ours by grace?" (*Inst*. 2.12.2).

Accordingly, because Calvin identified sin with disobedience, he placed Christ's obedience to the Father at the center of Christ's mission. If the first requirement of atonement is that the Mediator be fully God and fully human, the second is that the Mediator would remedy human disobedience through his obedience (*Inst*. 2.12.3). Calvin's emphasis on Christ's *human* obedience is thus a "noteworthy" aspect of his account of the atonement.[15] It means that Calvin extends atonement to the entire life of Christ:[16] "How has Christ abolished sin, banished the separation between us and God, and acquired righteousness to render God favorably and kindly toward us? . . . He has achieved this for us by the whole course of his obedience. . . . From the time when he took on the form of a servant, he began to pay the price of liberation in order to redeem us" (2.16.5).

Calvin acknowledges that Scripture focuses on Christ's death and that Christ's obedience is fundamentally oriented to the cross. This does not detract from Christ's entire life of obedience; rather, Christ's death on the cross is the most important aspect of that life of obedience. For it was there that he offered a sacrifice for sin: "And truly, even in death itself his willing obedience is the important thing because a sacrifice not offered voluntarily would not have furthered righteousness" (*Inst*. 2.16.5). Calvin's atonement theology is not simply a theology of the crucifixion.

These three themes—salvation from sin, exchange, and obedience—are the fundamental presuppositions of Calvin's theology of the atonement. He begins his discussion of atonement with a summary that displays these themes through a variety of metaphors:

15. Jones, "Fury of Love," 227; Wendel, *Calvin*, 226; Van Buren, *Christ in Our Place*, 27.
16. Van Buren, *Christ in Our Place*, 29.

Our Lord came forth as true man and took the person and the name of Adam in order to take Adam's place in obeying the Father, to present our flesh as the price of satisfaction to God's righteous judgment. In short, since neither as God alone could he feel death, nor as man alone could he overcome it, he coupled human nature with divine that to atone for sin he might submit the weakness of the one to death; and that, wrestling with death by the power of the other nature, he might win victory for us. . . . Our common nature with Christ is the pledge of our fellowship with the Son of God; and clothed with our flesh he vanquished death and sin together that the victory and triumph might be ours. He offered as a sacrifice the flesh he received from us, that he might wipe out guilt by his act of expiation and appease the Father's righteous wrath. (*Inst.* 2.12.3)

The above account contains elements of (1) obedience, (2) satisfaction, (3) penal substitution, and (4) Christus Victor. One might infer from this that Calvin embraces no single model or metaphor of the atonement. However, as we saw above, Calvin's discussion of Christ's priestly office concludes with a summary of penal substitution. And while Calvin's theology draws on numerous metaphors, these are explained *in terms of* penal substitution. For Calvin "substitution" is the "very centre of the work of Christ," and "Christ in our place" is the point from which the rest of Calvin's theology must be understood.[17] What are the distinctive characteristics of Calvin's theology of penal substitution?

Satisfaction

Western theology following Anselm tended to use satisfaction language, so it should not be surprising to find this language in Calvin. In contrast to Anselm, however, for whom satisfaction and punishment are exclusive alternatives, Calvin identifies satisfaction directly with punishment: "For unless Christ had made satisfaction for our sins, it would not have been said that he appeased God by taking upon himself the penalty to which we were subject" (*Inst.* 2.17.4). In an account that begins with the experience of personal guilt, Calvin couples satisfaction with the appeasement of divine wrath and punishment: "No one can descend into himself and seriously consider what he is without feeling God's wrath and hostility toward him. Accordingly, he must anxiously seek ways and means to appease God—and this demands a satisfaction. . . . God's wrath and curse always lie upon sinners until they are absolved of guilt. Since he is a righteous Judge, he does not allow his law to be broken without punishment, but is equipped to avenge it" (2.16.1).

17. Van Buren, *Christ in Our Place*, 51, 141.

Another distinctive of Calvin's atonement theology seen in this quote is the object of satisfaction. For Anselm and Aquinas, it is God's justice that must be satisfied. For Calvin, the object of satisfaction is God's "wrath."

Substitution

The legal and substitutionary nature of Calvin's atonement theology is shown in his discussion of Jesus's trial before Pontius Pilate. Though Jesus was innocent, he took our place, "became" sin, and was condemned as a criminal instead of us. In doing so, Jesus transferred our guilt and condemnation to himself: "We could not escape God's dreadful judgment. To deliver us from it, Christ allowed himself to be condemned. . . . To take away our condemnation, it was not enough for him to suffer any kind of death: to make satisfaction for our redemption a form of death had to be chosen in which he might free us both by transferring our condemnation to himself and by taking our guilt upon himself" (*Inst.* 2.16.5).

In being condemned as a criminal, Jesus thus "took our place to pay the price of our redemption" (*Inst.* 2.16.7). While our guilt was transferred to him, his innocence was transferred to us. Thus, Jesus's death was in the literal sense a substitution: "This is our acquittal: the guilt that held us liable for punishment has been transferred to the head of the Son of God. We must, above all, remember this substitution" (2.16.5).

Punishment

As noted above, satisfaction for Calvin is not an alternative to punishment but *is* punishment. In listing three requirements for reconciliation with God, Calvin identifies satisfaction with the payment of penalty: "Man, who by his disobedience had become lost, should by way of remedy counter with obedience, satisfy God's judgment, and pay the penalties for sin" (*Inst.* 2.12.3). Calvin's atonement theology is thus a theology of satisfaction as penal substitution: "For when we say that he bore all our sins in his body upon the tree, we mean only that he bore the punishment and vengeance due for our sins" (3.4.30).

Divine Wrath

Just as Calvin's version of satisfaction entails punishment, it also entails the appeasement of God's wrath: "When he himself appeared, he declared that the reason for his advent was by appeasing God to gather us from death unto life" (*Inst.* 2.12.4). Calvin insists that the word "appeasing" is "very important. For in some ineffable way, God loved us and yet was angry toward us at the same time, until he became reconciled to us in Christ" (2.17.2). While some claim that Calvin's atonement theology is strictly about our reconciliation to God, the above quote makes clear that God also needs to be reconciled to us. This raises the question as to whether the death of Christ changes God's attitude toward us. Is the death of Christ the precondition of God's love for us, or is God's love for us the cause of Christ's death for us? We will address this question below.

At the same time, Calvin is clear that this does not mean God was angry toward Christ: "Yet we do not suggest that God was ever inimical or angry toward him. How could he be angry toward his beloved Son?" (*Inst.* 2.16.11). At least one popular caricature of Calvin's theology of atonement is therefore incorrect. Calvin did not create a "division" within the Trinity in which an angry Father inflicts his anger upon his Son rather than us. Calvin's version of penal substitution is not "divine child abuse."[18]

Sacrifice and Redemption

While sacrifice, imputation, redemption, and penal substitution arguably represent four distinct metaphors for atonement, Calvin conflates the first three with penal substitution. In discussing sacrifice, he imports imagery of satisfaction, appeasement of divine wrath, and substitution ("transferred imputation"): "The Father destroyed the force of sin when the curse of sin was transferred to Christ's flesh. . . . Christ was offered to the Father as an expiatory sacrifice that when he discharged all satisfaction through his sacrifice, we might cease to be afraid of God's wrath. . . . He who was about to cleanse the filth of those iniquities was covered with them by transferred imputation" (*Inst.* 2.16.6).

Calvin also interprets the metaphor of redemption in terms of satisfaction and penal substitution: "The apostles clearly state that he paid the price to redeem us from the penalty of death. . . . Satisfaction had been made for our sins with this price. . . . The penalty that we deserved had been cast upon him" (*Inst.* 2.17.5). Calvin never specifies what we owed to God's justice or what the penalty was that Christ paid.[19] Yet insofar as Calvin's model is one of penal substitution, "payment" consists in Jesus having received the punishment we deserved.

Merit

Finally, Calvin's theology of penal substitution is not limited to Christ's death paying the penalty of our sins. In addition to this negative aspect of

18. Van Buren, *Christ in Our Place*, 58.
19. Zachman, "Christology of Calvin," 289

merit (*Inst.* 2.17.4), Calvin asserts that Jesus's own positive righteousness is "imputed" to us: "By his obedience, however, Christ truly acquired and merited grace for us with his Father. . . . If Christ made satisfaction for our sins, if he paid the penalty owed by us, if he appeased God by his obedience . . . then he acquired salvation for us by his righteousness, which is tantamount to deserving it" (2.17.3).

Calvin interprets Romans 4 in terms of "imputation of righteousness." He writes that "the righteousness found in Christ alone is reckoned as ours" (*Inst.* 2.17.5). As mentioned above, Calvin's atonement theology includes the "whole course" of Christ's obedience, and the discussion of merit seems to point in that direction. Atonement includes the positive righteousness of Christ's entire life of obedience, an "acquired righteousness" that is "imputed" to redeemed sinners.[20]

Resurrection, the Holy Spirit, and Union with Christ

As Calvin insists that atonement is not exclusively tied to the death of Christ but includes his entire life of obedience, so he refuses to separate Jesus's death from his resurrection: "So, then, let us remember that whenever mention is made of his death alone, we are to understand at the same time what belongs to his resurrection." Conversely, whenever Jesus's resurrection is mentioned, "we are to understand it as including what has to do especially with his death" (*Inst.* 2.16.13).

While Christ's death accomplishes forgiveness of sins and justification, Christ's resurrection is associated with sanctification and newness of life: "We divide the substance of our salvation between Christ's death and resurrection as follows: through his death, sin was wiped out and death extinguished; through his resurrection, righteousness was restored and life raised up, so that—thanks to his resurrection—his death manifested its power and efficacy in us" (*Inst.* 2.16.13). The crucifixion has to do with Christ's extrinsic "alien righteousness" (Christ "outside us"), while resurrection (and ascension) has to do with the intrinsic spiritual and moral transformation that takes place through union with the risen Christ through the Holy Spirit (Christ "within us").[21]

Christ's resurrection thus makes possible our union with Christ without which his atoning work can be of no value to us: "As long as Christ remains

20. Van Buren, *Christ in Our Place*, 64.
21. Zachman, "Christology of Calvin," 293.

outside of us, and we are separated from him, all that he has suffered and done for the salvation of the human race remains useless and of no value for us" (*Inst.* 3.1.1). Because the resurrected Jesus has ascended bodily into heaven, Christ unites us to himself through the Spirit. Union with the risen Christ takes place through "incorporation." The Holy Spirit makes us "members of Christ": "The Holy Spirit is the bond by which Christ effectually unites us to himself. . . . By the grace and power of the same Spirit we are made his members, to keep us under himself and in turn to possess him" (3.1.1, 3).[22]

Assessment of Penal Substitution in Calvin

At least three tensions lie at the heart of Calvin's atonement theology. First is the tension between God's love and God's justice. Calvin is "consistently at pains to claim that the death of Christ appeases the wrath of God and changes God's attitude toward us from hatred and anger to love and mercy." What do we make of this kind of language? "Does God love us because Christ died for us? Or did Christ die to show us how much God already loves us?"[23]

Second is a tension between literal and metaphorical language in Calvin's use of "wrath" and "punishment." How literally should we take this language? Though it has been challenged in recent centuries, the ancient tradition in Christian theology holds that God has no "passions."[24] While this might lead us to assume that Calvin's language of "divine wrath" is metaphorical, he employs it quite literally. Is it literally true, as a popular contemporary worship song puts it, that "on that cross as Jesus died, the wrath of God was satisfied"?

Finally, and related, is the matter of punishment understood in terms of retributive justice the crucial element in Calvin's doctrine of the atonement? Is there biblical warrant for such a notion? Even within a model of *substitutionary* atonement, is the notion of *penal* substitution theologically or ethically incoherent?

What follows will address the first concern and to some extent the second: the tension between love and divine justice, and the meaning of God's "wrath." The question of theological coherence and adequacy of the model itself will be addressed in the chapter's conclusion.

There is among Calvin scholars no single agreed-upon resolution to the first tension. All interpreters of Calvin agree that God's love cannot be the result

22. Van Buren, *Christ in Our Place*, 95–99.
23. Zachman, "Christology of Calvin," 289, 292.
24. E.g., Thirty-Nine Articles of Religion, art. 1: "There is but one living and true God, everlasting, *without body, parts, or passions*; of infinite power, wisdom, and goodness; the Maker, and Preserver of all things both visible and invisible" (emphasis added).

of Christ's death on the cross and that Christ's death should not be thought to "change" God's mind. Rather, "*The free love of God in Jesus Christ* is the starting point of Calvin's doctrine of the atonement."[25]

Scholars have suggested two ways of resolving the tension. First, some contend that the point of Calvin's language is to tell us something about ourselves. The language of divine wrath should not be interpreted to mean that God is propitiated *toward* us but rather that God has laid on Christ all of that evil we have brought on ourselves in order to free us from it.[26] This would be an interpretation of Calvin that brings him closer to the incarnational or Christus Victor models of atonement.

A second way of resolution lies in Calvin's use of "accommodation language."[27] In a frequently cited passage, he writes about "appeasing God's wrath": "Expressions of this sort have been accommodated to our capacity that we may better understand how miserable and ruinous our condition is apart from Christ. For if it had not been clearly stated that the wrath and vengeance of God and eternal death rested upon us, we would scarcely have recognized how miserable we would have been without God's mercy, and we would have underestimated the benefit of liberation" (*Inst.* 2.16.2).

However, other scholars claim that the language of accommodation is not a sufficient solution to resolve this tension because Calvin himself acknowledges that God's wrath is not mere metaphor: "Accommodation is not the final answer. It cannot be, because Calvin took the holiness of God and the sinfulness of men and women with utter seriousness."[28]

Calvin brings us closer to a resolution when he expands on what he means by accommodation. Although God loves us, since God is the "highest righteousness" he cannot love the unrighteousness that is in us because of sin. Insofar as we are creatures, God loves what he has created and is moved by "pure and freely given love" to receive us through grace. However, as long as there is a division in us between righteousness and unrighteousness, as long as we remain sinners, he cannot receive us. "Therefore, by his love God the Father goes before [us] and anticipates our reconciliation in Christ. Indeed, 'because he first loved us,' he afterward reconciles us to himself. But until Christ succors us by his death, the unrighteousness that deserves God's indignation remains in us, and is accursed and condemned before him. . . . Through Christ alone

---

25. R. Peterson, *Calvin's Doctrine of the Atonement*, 1 (emphasis original).

26. Zachman, "Christology of Calvin," 291–92.

27. Zachman, "Christology of Calvin," 292–93.

28. R. Peterson, *Calvin's Doctrine of the Atonement*, 8. For a further comparison of views, cf. Van Buren, *Christ in Our Place*, 58, 59, 65; Jones, "Fury of Love," 214, 222, 223; Wendel, *Calvin*, 229, 231.

we escape the imputation of our sins to us—an imputation bringing with it the wrath of God" (*Inst.* 2.16.3).

If we were to read the rest of Calvin in light of this passage, we might understand his doctrine of penal substitution *not* to mean that Christ's death made it possible for God to love us because God poured out his wrath on Christ instead of us. Instead, it would mean that from eternity God had loved us and created us for union with himself. God did not hate us; it is not against us but against the evil of sin that God's anger is directed. This is made difficult, however, by the aforementioned passages in which Calvin writes of Christ's death "appeasing" God's wrath and that atonement demands the "paying of a penalty" and a "punishment."

Thus, the tensions between divergent readings of Calvin are found in Calvin's own texts. These tensions have led to two kinds of readers, both of which claim to follow Calvin: The tradition of "federal Calvinism" finds its purest expressions in theologians such as Jonathan Edwards and Charles Hodge. The other reading ultimately leads to Karl Barth and his followers. "Federal Calvinism" will be illustrated by the following examination of the theology of Princeton theologian Charles Hodge. We will address the second reading in the chapter on Barth.

Charles Hodge

Some contemporary Reformed scholars make a distinction between "evangelical Calvinism" and "rationalistic Calvinism." Evangelical Calvinism is "more biblical and less scholastic." In its doctrine of God, evangelical Calvinism focuses more on the Trinity and the incarnation and tends toward an inductive rather than deductive theological method. In rationalistic Calvinism, the "legal [is] prior to the filial, the deductive to the inductive, and the propositional to the personal." It has a tendency to draw rationalistic conclusions from propositions and to reason from concepts to subject matter rather than from subject matter to concepts.[29]

An example of such a rationalist approach may be found in federal Calvinism, which developed at the end of the sixteenth and particularly the seventeenth century in England and Scotland, as well as in the Netherlands and New England. Federal Calvinism gave central place to the concept of covenant, distinguishing between various covenants that constitute humanity's relation to God. It especially made a distinction between a "covenant

29. Hunsinger, *Reading Barth with Charity*, xiv–xv. See also T. F. Torrance, *Scottish Theology*, 125–53.

of works" and the "covenant of grace." Adam was the "federal head" of the human race who represented all of humanity under a "covenant of works." When Adam disobeyed God, he thus brought a curse not only on himself but also on all his descendants. God elected a number out of this fallen group and made a covenant of grace with them in Christ, who in the same manner as Adam is their "federal head."

James Torrance asserts that this distinction between a covenant of works and a covenant of grace is unknown in Calvin's own theology. Calvin has only one eternal covenant of grace promised in the Old Testament and fulfilled in Jesus Christ in the New Testament.[30] The following distinctive characteristics of federal Calvinism are adapted from Torrance:

1. Federalism conflates covenant and contract. In Scripture, a covenant is a "promise" between two persons, whereas a contract is a legal relationship based on mutual conditions.
2. Federalism is predicated on a dichotomy between the sphere of nature and the sphere of grace. All people by nature have a relationship to God as a judge. Only the elect are related to God in grace through Christ the Mediator.
3. Limited atonement means that Christ is not head over all humanity and does not have solidarity with all humanity.
4. Attention moves from what Christ has done for us to what we must do if we want to be in covenant with God.[31]

Charles Hodge (1797–1878) was a Presbyterian theologian who taught at Princeton Theological Seminary (1851–78). His work belongs to a tradition known as Princeton theology, which also includes the work of Archibald Alexander, B. B. Warfield, and his son A. A. Hodge. The elder Hodge's discussion of atonement occurs in the second volume of his three-volume *Systematic Theology*. Hodge both articulates a theology of penal substitution and places it firmly within a framework of federal Calvinism.

The Covenant of Grace and the Covenant of Works

Hodge embraces the understanding of covenant as a contract in which God's relation to humanity is consistently based on the performance of certain

---

30. J. B. Torrance, Introduction to Campbell, *Nature of the Atonement*, 5.
31. J. B. Torrance, Introduction to Campbell, *Nature of the Atonement*, 6–7.

conditions. The chief difference between the covenant of works and the covenant of grace is the specific conditions that obtain. All covenants have two partners, are established by a condition, and result in either reward or punishment depending on whether the conditions are met. Reward and punishment are matters of strict obligation. If the conditions of the covenant are met, God *must* reward as a matter of obligation. If the conditions are not met, justice requires punishment. All covenants are also mediated by a legal representative, a "head" whose relationship to the represented is extrinsic rather than intrinsic. The representation is a juridical relation rather than an ontological or participatory union.

Thus, "God made to Adam a promise suspended upon a condition, and attached to disobedience a certain penalty. That is what in Scriptural language is meant by a covenant, and that is all that is meant by the term as here used."[32] The covenant with Adam is a "covenant of life" because life is attached to its obedience. It is a "covenant of works" because works are the condition of its fulfillment. Because God is just, it follows of "necessity" that rational creatures are dealt with justly. Obedience will result in life, but failure to keep the conditions of the covenant eventuates in death.[33] The original parties to the covenant were God and Adam, with Adam acting as "head and representative" of the entire human race. Because Adam acted representatively, all are included in the consequences of his disobedience: "Men are all involved in the penal and natural consequences of Adam's transgression."[34]

As God entered into a covenant with Adam, so even prior to creating the world God the Father entered into a covenant with the preexisting Son of God.[35] The Father has given Christ certain tasks to perform: to become incarnate; to "fulfill all righteousness" by obeying the law; to provide a "propitiation to God in the expiation of the sins of men." In return, God rewards Christ by (among other things) raising him from the dead and giving him a kingdom and a church.[36]

Finally, a third covenant, the "covenant of grace," is also patterned on a new condition to be met out of justice with reward and punishment. Thus, it is also a kind of "covenant of works," but its conditions are different from those of the original covenant. Because Christ has met the conditions of the covenant made between the Father and the Son, salvation can now be offered to human beings under a new condition: faith in Jesus Christ, which God

32. Hodge, *Systematic Theology*, 2:117.
33. Hodge, *Systematic Theology*, 2:118, 120.
34. Hodge, *Systematic Theology*, 2:122.
35. Hodge, *Systematic Theology*, 2:360.
36. Hodge, *Systematic Theology*, 2:361–62.

gives by grace to his elect. However, as with the initial covenant of works, the reward of this covenant of grace remains a matter of strict justice. If human beings fulfill the condition of faith in Jesus Christ, they will necessarily receive the reward: "In virtue of what the Son covenanted to perform . . . salvation is offered unto all men on the condition of faith in Christ. . . . The gospel . . . is the offer of salvation upon the conditions of the covenant of grace."[37]

Retributive Justice

As stated previously, retributive justice presupposes that those who do wrong deserve proportionate punishment and that such punishment is intrinsically good. Hodge calls this "vindicatory justice" and assumes this principle to be self-evident. God is "determined by his moral excellence to punish sin"; justice is a "perfection of the divine nature which renders it necessary that the righteous be rewarded and the wicked punished."[38] It would not be possible for God simply to forgive sin, for if God were not to punish sin, he would not be just: "If sin be pardoned it can be pardoned in consistency with the divine justice only on the ground of a forensic penal satisfaction."[39]

Penal Substitution

Where Hodge differs from the traditional account of retributive justice is in the third point discussed at the beginning of this chapter—that it is immoral to inflict punishment on the innocent or to inflict disproportionate punishment on wrongdoers. The basic claim of the penal substitution model is that the innocent Jesus Christ has received the punishment that sinners deserve instead of the sinners themselves. However, because justice demands punishment of actual wrongdoers, punishing the innocent creates a disproportion of justice. The wrongdoers who deserve punishment receive *no* punishment, while, by definition, the punishment of the innocent is disproportionate and therefore a miscarriage of justice.

Hodge responds by simply dismissing the third principle of retributive justice. Punishing the innocent for the guilty "has been admitted not only as possible, but as rational, and recognized as indicating the only method by which sinful men can be reconciled by a just and holy God."[40]

37. Hodge, *Systematic Theology*, 2:362–63.
38. Hodge, *Systematic Theology*, 2:490, 492, 493.
39. Hodge, *Systematic Theology*, 2:488.
40. Hodge, *Systematic Theology*, 2:532.

Hodge's theology of penal substitution thus rests on two principles: (1) the satisfaction of justice through punishment and (2) the substitution of the innocent for the guilty. He distinguishes between personal guilt and guilt as a legal obligation to satisfy justice. Personal guilt is "inseparable from sin" and cannot be removed; "it personally attaches to all who have sinned." However, as a legal obligation to satisfy justice, guilt may be removed either "personally" or "vicariously." As a judicial obligation, guilt "may be transferred from one person to another." Thus, the guilt of Adam's sin may be "imputed" to us, and Christ likewise can assume our guilt. Guilt in this sense can be removed *only* by punishment: either the sinner must be punished, or a substitute must be provided to assume the guilt and bear the punishment. "This is the fundamental idea of atonement or satisfaction."[41]

The death of Christ is thus "vicarious" or a "substitution." In dying on the cross, Christ received the punishment we deserved and thus satisfied justice: "When, therefore, it is said that the sufferings of Christ were vicarious, the meaning is that He suffered in the place of sinners. He was their substitute. He assumed their obligation to satisfy justice. What He did and suffered precluded the necessity of their fulfilling the demands of the law in their own persons."[42] Hodge uses Anselm's language of "satisfaction of justice," but, in contrast to Anselm, he explicitly identifies justice with punishment. The work of Christ for our salvation was a satisfaction "to [God's] distributive and vindicatory justice which renders necessary the punishment of sin."[43] Unlike Calvin, however, Hodge writes not of Christ satisfying the "wrath of God" but of his "satisfying justice."[44]

According to Hodge, "expiation" and "propitiation" are reciprocal. On the one hand, the sinner's guilt is "expiated" in that justice is satisfied through vicarious punishment. On the other hand, God is "propitiated"—the penal conditions of justice have been met, and pardoning the sinner is now consistent with God's justice. The sufferings of Christ satisfy justice and pardon sin because their worth is attached to the "infinite dignity of his person": "The satisfaction of Christ has all the value which belongs to the obedience and sufferings of the eternal Son of God, and his righteousness, as well active as passive, is infinitely meritorious."[45] Other than the earlier discussion of the eternal covenant between the Father and the Son, this passage is the extent of what Hodge writes about the necessity of Christ's deity for the doctrine of the atonement.

41. Hodge, *Systematic Theology*, 2:476, 477.
42. Hodge, *Systematic Theology*, 2:475.
43. Hodge, *Systematic Theology*, 2:495.
44. Hodge, *Systematic Theology*, 2:528.
45. Hodge, *Systematic Theology*, 2:483.

Hodge mentions other metaphors of atonement besides penal substitution, such as sacrifice and redemption. But in each case he makes clear that these are simply different terms to describe the same thing. Jesus Christ's death is an "offering for sin" in the same way that Old Testament sacrifices saved the Israelites: "He bore the guilt of our sins and endured the penalty in our stead."[46] Hodge interprets the metaphor of "redemption" to mean that "Christ saves us . . . as a satisfaction to divine justice, as an expiation for sin and as a ransom from the curse and authority of the law, thus reconciling us to God, by making it consistent with his perfections to exercise mercy toward sinners."[47] That is, Christ "redeems" us by making it possible for God the Father to pardon sin.

Finally, Hodge addresses the issue of the tension between divine justice and divine love. He writes: "God is love. He loved us while sinners, and before satisfaction was offered. Satisfaction or expiation does not awaken love in the divine mind. It only renders it consistent with justice that God should exercise his love towards transgressors of his law."[48] Hodge elaborates on his meaning toward the end of the paragraph: "In the Old Testament and the New, God is declared to be just, in the sense that his nature demands the punishment of sin; that therefore there can be no remission without such punishment, vicarious or personal; that the plan of salvation . . . involves the substitution of the incarnate Son of God in the place of sinners who assumed their obligation to satisfy divine justice, and that he did in fact make a full and perfect satisfaction for sin, bearing the penalty of the law in their stead."[49]

In another passage, Hodge states, "The Scriptures, in representing the gift of Christ as the highest conceivable exhibition of the divine love, do thereby teach, first, that the end to be accomplished was worthy of the sacrifice; and, secondly, that the sacrifice was necessary to the attainment of that end. If the end could have been otherwise attained there would have been no exhibition of love in the gift of Christ for its accomplishment."[50] And finally, "It is true God is love. But it is no less true that love in God is not a weakness, impelling Him to do what ought not to be done. If sin ought to be punished, as conscience and the word of God declare, then there is nothing in God which impels Him to leave it unpunished. His whole nature is indeed harmonious, but it has the harmony of moral excellence, leading with absolute certainty to

46. Hodge, *Systematic Theology*, 2:506.
47. Hodge, *Systematic Theology*, 2:520.
48. Hodge, *Systematic Theology*, 2:478.
49. Hodge, *Systematic Theology*, 2:478–79.
50. Hodge, *Systematic Theology*, 2:488.

the judge of all the earth doing right; punishing or pardoning, just as moral excellence demands."[51]

The above quotations may at first suggest a similarity to Calvin's position. However, a careful reading makes clear that the tension acknowledged in Calvin's theology is not resolved in Hodge but simply eliminated. God is love, but God's primary nature is that of justice, and love can be expressed only within the parameters of justice. Justice demands punishment for sin, and if sin exists, love can be expressed only after justice has been satisfied. There is no reference to "accommodation" here. What Calvin recognized as a tension is no longer so for Hodge, who resolves the tension by coming down firmly on the side of justice, specifically retributive justice, as the only context in which divine love can be expressed toward sinful humanity.

Evaluation of Hodge

Although Hodge, like Calvin, endorses a model of penal substitution, Hodge departs significantly from Calvin's own theological approach. Hodge's federal theology is a prime example of rationalistic Calvinism. While all atonement paradigms are rational in the sense that they are exercises in faith seeking understanding, rationalistic paradigms are deductive rather than inductive. They impose a preestablished interpretive system on the narratives and symbolic aspects of Scripture, forcing them to fit within that structure.[52]

In the initial chapter it was acknowledged that Scripture contains numerous metaphors for atonement. Images that refer to the work of Christ as military victory, ransom, redemption, and sacrifice are clearly metaphorical. Judicial and satisfaction metaphors provide a useful counterbalance in that they focus on the legal and moral dimensions of atonement rather than the "cosmic aspects" found in incarnational and Christus Victor models. As in Anselm, they ground the atonement in both God's justice and the ordered structure of the universe.[53]

However, rationalism tends to flatten or literalize such metaphors, such that they are either reduced to "mere metaphors" or taken to be literal and univocal descriptions of reality. Hodge's understanding of penal substitution both tends to a deductive rationalism and reduces divine justice to a literal and univocal "retributive justice," through which he interprets the entire economy of salvation.

51. Hodge, *Systematic Theology*, 2:540.
52. Gunton, *Actuality of Atonement*, 1–25.
53. Gunton, *Actuality of Atonement*, 95.

For Hodge, federalism is the all-explaining rational interpretive lens. Adam and Christ are equally federal heads who legally represent either fallen humanity or the church. Scripture includes covenants between God and Israel and between Christ and the church. Despite the lack of biblical precedent, Hodge even postulates an eternally existing covenant between the trinitarian persons of God the Father and God the Son.

Hodge also assumes that retributive justice is self-evidently true and accounts for all examples of justice in Scripture. However, as we have seen, equally valid models of justice have been adopted by other theologians. While retributive justice is evident in Anselm's satisfaction model, his focus on the restoration of created order also points to restorative justice. Likewise, justice as redemption from slavery is operative in Christus Victor models of atonement, and justice as re-creation appears in incarnational models.

Although Hodge insists that Scripture is the final authority and appeals to the same biblical passages cited by other interpreters, he invariably interprets those passages in terms of penal substitution. Should we presume that biblical metaphors of "redemption," "victory," "sacrifice," and "ransom" are all really about penal substitution? At the very least, Hodge's rationalist hermeneutic contrasts sharply with Calvin's own Christocentric, ecclesial, and typological reading of Scripture.

As noted above, Hodge's federal schema eliminates any tension between love and justice by subordinating love to justice. By giving priority to justice over love, federalism gives priority to the judicial over the filial.[54] Hodge eliminates the tension in Calvin's own theology by affirming that justice is the single determining divine attribute.[55]

Perhaps most critically, Hodge's federal Calvinism inverts the order of the relationship between forgiveness and atonement. In historic Christian atonement theologies, God the Father first loves the world; and because God forgives sin, he makes a way of atonement in Jesus Christ. By contrast, because of the priority of retributive justice in Hodge's federalism, Christ must fulfill the just penalty for sins before forgiveness can be given as a *reward*. God must be conditioned to be gracious.[56]

In addition, because for Hodge atonement takes place through the fulfillment of a legal contract, there is, strictly speaking, no forgiveness or mercy involved. Justice demands that punishment take place, and there can be no forgiveness without punishment. Because Christ has fulfilled his part of the

54. J. B. Torrance, Introduction to Campbell, *Nature of the Atonement*, 10.
55. Schmiechen, *Saving Power*, 110.
56. J. B. Torrance, Introduction to Campbell, *Nature of the Atonement*, 9.

conditions of the eternal covenant, God the Father is obligated to fulfill his side. God does not actually have mercy on sinners because this would violate the principles of justice. Rather, God fulfills the conditions of penal justice by punishing Christ instead of sinners, and because strict justice has been met, no further penalty against sinners remains.

Thus, while Hodge contrasts a covenant of works with a covenant of grace, the only distinction between the two covenants is their conditions of fulfillment. By placing faith as the condition of the fulfillment of the covenant of grace, rather than as a response to the good news of salvation in Christ, Hodge moves the focus away from what Christ has done for us to what *we must do* to fulfill the conditions.[57]

Because it is almost exclusively focused on juridical categories, Hodge's federal Calvinism also misses the significance of the vicarious humanity of Jesus Christ in his resurrection and ascension. Christ's vicarious humanity is crucial for a theology of participation, which arguably should be at the center of a theology of Christ's priesthood rather than the notion of the "satisfaction of justice."[58] Yet Hodge has no theology of participation or union with Christ in his risen humanity apart from federal headship.[59]

Finally, the trinitarian and incarnational themes so important to patristic and medieval atonement theologies effectively disappear in Hodge's theology. Hodge certainly affirms that God is Trinity and that Jesus Christ is fully God and fully human, but the doctrine of the Trinity is significant for Hodge mainly because it allows the Father and the Son to enter an eternal contract. And the incarnation is significant mainly because as the Son of God, Jesus Christ is an infinite divine person who is able to fulfill the demands of penal justice regardless of the number of sins that have been committed.

Conclusion

Penal substitution is the atonement model most associated historically with conservative Protestant theology and is also (with the moral exemplarist model) one of the most controversial. It is preached from countless pulpits and celebrated in hymnody but is also vehemently opposed. Some claim it to be essential, even the very heart of the Christian gospel, while others reject it as the equivalent of "divine child abuse."

57. J. B. Torrance, Introduction to Campbell, *Nature of the Atonement*, 7–8.
58. J. B. Torrance, Introduction to Campbell, *Nature of the Atonement*, 11–16.
59. Wallace, "History and Sacrament."

A positive assessment of penal substitution would include the following: First, penal substitution rightly upholds an essential forensic or judicial aspect of atonement. Any adequate doctrine of atonement needs to take seriously both the notion of sin as an offense against divine righteousness and God's proper response of judgment. God is portrayed as righteous in Scripture, and divine judgment is a major theme throughout the canon, including Jesus's teaching. "Jesus died for our sins" is both a statement of God's love and a judgment of human guilt, for it is the sin of human beings that made the cross necessary. Legal metaphors also have a sound basis in Scripture, and Pauline imagery of justification evokes forensic imagery of pardon from guilt.

Second, the notion of substitution means that Jesus Christ does not merely act on our behalf; he does for us what we ourselves cannot do. Positively speaking, penal substitution addresses the issue of guilt by making clear that we no longer face judgment as sinners because Jesus Christ has borne the judgment for sin in our place.

Third, penal substitution is perhaps the most objective of all the atonement models. It makes clear that atonement is entirely the work of God on our behalf. We do not justify or forgive ourselves; rather, in the cross of Jesus Christ, God has forgiven us freely and without condition. Our response to the atonement is just that—a *response* of faith and gratitude, not a positive contribution that earns salvation or forgiveness.

However, each of these positive aspects of penal substitution is also subject to correction or at least modification. A forensic notion of divine judgment that focuses exclusively on Jesus's death on the cross misses the eschatological notion of judgment with its accompanying *positive* emphasis found in Jesus's resurrection. By focusing on the cross as a punishment of Jesus and not including an anticipation of the eschatological judgment, penal substitution misses the dimension of Jesus's resurrection and our justification. Instead, penal substitution becomes a timeless focus on the negative judgment on sin in the death of Jesus.

As noted above, while penal substitution is an example of retributive justice, there are other kinds of justice by which to address atonement. Aulén writes of the law as one of the enemies defeated in a Christus Victor atonement theology. For Aquinas, divine love is the key to a modified version of Anselm's theory of satisfaction. As will be seen in a later chapter, Barth develops a rich theology of atonement focusing on Jesus Christ as the "Judge Judged in our Place." None of these literalize forensic language as a straightforward account of how God judges our sins on the cross.

Granted the use of the forensic language of judgment in both the Old and New Testament, does Scripture actually teach penal substitution? Numerous scholars argue that the New Testament does not teach that God punished Jesus or that God poured out his wrath on Christ on the cross.[60] Contemporary biblical scholars do not tend to consider Old Testament sacrifices as a form of divine appeasement. Key passages in the New Testament speak of Jesus dying "for us" and "in our place" and speak of deliverance from sin, but they nowhere suggest that Jesus's death was a punishment intended to satisfy God's justice or, even more, God's wrath.[61] The notion of penal satisfaction arguably conflates Old Testament sacrifice with (secular) notions of legal satisfaction.

As noted in the initial chapter, Scripture uses numerous atonement metaphors, and it is important to distinguish between metaphors and literal descriptions. However, penal substitution interprets one of these, the legal metaphor, as a *literal* description and then utilizes that as the single necessary and logically rational theological *explanation* for the whole of the atonement. Certain concepts from the Western legal tradition, combined with a notion of necessity, become a rational framework into which the legal metaphors of Scripture are reductively forced to fit rather than following the narrative logic of the biblical texts.

Relatedly, penal substitution presupposes that the law of "distributive" or "retributive justice" is "immutable." God *cannot* relate to sinful humanity until God's justice has been satisfied, and (especially in theologians like Hodge) divine love becomes subordinate to divine justice.[62]

As noted above, penal substitution also tends to miss the significance of Jesus's earthly mission and resurrection. Calvin does point to Jesus's obedience to the Father to make clear that penal substitution does not focus *exclusively* on Christ's death. However, even for Calvin, Jesus's obedience is primarily interpreted forensically—Christ fulfills the law's righteousness—rather than, for example, in terms of the recapitulation of Adam's disobedience. Calvin does speak of Christ's "entire life" and tries to hold together cross and resurrection, but in the end he assigns justification (forensic judgment) to the cross and sanctification (moral transformation) to the resurrection. Calvin claims that Jesus's resurrection cannot be separated from crucifixion, but in terms of his soteriology, resurrection functions in a different category than atonement. Atonement deals with justification and forgiveness. Resurrection deals with sanctification.

Concerning the notion of *substitutionary* atonement, the key question is whether Jesus Christ's atoning work is something he does *instead of* us or

---

60. O'Collins, *Jesus Our Redeemer*, 133–60; Fee, "Paul and the Metaphors"; Dunn, *Theology of Paul*, 212–33.

61. Schmiechen, *Saving Power*, 111; T. F. Torrance, *Atonement*, 72.

62. Schmiechen, *Saving Power*, 110.

something he does *on behalf of* us. An adequate understanding of atonement should include aspects of both vicariousness and participation. Substitution is important to make clear that Jesus Christ has done for us what we cannot do for ourselves. At the same time, our participation and union with Christ clarifies that we also share in the resurrected life of Jesus Christ. For Calvin, there can be no substitution without union with Christ as well—thus, participation appears to be a corollary of substitution. By contrast, in Hodge's federal Calvinism the union between Christ and the church appears to be entirely extrinsic. It is a legal contract first between the Father and the Son, then between God and Adam, and finally between God and the church. Even the church's union with Christ has been rendered a legal relation.

As noted above, penal substitution is probably the most objective of the theories of atonement. However, historically, penal substitution has also had a strongly exemplarist dimension. Calvin's theology is usually designated as objective, but "Calvin consistently balances this with a more 'subjective' approach . . . that Christ, as priest, also reconciles humanity to God through his Atonement by drawing humanity back to God, reawakening us to God's fatherly love." "We are made to see the depth of Christ's love for us."[63]

Such devotion to the sacred humanity of Christ in the crucifixion first appeared in the medieval spirituality of Bernard of Clairvaux, who viewed the cross as the revelation of divine love.[64] This cross-centered piety is echoed (among other places) in the stigmata of Saint Francis of Assisi as well as the mystical visions of the anchorite Julian of Norwich.[65] Devotion to the cross as part of a theology of penal substitution also found expression in Protestant spirituality. Thus, the Puritan Richard Baxter could write in *The Saints Everlasting Rest* (1650): "Look well upon him. Dost thou not know him! It is he that brought thee up from the pit of hell, reversed the sentence of thy damnation, bore the curse which thou shouldst have borne, restored thee to the blessing thou hadst forfeited, and purchased the advancement which thou must inherit for ever. And dost thou not yet know him? Why, his hands were pierced, his head, his side, his heart were pierced, that by these marks thou mightest always know him."[66]

This devotional aspect of penal substitution appears repeatedly in the history of Protestant hymnody. An earlier chapter discussed the theology and hymnody of the brothers John and Charles Wesley. A cross-centered piety appears in Charles's hymn "And Can It Be?": "Amazing love! How can it be / That

63. Edmondson, *Calvin's Christology*, 93, 105.
64. Prestige, *Fathers and Heretics*, 187.
65. Prestige, *Fathers and Heretics*, 189, 194; Julian of Norwich, *Showings*, 275, 276.
66. Baxter, *Saints' Everlasting Rest*, 14.11.

Thou, my God, should die for me?"[67] Likewise, Isaac Watts's hymns "When I Survey the Wondrous Cross" and "Alas and Did My Savior Bleed" provide parallels, as does the revivalist spirituality of "The Old Rugged Cross" and spirituals such as "Were You There?" If penal substitution is the atonement model that has met with some of the harshest criticism, it is also a theology that has produced some of the most profound and enduring spiritual devotion.

67. Wesley, *Works of John Wesley*, 7:323 (Hymn 193).

7
· · ·

Atonement as Moral Example

Hastings Rashdall

Our introduction to this book made a distinction between constitutive and illustrative models of atonement. Constitutive models presume that Jesus Christ's life, death, and resurrection—or some aspect thereof—uniquely create or constitute a salvation that is available exclusively through Jesus. By contrast, illustrative models presume that Jesus does not actually create salvation but illustrates or is the prime example of a salvation already available to all. For illustrative models, the significance of Jesus's work or mission is primarily epistemological rather than ontological. That is, the primary purpose of Jesus's life, death, and resurrection (if such indeed happened) is to *teach* us something about God that we did not know before, to *illustrate* the love of God such that we are inspired to emulate it, or to provide a *moral example* that we are expected to follow. The primary effect of Jesus's mission is thus psychological and moral: inspired by love or gratitude, we try to live as Jesus lived. Such models are usually labeled exemplarist in that Jesus is the supreme example of this universally available salvation or is the first person to attain it (that we know of). This chapter will examine the influential exemplarist theology of modernist Anglican theologian Hastings Rashdall (1858–1924).

Hastings Rashdall may be the theologian most closely associated with the modern exemplarist theory of the atonement, which he referred to as the

"Abelardian Doctrine of the Atonement." Rashdall expounded his atonement theology most fully in his 1915 Bampton Lectures.[1] Rashdall is also the
theologian most closely associated with the modernist movement in the early
twentieth century in the Church of England. He was the "leading theological
liberal of his generation," an initial founder of the Churchmen's Union for
the Advancement of Liberal Religious Thought in 1898, renamed the Modern
Churchmen's Union in 1928.[2] Until his death, Rashdall remained a major
contributor to their journal *The Modern Churchman*. His theology remained
consistent from the early publication of his university sermons to his post-
humous *God and Man*.[3]

Rashdall's "liberal" or "modernist" theology must be understood in the
light of cultural and historical changes associated with the rise of modernity.
Depending on its ecclesial context, liberal theology, modernism, or revisionism
is a theology characterized both by a concern for methodological problems
and by an emphasis upon the significance of modernity for theology.[4] In
particular, liberalism is concerned that contemporary theology be expressed
in a manner intelligible to modern people.

As a rule, theological liberalism believed it paramount that Christian
theology respond to certain characteristics of modernity. The first of these
characteristics was modern science. The most significant contribution of modern science in the nineteenth century was arguably the discovery of the ancient
age of the earth. Combined with Charles Darwin's theory of evolution, this
appeared to place the natural sciences in conflict with a literal reading of the
creation and primeval narratives of the first chapters of Genesis.

Second was biblical criticism. The modern science of history arguably began
in the nineteenth century. The "historical critical method" applied modern
historical methods to the study of biblical texts. Many of its "assured results"
are now considered uncontroversial, such as the priority of the Gospel of Mark
and the two-source theory of synoptic authorship. However, liberal theologians such as Rashdall, influenced largely by German scholars such as Julius
Wellhausen, Adolf von Harnack, and Albrecht Ritschl, embraced more radically skeptical conclusions about the historical trustworthiness of the Bible.

Third was philosophy, specifically the modern "turn to the self." Following
René Descartes (1596–1650), the primary focus of modern philosophy shifted
from metaphysics and ontology to questions of epistemological certainty:

1. Rashdall, *Idea of Atonement*.
2. Dorrien, "Idealistic Orderings," 316. The name was changed to The Modern Church-
people's Union in 1986 and to Modern Church in 2010.
3. Rashdall, *Doctrine and Development*; Rashdall, *God and Man*.
4. Markham, "Revisionism," 600.

How do I know what I know? The "idealist" philosophy following Immanuel Kant dominated nineteenth-century philosophy, especially as developed by Georg Wilhelm Friedrich Hegel. Hegelianism combined a modern focus on history with post-Kantian idealism in an attempt to articulate a comprehensive "philosophy of history," sometimes referred to as "historicism."

In theology, liberalism followed in the train of earlier deists such as Lord Herbert of Cherbury, Matthew Tindal, and John Tolland. Schleiermacher, the "father" of liberal theology, combined post-Kantian idealism with pietist spirituality to formulate a theology that restricted theological knowledge of God to the dimension of human "experience of dependence" on the divine.

Modernity

From the beginning of Rashdall's career to its end, his theology is marked by a commitment to the modern theological project. In the first sentence of the preface to his first collection of sermons, he writes, "This volume is intended as a modest attempt to translate into the language of modern thought some of the leading doctrines or ideas of traditional Christianity."[5] Rashdall introduced *The Idea of Atonement* in a similar manner: "One of the most crying needs of the Church at the present moment is a serious attempt at re-thinking its traditional Theology. A large part of that theology has obviously become more or less unintelligible for modern men who do not possess technical knowledge of its history and contents. It needs to be re-examined, and (where necessary) reconstructed in the light of modern philosophy, modern science, and modern criticism."[6]

For Rashdall, modernity was not simply a contemporary context that theology needed to address or a social setting within which it had to function. Modernity was a filter that determined which elements of traditional theology were rationally acceptable. It was not simply that theologians had to communicate in a manner intelligible to moderns. Anything in traditional theology that was deemed "irrational" or "arbitrary" by modern standards had to be either translated into modern categories or discarded.

Subjective Idealism

Rashdall was deeply influenced by idealism, which served as a kind of natural theology and interpretive lens for his theological enterprise. While Rashdall was

---

5. Rashdall, *Doctrine and Development*, vii.
6. Rashdall, *Idea of Atonement*, vii–viii.

aware of the influence of Hegel, he appealed to the earlier position of eighteenth-century philosopher George Berkeley, with some correction from Kant.[7]

Following Berkeley, Rashdall denied the existence of "matter in itself" or "things in themselves." He held that the only realities that exist are minds and their perceptions. Space and "relations" exist only for minds, and since there can be no matter without space, there can be no matter without mind.[8] By "object" or "thing," we mean only what the mind thinks or feels. "No independence or self-existence can be attributed to the thing," and the distinction between "mind" and "thing" is only a mental one. That there are realities that human beings do not perceive does not mean that such realities exist apart from perception but rather that it is God as the Universal Mind who perceives reality.[9]

Personalism

In contrast to pantheistic and impersonalist forms of idealism, Rashdall embraced a form of "personal" idealism. The mind craves a "personal God"—a "God who really thinks, feels, wills, loves," a God whose nature is analogous to human consciousness.[10] All things exist as eternally present in the mind of God, but it would be meaningless to attribute knowledge to a reality without consciousness. What then do we mean by "God"? According to Rashdall, God is "a Spirit who knows, and in some sense experiences all reality." God must be a "causative intelligence" and thus a "Will." When we attribute "Personality" to God, this includes "self-consciousness" as well as morality: "The idea of Personality which we ascribe to God is complete when we regard Him as not only a Reason and a Will, but as moral, as objectively good."[11] Complete personality is "never fully attained by human consciousness"; "God is the only being who is in the fullest and completest sense a Person."[12]

Besides God, there exist only other personal beings. Other spirits can be distinguished from God in that (unlike God) they have a beginning in time. Rashdall applies to knowing subjects the substantival reality that he denies

7. Rashdall, *God and Man*, 17–18. On the influence of idealism on not only Rashdall but also nineteenth- and early twentieth-century English theology, see Dorrien, "Idealistic Ordering"; Dorrien, *Kantian Reason*, 378–453; Langford, *In Search of Foundations*, 55–87; Ramsey, *From Gore to Temple*, 60–76.
8. Rashdall, *God and Man*, 19–20; Rashdall, *Philosophy and Religion*, 14.
9. Rashdall, *God and Man*, 29–31.
10. Rashdall, "Theism or Pantheism?," 398.
11. Rashdall, *God and Man*, 32–34, 41, 42, 51.
12. Rashdall, *God and Man*, 42.

to extra-mental realities. While human beings are personally distinct from God's own Personality, Rashdall suggests that human nature is "the same in principle with the divine": "Every human soul is an emanation from the divine, a reproduction of the divine." A human soul is a "spark" or "emanation of the divine," a "limited mode of the divine self-consciousness."[13]

God and the World

In holding such a view—that the Person of God (and God's ideas) and other persons (with their perceptions) who are "sparks" of the divine are all that exist—Rashdall's theology is more reminiscent of panentheistic emanationist ontologies of the God-world relation (such as Neoplatonism) than the traditional Christian understanding of the divine and creation from nothing (*creatio ex nihilo*). According to Rashdall, "the world must be thought of as perpetually existing in some sense in the mind of God." Since there can be no subject without an object, "the world is as necessary to God as God to the world." Nonetheless, such a position is not pantheistic in that "this world is what it is by reason of the will of God."[14]

Rashdall is ambivalent concerning divine infinity. Contrary to traditional Christian doctrine, he insists that God is "finite inasmuch as He is not man." He also appeals to the notion of divine finitude as an explanation for the existence of evil in the world. If God is good, the ultimate purpose of the universe must be good; however, the fact that evil exists necessarily involves a "certain limitation of power."[15] That so much evil exists can be reconciled with God's goodness only if we suppose that "evil is in some way a necessary means to the utmost attainable good."[16] Rashdall suggests that "the term 'infinite' would seem more properly to belong to that Absolute which includes God and other spirits."[17]

Revelation

There is a direct correlation between Rashdall's idealist philosophy and his understanding of revelation. He posits reason (by which he means philosophy)

13. Rashdall, *God and Man*, 44, 58–59.
14. Rashdall, *God and Man*, 43.
15. Rashdall, *God and Man*, 53, 55; Rashdall, *Theory of Good and Evil*, 2:236–37.
16. Rashdall, *Idea of Atonement*, 452.
17. Rashdall, *Theory of Good and Evil*, 2:240.

and revelation as two distinct but equal sources of knowledge about God, the contents of which exactly overlap. Indeed, we believe in revelation precisely to the extent that it accords with reason and not otherwise: "All religious truth," writes Rashdall, "depends logically upon inference. . . . The truth of Theism is in that sense a truth discernible by Reason. . . . In its essentials the Monotheism of Isaiah is a reasonable belief; we accept it because it is reasonable, not because Isaiah had an intuition that it was true."[18]

Rashdall did not believe in revelation as a verbal communication from God and seems to have held that notion in contempt. A view of revelation in which God "supplied various pieces of information about himself" is "impossible for modern man." Rashdall also did not believe in miracles. Neither the virginal conception nor the bodily resurrection of Jesus is necessary to Christian faith. Rather, what is important is whether the moral teaching of Jesus is true: "The Conscience that accepts the moral ideal represented by Christ's teaching and personality as the true and final moral ideal . . . will recognize the Person from whom the teaching proceeds . . . as the highest and fullest Revelation."[19]

Rashdall accordingly conflates revelation with other knowledge, including both canonical and extra-canonical sources. If the human soul is a "spark of the divine," there can be no "merely natural reason." All true thoughts come from God, and "we must school ourselves to see revelation everywhere, or we shall end by seeing it nowhere."[20] From the point of view of idealism, "all knowledge may be looked upon as a partial communication to the human soul of the thoughts or experiences of the divine mind."[21] Rashdall refers to those with especially developed moral or religious faculties as "religious geniuses."[22] The Old Testament prophets were "religious teachers of the intuitive order," but they should not be distinguished too greatly from philosophers such as Socrates or Plato.[23]

Accordingly, Rashdall writes that there can be no "hard and fast distinction between revealed and unrevealed, inspired and uninspired, mere natural knowledge and wholly supernatural knowledge."[24] Similarly, we should not distinguish too sharply between the writings of the New Testament and post–New Testament writings.[25] "Revelation is gradual. Revelation is progressive.

18. Rashdall, *Philosophy and Religion*, 138.
19. Rashdall, "Miracles," 375–76, 384; cf. Rashdall, "Fighting against God," 703.
20. Rashdall, *Christus in Ecclesia*, 238.
21. Rashdall, *Philosophy and Religion*, 141.
22. Rashdall, *Christus in Ecclesia*, 247.
23. Rashdall, *Philosophy and Religion*, 143–44.
24. Rashdall, *Christus in Ecclesia*, 261.
25. Rashdall, *Christus in Ecclesia*, 269.

Revelation admits of degrees."[26] In comparison to other religions, Christianity has taught the "great [religious] truths in all their fullness. . . . The claim of Christianity to be the supreme, the universal, in a sense the final Religion, must rest mainly, in the last resort upon the appeal which Christ and his Religion make to the moral and religious consciousness of the present."[27]

While he identifies the highest truths of Christianity with the highest moral teaching found in philosophy and non-Christian religions, Rashdall introduces a hermeneutic of discontinuity between the Old Testament and Jesus but also between the Old Testament and the church, and even between Jesus and the church. What made Israel's faith unique was the "intrinsic value" of monotheism: "Judaism was the first great monotheistic religion." At the same time, Rashdall refers to "elements of imperfection [that] clung to Jewish monotheism," especially the Old Testament emphasis on "ritual" and "legal ordinances." He warns: "We must know the limitations of Judaism, the narrowness and exclusiveness of its creed." We are "no longer bound to accept as historical facts narratives presupposing conceptions of the divine nature which all Christians have abandoned." One of Jesus's purposes was to deliver the church from the limitations of Judaism: "To set Judaism free from these fetters and restrictions, to moralise, to spiritualise, to universalise the teaching of Judaism, was the work of our Lord Jesus Christ."[28]

While Rashdall's attitude toward the Old Testament inclines toward Marcionism and even antisemitism,[29] he finds similar imperfections in the New Testament. On the one hand, it is true that a "recognition of the imperfection of the Old Testament has only thrown into relief the spirituality and completeness of the New." On the other hand, the importance of the New Testament lies not in its words but in the "moral and spiritual truths contained in it, that constitute the measure of its inspiration." We need to recognize "degrees of inspiration" within the New Testament. We must distinguish between the words of Jesus and the comments and interpretations of the Evangelists.[30] We should recognize that Paul's universalism is more important than his views on marriage and that the book of Revelation is less in the Spirit of Christ than are the Johannine Epistles.[31]

---

26. Rashdall, *Christus in Ecclesia*, 247; cf. 243.

27. Rashdall, *Philosophy and Religion*, 154, 156.

28. Rashdall, *Christus in Ecclesia*, 250–56.

29. Ironically, yet consistent with Hegelian idealism, Rashdall was a white supremacist. See Rashdall, *Theory of Good and Evil*, 1:238–39, and discussion of Rashdall's uncritical racism in Dorrien, "Idealistic Ordering," 303–9.

30. Rashdall, *Christus in Ecclesia*, 262–65.

31. Rashdall, *Christus in Ecclesia*, 268.

The Historical Jesus

It follows that, for Rashdall, the historical figure Jesus of Nazareth is revelatory primarily because of Jesus's moral sensibilities. Jesus is the summit of revelation because of his moral teaching, but what Jesus teaches are timeless moral truths.[32] Accordingly, Rashdall displays ambiguity as to whether the historical figure of Jesus is actually necessary to bring about human salvation: "If it could be shown that there never was an historical Jesus or that we know nothing to speak of about his teaching, the truth and the value of the teaching attributed to our Lord in the Gospels would not be one whit diminished. . . . And what is true of the ethical teaching is true equally of the religious teaching of Jesus—if we put aside those few genuine sayings which speak of His own divine Sonship or Messiahship."[33]

Rashdall's sympathies lie with German writers such as Harnack and Ritschl who sought to reconstruct a non-dogmatic "historical Jesus." Rashdall's summary of the heart of Jesus's message clearly echoes Harnack: "Christianity is the religion which for the first time proclaimed in all its fullness those twin-truths which are best expressed in the simple phrases—the fatherhood of God and the brotherhood of man."[34] Rashdall was aware of the challenge posed to liberal reconstructions of the "historical Jesus" by Albert Schweitzer's (1875–1965) claim that eschatology was at the heart of Jesus's ethic.[35] In a manner later echoed by the Jesus Seminar of the 1990s, Rashdall responded against Schweitzer that much of the eschatological language of the Gospels is of "doubtful authenticity." Perhaps Jesus did look forward to some kind of "catastrophic judgment" in which he would be recognized as the Messiah or King of Israel. However, for modern purposes, "all this eschatological language must be treated as the accidental historical dress in which the ethical and religious ideas of Jesus would appear to have clothed themselves."[36]

What is crucial about Jesus's message is its timeless and universal truth. The emphasis in Jesus's teaching is on "moral righteousness, love of God and one's neighbour, the state of the heart."[37] Consistent with his focus on the universal implications of Jesus's moral teaching, Rashdall says little about Jesus's physical actions. He interprets the Gospel accounts of Jesus's miracles in accord with his idealist assumptions: it is probable that Jesus healed people

32. Rashdall, *Idea of Atonement*, 456.
33. Rashdall, *Conscience and Christ*, 275.
34. Rashdall, *Idea of Atonement*, 49; cf. Rashdall, *Philosophy and Religion*, 153.
35. Schweitzer, *Quest of the Historical Jesus*.
36. Rashdall, *Idea of Atonement*, 8–10, 11.
37. Rashdall, *Idea of Atonement*, 19. For detailed discussion, see Rashdall, *Conscience and Christ*, 36–133.

through the power of suggestion, but any nature miracle would be a "violation of divine law" and "essentially incredible." That Jesus persisted beyond death in some manner and appeared to his disciples in a vision is compatible with belief in the "Immortality of the Soul," but Rashdall seems to think that bodily resurrection would be a violation of the laws of nature.[38]

Given that Rashdall identified the heart of Jesus's mission as a timeless moral proclamation of "the fatherhood of God and the brotherhood of man," it should not surprise us that his Christology is Nestorian or adoptionist, and his doctrine of God is Unitarian. These same themes are repeated from his earliest collection of sermons through the papers he delivered at the end of his career.[39]

Rashdall's goal was to "translate" the traditional terminology into "modern thought and speech." Terms such as "substance," "essence," "nature," "hypostasis," "person," "eternal generation," "procession," and "hypostatic union" were not immediately intelligible to modern people. They are couched in the language of "Greek Metaphysics . . . simply pieces of metaphysical thinking, some of them valuable, and successful pieces of thinking, others less so."[40] What matters is our attitude toward Christ and his teaching, not particular terminology as to his nature. If we simply believe what Jesus taught about God's fatherhood and human brotherhood, then we are Christians "in the fullest sense of the word."[41]

Despite claiming a disinterest in speculation about such things, Rashdall did have a working Christology, which had the following characteristics: First, there is a blurring of the distinction between God and creatures; every human being in some sense shares in God's being. Rashdall's writings include statements such as the following: "We cannot say intelligibly that God dwells in Christ, unless we have already recognized that in a sense God dwells and reveals Himself in humanity at large, and in each particular soul."[42] "Every human being is admitted to be in some measure a Son of God. . . . Every human consciousness is derived from God, and has in it something of the Divine . . . a partial reproduction of the Divine Mind."[43]

---

38. Rashdall, *Doctrine and Development*, 72, 177–89; Rashdall, *Philosophy and Religion*, 158–60; Rashdall, "Miracles"; Rashdall, "Fighting against God," 702–6; Rayner, "Hastings Rashdall on Immortality."

39. Rashdall, *Doctrine and Development*, 79–81, 95, 97; Rashdall, *Philosophy and Religion*, 172–81; Rashdall, "Creeds," 211–12; Rashdall, "Miracles," 381–84; Rashdall, *Idea of Atonement*, 444, 446, 448–55; Rashdall, "Christ as Logos"; Rashdall, *God and Man*, 68–78.

40. Rashdall, *Philosophy and Religion*, 171–72, 176–77.

41. Rashdall, *Philosophy and Religion*, 173.

42. Rashdall, *Philosophy and Religion*, 180.

43. Rashdall, "Miracles," 382.

Second, while God is present in everyone, God is present in some more than in others: "The highest developments of the religious consciousness have been the especial privilege of few nations and few individuals."[44] A higher and more developed moral consciousness reveals God more.[45] Every human soul "incarnates God *to some extent*," but this occurs more so in great religious personalities, reformers, prophets, and saints.[46]

Third, it follows that the presence of God in Jesus Christ is not unique. Given that the "spark of divinity" is present in every human being, God is not uniquely incarnate in Jesus Christ: "We ought most strongly to assert, that Jesus Christ is not the only Son of God. All men are born sons of God in one sense; in another all men are called to be sons of God."[47] "It is impossible to maintain that God is fully incarnate in Christ and not incarnate at all in anyone else."[48]

In light of the above, Rashdall clearly embraces a Nestorian, adoptionist, or what might be called a "degree" Christology. God is not present in Jesus Christ in a categorically different *way*; rather, God is *more* present in Jesus than in anyone else—and therefore Jesus is most revelatory of God's nature. Rashdall uses the language of "indwelling" and "revelation," but he distinctly rejects any suggestion that Jesus's personal identity is that of the Son of God incarnate *as*, or living *as*, a human being: "What can this word 'better' mean to us but a higher degree of the goodness which we have learned to reverence in men? In Jesus Christ Humanity attained its highest moral development, and just because of that perfect Humanity the conscience of mankind has recognised in him a supreme, a unique, in a sense, a final revelation of that God who all through the world's history had been, by slow, successive states, revealing Himself more and more fully to the human spirit."[49]

Rashdall speculates that if there is something of the image of God in all humanity, and if human beings represent God to the "degree" of their moral and spiritual insight, "then it becomes possible to conceive that One Man was supremely uniquely a Revealer of God."[50] Thus, we are justified in saying that God is like Christ, "that the character and teaching of Christ contains the fullest disclosure both of the character of God Himself and of His will for man." This, Rashdall claims, is "the true meaning for us of the doctrine of Christ's Divinity."[51]

44. Rashdall, *Christus in Ecclesia*, 240.
45. Rashdall, *Philosophy and Religion*, 180.
46. Rashdall, *God and Man*, 74.
47. Rashdall, *Doctrine and Development*, 79.
48. Rashdall, "Christ as Logos," 647.
49. Rashdall, *Doctrine and Development*, 80–81.
50. Rashdall, "Creeds," 212.
51. Rashdall, "Christ as Logos," 648.

Rashdall undergirds his adoptionist Christology with an ultimately Unitarian (and misleading) interpretation of the doctrine of the Trinity that he held throughout his career: "For Aquinas, as for St. Augustine, the Son is the knowledge by which God knows Himself, and the Holy Spirit is the love by which God loves Himself." There is no trace in Aquinas, he writes, of the "three-mind view of the Godhead." Concerning the Son, Rashdall writes, "What can be plainer? The Word is a name for God's thinking, including the object of His thought, which is also Himself, and includes in a sense potentially or actually all that He creates." And of the Holy Spirit, he asks, "How can the love which impels a man to do anything be thought of as a separate consciousness from the man?" Indeed, "That God is Power, Wisdom and Love is surely a doctrine which most genuine Theists would accept." Some might object that Unitarians could also accept this position, says Rashdall, but that "ought to be no objection to a reasonable Trinitarian." Rashdall concludes, however, "I do not believe that the patristic and scholastic formulations of the doctrines of the Holy Trinity and of the Divinity of Christ are of very much spiritual value."[52]

As noted in the earlier chapter on Irenaeus and Athanasius, a fundamental distinction in historic trinitarian theology and Christology is the distinction between "person" and "nature." While Jesus's personal identity is that of God ("who" Jesus is), he has two natures ("what" Jesus is)—one fully divine ("of one substance with the Father as regards his Godhead") and one fully human ("of one substance with us as regards his humanity"). In the words of the Chalcedonian Definition, Jesus Christ is "truly God, and truly human." Thus, Jesus Christ is one (divine) person with two natures (one uncreated and one created), while the triune God is three eternal persons (the Father, the Son, and the Holy Spirit) with one divine (uncreated) nature. Without this fundamental distinction between person and nature, it is impossible to formulate the doctrines of either the incarnation or the Trinity.

However, Rashdall's philosophical idealism erases this distinction. Rashdall applies the traditional definition of "nature" (that which exists "for itself") only to "Personalities." Moreover, the distinction between divine and human personalities is not a hard and fast one in Rashdall's theology, since all human persons are "sparks" of the divine Personality. Given that for Rashdall there are no natures that can be distinguished from personalities, the traditional doctrine of the Trinity can only be understood as either "tritheism" (three distinct and separate personalities) or Unitarianism (Rashdall's preferred option). In terms of Christology, the doctrine of the incarnation could only then mean either

52. See Rashdall, *Philosophy and Religion*, 182–85; Rashdall, *God and Man*, 113–14, 117–18, 121.

something like Apollinarianism (a divine Personality with a human body) or some version of adoptionism/Nestorianism (a human personality in whose life the divine Personality was especially present—Rashdall's preferred option). What Rashdall could not accept was the traditional christological doctrine that the personal subject of the incarnation is a divine person (the eternal Son of God) living *as* human (in a human nature) with a complete human mind and will.

Rashdall on the Atonement

Rashdall's first discussion of an exemplarist understanding of atonement occurs in his essay "The Abelardian Doctrine of the Atonement."[53] Here Rashdall asks, "To what, if the idea of appeasing an offended Deity be rejected, can the sacrifice [of Christ] be conceived of as owing its acceptability or validity, except to its actual effects of awakening the love of Christ and of all good, and the hatred of evil?"[54] He concludes: "The task which Abelard set before himself is precisely the task to which the Church of our day is imperatively called."[55]

Rashdall develops his more complete case in *The Idea of Atonement in Christian Theology*. Here he lays out "clearly what the theory is" by summarizing the teaching of Peter Abelard: "So great a pledge of love having been given us, we are both moved and kindled to love God who did such great things for us; and by this we are justified, that is, being loosed from our sins we are made just. The death of Christ therefore justifies us, inasmuch as through it charity is stirred up in our hearts." As stated, few would dispute this. However, Rashdall goes further to assert that it is "not the truth [so much] as the sufficiency" of the "Abelardian doctrine" as the "*sole* explanation" of the atonement that is at stake.[56]

Rashdall's exemplarist account of the atonement is a direct corollary of his commitment to idealist philosophy, combined with a modernist Protestant appropriation of a historical-critical reading of the Bible. Given his views on God, creation, Jesus Christ, and humanity, an exemplarist reading is likely the only possible interpretation of the atonement available to Rashdall. His combination of an idealist philosophy and the "historical Jesus" of nineteenth-century liberalism, along with a hermeneutic of discontinuity, leads him inevitably to exemplarism.

Rashdall begins his argument with the claim that any theology of atonement must be based on the teaching of Jesus, and not on later Christian thought.

53. In Rashdall, *Doctrine and Development*, 128–45.
54. Rashdall, *Doctrine and Development*, 141.
55. Rashdall, *Doctrine and Development*, 143.
56. Rashdall, *Idea of Atonement*, 438 (emphasis added).

The substance of Jesus's teaching is found in his proclamation, "Repent, for the kingdom of heaven is at hand."[57] According to Rashdall, the kingdom is neither a "political institution" nor (contrary to Schweitzer) a "cosmic catastrophe." The kingdom rather corresponds to a Harnackian reading of an immanent moral transformation: a "state of society in which God's will should be perfectly done—as it is in heaven."[58]

According to Rashdall, Jesus taught a doctrine of justification by good works: "The clear, unmistakable, invariable teaching of Jesus was that men were to be judged according to their works, including in the conception of works the state of the heart and intentions as scrutinized by an all-seeing God."[59] The crucial difference for Rashdall between Jesus's teaching and that of Pharisaic Judaism is that Jesus's teaching was "universalistic" and focused on the intentions of the heart rather than mere external observance of the law: for Jesus, forgiveness depends on nothing except "sincere repentance" and the necessary "amendment" that follows.[60] No doctrine of the atonement is permissible except that which Jesus himself taught, and Jesus did not teach any condition for forgiveness except repentance: "There is not the slightest suggestion that anything else but repentance is necessary—the actual death of a Saviour, believing in the atoning efficacy of that death or in any other article of faith, baptism, confession to any but God, absolution, reception of the holy eucharist, Church membership—not a hint of any of these."[61]

Rashdall recognizes two possible obstacles to his claim that Jesus never connected forgiveness of sins to his death. The first is Jesus's statement about his death being a "ransom for many" (Mark 10:43–45; Matt. 20:26–28), and the second is the Last Supper narrative in which Jesus compares bread and wine to his body and blood "given for you." Given that it does not appear in Luke's Gospel, Rashdall first suggests that the "ransom" saying does not represent authentic words of Jesus. However, if the saying is genuine, Rashdall suggests that Jesus meant it literally: he was going to die for his disciples by surrendering to the Jewish authorities so his followers would not have to die. Yet no matter how Jesus's death might benefit others, "there is nothing to suggest that the particular benefit which His death would win was the forgiveness of sins . . . or that the way in which it was to operate was by constituting an expiatory or substitutionary sacrifice."[62]

57. Rashdall, *Idea of Atonement*, 5.
58. Rashdall, *Idea of Atonement*, 7.
59. Rashdall, *Idea of Atonement*, 12, 14.
60. Rashdall, *Idea of Atonement*, 19, 23, 25.
61. Rashdall, *Idea of Atonement*, 26.
62. Rashdall, *Idea of Atonement*, 29–37.

Concerning the Last Supper narratives, Rashdall asserts that if the reference to a "covenant in my blood" echoes Jeremiah's new covenant, "there is nothing sacrificial about such a covenant as this." Jesus was thinking of his coming death as sacrificial "only in the sense in which any great leader of men might regard a martyr's death as an act of self-sacrifice on behalf of his followers."[63] Rashdall concludes that nothing in either the "ransom" reference (Mark 10:43–45) or the "new covenant" reference of the Last Supper narratives indicates that Jesus thought his death was necessary for the forgiveness of sins. The only notion of sacrificial atonement that can thus be traced back to Jesus was that his death would be a self-sacrifice for his followers that would inspire the same devotion in them.[64]

Assuming that the notion of an objective atonement cannot be traced to Jesus, Rashdall suggests Paul as the likely source. Rashdall's hermeneutic of discontinuity is most evident in his analysis of Paul. On the one hand, Paul's theology contains undeniable language of "expiation" and "substitution." On the other hand, Paul's ideas cannot be reconciled with either the teaching of Jesus or the demands of modern moral consciousness.[65] Rashdall suggests that Paul tried to reconcile two incompatible ideas: "the eternal and unchangeable love of God"[66] and the God of the Old Testament who is the "stern promulgator of the law with all its terrible penalties." Paul attempted to reconcile these two "incompatible" notions with the "theory of the substituted death of an innocent Son of God." However, "there is a real contradiction between the spirit of the Old Testament and the spirit of Christ, which St. Paul's theories fail to bridge." Nonetheless, "we can bridge that gulf by methods which were not open to St. Paul"—that is, by adopting an attitude toward the Old Testament made possible by modern theologians.[67]

Rashdall's historical discussion ranges from the Apostolic Fathers through Luther and the Reformation. Irenaeus was the first, he claims, to hold a theory of "objective redemption." Rashdall regards Irenaeus's recapitulation theory as "a sort of metaphysical or almost physical effect," which Rashdall considers "in the region of pure myth."[68] In the end, Irenaeus offers "vague and crude metaphysical theories" that no modern mind could adopt without translation into "more intelligible equivalents."[69] Similarly, Athanasius's understanding

63. Rashdall, *Idea of Atonement*, 41–45.
64. Rashdall, *Idea of Atonement*, 45.
65. Rashdall, *Idea of Atonement*, 98.
66. Rashdall, *Idea of Atonement*, 100.
67. Rashdall, *Idea of Atonement*, 103–4.
68. Rashdall, *Idea of Atonement*, 240, 241.
69. Rashdall, *Idea of Atonement*, 246.

of the incarnation is dismissed as a "sort of direct, physical, or metaphysical effect of the incarnation upon the soul," as resembling the "sympathetic magic" of "primitive man."[70]

Rashdall credits Anselm and Abelard with the "emancipation" of the church from the "hideous theory" of a ransom paid to the devil. However, insofar as humanity is obligated to repay a debt of satisfaction, Anselm is guilty of "the old bastard Platonism," which makes "universal human nature" something separable from individual human beings. Anselm appeals to justice, but his notions of justice are the "barbaric ideas of an ancient Lombard king." The fundamental defect of his theology is that "no civilized system of law permits the attribution of guilt to all humanity for the sin of one; nor can the penalty of the sinless Christ rationally or morally be considered to make any easier or any juster the remission of the penalty which man owes for his own sin."[71] As for Aquinas, "no new idea emerges" in his treatment.[72]

Rashdall saves his most bitter criticisms for Calvin and Luther. In Luther, the breach between theology and morality reaches the point of "formal divorce." Luther's theology is the "most exaggerated expression" of the substitutionary view. The substitutionary doctrine implies the "retributive theory of punishment," a "survival of primitive modes of thought" originating in the desire for revenge. However, even the retributive view renders unjust the punishment of the innocent in the place of the guilty. And vicarious punishment is not made "more rational" by vague terms such as "expiation" or "satisfaction." At bottom, medieval satisfaction theories as well as their Reformation developments involve the same "fundamental immorality."[73] And "Greek" (patristic) theories of the atonement are no better insofar as they presuppose the "same erroneous theory of punishment." In the end, "no juggling with universals will make it true to say that an individual who has in point of fact not been punished may nevertheless be deemed to have been punished."[74]

Rashdall summarizes his critique of any objective or constitutive notion of atonement by asserting that the doctrine was not part of Jesus's own teaching. Rather, it originated as an explanation of the scandal of a crucified Messiah using Old Testament prophetic statements that seemed to explain the scandal.[75]

70. Rashdall, *Idea of Atonement*, 297.
71. Rashdall, *Idea of Atonement*, 350, 353, 355.
72. Rashdall, *Idea of Atonement*, 373, 375, 377.
73. Rashdall, *Idea of Atonement*, 411, 420–23.
74. Rashdall, *Idea of Atonement*, 423–24.
75. Rashdall, *Idea of Atonement*, 435.

The Argument for Exemplarism

Despite his strong rejection of the traditional mainstream of atonement theology, Rashdall hopes that "a little selection among the rich materials accumulated by previous Christian thought may . . . present us with an interpretation of the doctrine which fully meets the demands of the most modern spirit." If we "put aside certain views of St. Paul," it would be possible to develop an atonement doctrine in which there is "no definite theory of substitution or expiation."[76] Rashdall claims that the "most definite and systematic expression which this subjective view of the atonement has found" is in the work of Abelard and those influenced by him. All discussions of the atonement offer a clear choice between substitutionary or expiatory accounts and some variation of subjective accounts. Thus, "the Abelardian view has more and more superseded the older substitutionary modes of representation."[77]

As seen in our chapter on Abelard, Rashdall appropriates the commonly accepted characterization of Abelard to identify characteristics of what he considers the "Abelardian" view. According to Rashdall, this view carries no notion of vicarious punishment, vicarious expiation, satisfaction, or objective sacrifice. It includes neither "mysterious guilt" that must be eliminated through death or suffering nor "pseudo-Platonic hypostasizing of the universal." The efficacy of Christ's death is explained exclusively through its "subjective influence" upon the sinner's consciousness leading to repentance and amendment of life. Jesus's voluntary death moves the sinner to gratitude and a response in love.[78]

As a corollary, the "atoning efficacy of Christ's work is not limited to his death." The whole life of Christ was one of love for his fellow human beings, and Jesus's love for humanity reveals in a unique way the heavenly Father's love for them as well: Jesus's entire life is atonement.[79]

In contrast to forensic accounts of the atonement or of justification, the justifying effect of Christ's work is a real effect, not a "legal fiction." Rashdall summarizes the exemplarist position on justification and sanctification concisely: "Christ's whole life was a sacrifice which takes away sin in the only way in which sin can really be taken away, and that is by making the sinner actually better."[80]

76. Rashdall, *Idea of Atonement*, 436–37.
77. Rashdall, *Idea of Atonement*, 437, 438.
78. Rashdall, *Idea of Atonement*, 358; cf. Rashdall, *Doctrine and Development*, 136.
79. Rashdall, *Idea of Atonement*, 443; cf. Rashdall, *Doctrine and Development*, 136.
80. Rashdall, *Doctrine and Development*, 137; Rashdall, *Idea of Atonement*, 454; cf. Rashdall, *Doctrine and Development*, 137.

Rashdall suggests that the exemplarist position is the real source of the implicit logic behind other atonement positions: "All through the Christian ages it has been the love of God revealed in Christ which really has won the heart of man." Although condemned in his own time, in the present day Abelard's "heresy" would be welcome. In Abelard, "at least we have found a theory of the atonement which thoroughly appeals to reason and to conscience."[81]

This is essentially the whole of Rashdall's positive presentation of his exemplarist view. Rashdall is simply spelling out the soteriological implications of his idealist philosophy concerning divine personalism, other minds, and "degree Christology." Most of his positive discussion of the "Truth of the Atonement" addresses criticism of his view, largely repeating his earlier affirmations.

Rashdall acknowledges that at the heart of traditional critiques of exemplarism is the claim that it is God himself who has taken on our sin in Christ: "We do not reach the real heart of the atonement doctrine unless we can see in the death of Christ without evasion or circumlocution the suffering and the death of God."[82] He addresses this critique first by questioning the coherency of and need for a traditional doctrine of the incarnation: "The love exhibited by Christ in life and in death might well be a source of spiritual life and death apart from all theories about Christ's nature."[83]

Rashdall's more detailed response appeals to what is clearly a Nestorian Christology. First, he denies any personal identity between God and the incarnate Jesus Christ in a manner resembling Nestorius's denial that Mary was the God-bearer (*theotokos*): "It was the divine Logos that preexisted, not the human Jesus." Rashdall also appeals to his Unitarian interpretation of Aquinas to claim that any juridical understanding of the atonement is impossible because it treats the relation between the Father and the Son as "distinct juridical Persons."[84]

Rashdall sums up what he believes to be the historical doctrine—but is actually a version of Nestorian Christology—by stating, "Christ reveals God because the Word or Logos of God was completely united to His human soul, and the human soul freely co-operated with the divine purposes. . . . Christ is the highest revelation of the divine character."[85]

Rashdall provides a concise summary of his exemplarist Christology in his paraphrase of John 14:6, a verse commonly understood to be a central New

81. Rashdall, *Idea of Atonement*, 360; cf. Rashdall, *Doctrine and Development*, 139, 140.
82. Rashdall, *Idea of Atonement*, 450.
83. Rashdall, *Idea of Atonement*, 446–47, 451
84. Rashdall, *Idea of Atonement*, 444, 446.
85. Rashdall, *Idea of Atonement*, 446.

Testament claim about Jesus's uniquely saving work: "I am the way, and the truth, and the life. No one comes to the Father except through me."

> The eternal meaning of the Christian doctrine of salvation through Christ alone is that in the acceptance of this supreme revelation lies the true way of being saved from sin and attaining the fullest deliverance from sin, and the highest perfection of which human nature is capable. . . . There is no other ideal given among men by which we may be saved except the moral ideal which Christ taught by His words, and illustrated by His life and death of love: and there is none other help so great in the attainment of that ideal as the belief in God as He has been supremely revealed in Him who so taught and lived and died.

Rashdall continues: "So understood, the self-sacrificing life which was consummated by the death upon the Cross has indeed power to take away sins of the whole world."[86]

What then does Rashdall make of the Pauline assertion that "God was in Christ" reconciling the world to himself? He does not so much answer this question as propose an alternative affirmation in its place: "In proportion as it is felt that *human* love reveals the love of God, the answering love which the self-sacrifice awakens will be love to God as well as love to man."[87] The key point of Christology for Rashdall is not the affirmation of the incarnation—that God himself is acting personally in the Second Person of the Trinity become human—but that just as *all* human beings reveal something to us about God, the strictly human Jesus reveals even more.

Another crucial claim of the traditional doctrine of the incarnation is that God himself has suffered and died for humanity. A reasonable objection to Rashdall's claim that the atonement reveals God's love is that we cannot claim that the cross is a revelation of the love of God "unless you are prepared to say that He who hung upon the cross was really a suffering God."[88] Did God suffer in Christ? As we saw in chapter 1, the crucial function of the *communicatio idiomatum* is to enable Christians to say literally and truthfully that in the person of Jesus Christ, God suffered, died, and rose again. It is because Nestorius was unwilling to say such things that his views were condemned at the councils of Ephesus and Chalcedon.

Rashdall's response to such questions effectively repeats the logic of Nestorius—and demonstrates that Rashdall missed the point of traditional incarnational theology. Rashdall correctly reminds his readers that Jesus did

---

86. Rashdall, *Idea of Atonement*, 463.
87. Rashdall, *Idea of Atonement*, 449–50 (emphasis added).
88. Rashdall, *Idea of Atonement*, 450.

not suffer in his divine nature: "I will only remind you that it is not orthodox to say that the divinity in Christ suffered." However, he qualifies this statement in the manner of Nestorian logic. The incarnation does not mean that Jesus Christ is God become human but means that Jesus is a human being who has a special relationship to God: "The man to whose human soul and flesh the Godhead became perfectly united suffered and died, and in virtue of that union we are allowed to ascribe to the man Jesus what is strictly and primarily true of the divinity which was united with His human nature, and to the Son of God what is strictly and primarily true only of the manhood in Christ." Rashdall complains that the "medieval language about God's blood and God's wounds has already become distasteful to modern Christians." "It is preferable to say 'The sufferings of Christ reveal to us the love of Christ, and the love of Christ reveals to us the love of God.'"[89]

Rashdall recognizes the pastoral significance of saying that God is present in human suffering. But instead of affirming the traditional doctrine that God literally suffered and died as a human in the divine person of Jesus Christ, he suggests that we say instead that God suffered in Christ insofar as "God must suffer with and in the suffering of all His creatures." If there is *some* revelation of God in all creatures and a supreme revelation of God in Jesus Christ, then "Christ represents in a supreme or unique way that sympathy or *suffering* with humanity which must needs be felt by a God of love. . . . If we cannot intelligibly say that the actual sufferings of Christ . . . are literally the sufferings of God, we may in quite earnest say that the suffering Christ reveals a suffering God."[90]

The crucial question to be asked here is the same one Cyril of Alexandria addressed to Nestorius: "Is Jesus Christ God become human or is Jesus Christ a human being in whom God was especially present?" While Rashdall repeatedly claims that his purpose is to expound a Christology and doctrine of the atonement that is intelligible to modern persons, he is in fact repeating the ancient Christology of Nestorius. Rashdall not only rejects the historic position but wrongly explains it. The *communicatio idiomatum* does not mean that we can ascribe to the man Jesus what is true of the divine nature to which he has become united. Rather, because Jesus Christ is a single divine person who is the subject of the incarnation, that person is also the subject of predication. We can therefore ascribe to the divine person that which belongs to either of his natures. That Rashdall finds medieval language about "God's blood" and "God's wounds, " as well as traditional hymnody, offensive demonstrates

89. Rashdall, *Idea of Atonement*, 450.
90. Rashdall, *Idea of Atonement*, 453–54.

that he really does not understand—or take the time to understand—historic incarnational theology.

Aftermath

Despite Rashdall's confidence in his modern liberal project, the decades immediately following saw the repudiation of his ideas. As we will see in the next chapter, Barth's theology explicitly repudiates both liberal theology and the modern epistemological "turn to the self" characteristic of idealist philosophy. However, despite this opposition and the collapse of idealist philosophy, new variations of liberal theology appeared, for example, in the writings of Rudolf Bultmann and Paul Tillich.[91]

Anglican Bishop of Woolwich John A. T. Robinson (1919–83) is best known for his controversial book *Honest to God*. In it he claims that language referring to a God "in heaven" is outdated mythology to be replaced with Tillich's description of God as the "Ground of our being."[92] Theology must be rewritten in order to speak to the concerns of contemporary culture, because theology's traditional concerns and language are "irrelevant to the burning issues of our day." Robinson's panentheist "degree" Christology echoes many of the themes in Rashdall's exemplarist soteriology.[93]

Other contemporary examples of exemplarism can be found in modern liberal theologians such as Sallie McFague, Elizabeth Johnson, and Marcus Borg. While not philosophical idealists, contemporary exemplarists often reject a realist account of knowledge and presume an epistemological agnosticism, especially regarding God. The historic Christian position is that God is in himself who he has revealed himself to be in his revelation. By contrast, the basic (Feuerbachian) premise of much modern theology is that knowledge of God is based on the projection of human aspirations. Such knowledge reflects how we relate to God but does not disclose God's own nature. Given the denial that God acts or speaks in the world in an "interventionist" manner, it would not make sense for modern exemplarists to affirm that God became a human being in Jesus Christ. As with Rashdall, their Christology is necessarily adoptionist.[94]

Such atonement theologies are thus illustrative, not constitutive, of atonement. Jesus's life, death, and resurrection do not create a salvation available

91. Dorrien, *Kantian Reason*, 454–529.
92. Robinson, *Honest to God*, 41, 59, 80.
93. Robinson, *Human Face of God*, 4, 14, 16–17, 203, 209–10.
94. McFague, *Models of God*, 136; Borg, *Heart of Christianity*, 88.

nowhere else but rather illustrate a salvation that is available elsewhere and perhaps everywhere. McFague perhaps states it best: "One can . . . understand the incarnation of God in Jesus of Nazareth to mean that Jesus' response as beloved to God as lover was so open and thorough that his life and death were revelatory of God's great love for the world. His illumination of that love . . . is paradigmatic of God the lover but is not unique. . . . Jesus is not ontologically different from other paradigmatic figures. . . . He is special to us as our foundational figure."[95]

Evaluation

The crucial theological question for evaluating Rashdall and all such exemplarist interpretations of atonement is *not* whether a theology of atonement contains a subjective aspect or includes some sort of human response of faith, hope, or love. The question is whether atonement is understood in an *exclusively* exemplarist manner and is therefore merely illustrative rather than constitutive of salvation. As Rashdall himself makes clear, it is the "sufficiency" of the subjective response as the "*sole* explanation" that makes for an exemplarist (or what he identifies as the "Abelardian") account of the atonement.

Ironically, as demonstrated in an earlier chapter, Abelard himself does not explain the atonement exclusively in terms of a subjective response but includes substitutionary and participationist elements as well. By Rashdall's own standards, Abelard was not actually "Abelardian"! As also discussed in previous chapters, Aquinas, John and Charles Wesley, and Calvin include elements of exemplarism in their atonement theologies, but each also affirms some version of a core constitutive theology of the atonement. An *exclusively* exemplarist interpretation of the atonement seems to be a uniquely modern phenomenon.

Perhaps most significantly, the modern exemplarist accounts of Rashdall and his followers are marked by a hermeneutic of suspicion and of "discontinuity" between the Old and New Testaments, between Jesus and Paul, and between the precrucifixion Jesus and the post-Easter resurrected Jesus. From the beginning of the New Testament era, Jesus's life, death, and resurrection were interpreted within the context of the Old Testament. However, modern exemplarists consistently downplay both the resurrection of Jesus and New Testament fulfillment of Old Testament promise. For Rashdall and other modern exemplarists, the resurrection of Jesus is barely significant. Of real

95. McFague, *Models of God*, 136.

concern is that his cause carries on and what that means *for us today*. Exemplarist accounts thus tend to be "Marcionite" not only in their dismissal of the Old Testament but also in divorcing Jesus of Nazareth from the incarnate and resurrected Jesus Christ of the creeds and ecumenical councils.

By contrast, in *The Riddle of the New Testament*, a book that had a significant impact in British theology in the generation following Rashdall, Edwin Hoskyns and Noel Davey demonstrate that no strand of New Testament teaching fails to interpret Jesus's life and death within the context of the Old Testament or to portray him as the Son of God and the Savior of the world who died on the cross for our sins and rose from the dead. Accordingly, the decision that must be made about Jesus is primarily a theological one and not reducible to a matter of historical criticism. Either we agree with the theological focus of the New Testament, or we assume that the New Testament writers provide a radically distorted account of Jesus's person and work.[96]

Thus, the choice between a strictly illustrative exemplarism and constitutive interpretations of the atonement is between a hermeneutic of trust and continuity versus one of suspicion and discontinuity. Either atonement is truly "at-one-ment"—a restored unity between God and sinful humanity effected through the person and work of the incarnate Son of God—or modern exemplarism's hermeneutic of discontinuity necessarily means that God is not in himself what Scripture portrays of Jesus Christ. If this verdict seems harsh, it is one that exemplarists themselves have claimed: theological metaphors are "projection" and "mostly fiction." Language of "incarnation" and "resurrection" does not refer to actual events that happened but to our own experiences of love or purpose that arise when we read the stories of Jesus in the Bible.[97]

If modern exemplarism insists that we can know nothing of God *in se*, it also necessarily implies the loss of Christian ontology, of the doctrines of the incarnation, of the Trinity, of the church's participation in Christ's risen humanity as the body of Christ, and of eschatology. For modern exemplarism, Jesus Christ is not God become a human being who saves us from sin; he merely gives us an example of how we might save ourselves. And if Jesus is primarily an example of a salvation that we could in principle have without him, is he really necessary?

By contrast, constitutive accounts of the atonement assume that Jesus Christ is still alive and that the risen Christ is present to the church through incorporation or participation. Christians do not merely imitate or become

96. Hoskyns and Davey, *Riddle of the New Testament*; Ramsey, *From Gore to Temple*, 131–40.
97. McFague, *Models of God*, 59–60, 182, 183, 192.

inspired by the example of the earthly Jesus. Rather, the church finds its corporate identity *in* Christ, the church is the community that is united *to* the risen Jesus Christ through the presence of the Holy Spirit, and the church is identified *as* the body of Christ. For constitutive accounts of atonement, this New Testament language refers to an ontological reality.

While there have been differences and disagreements in the various accounts of the atonement up to this point, all the theologians we have discussed prior to this chapter have shared the assumption that the person and work of Jesus Christ are constitutive of human salvation—that Jesus Christ and Jesus alone saves sinners who cannot save themselves. By contrast, when we come to modern exemplarism, we must ask whether its accounts are simply another way of attempting to explain the atonement, or whether exemplarism is actually a rejection of atonement theology. In the end, it appears that an ultimate and unavoidable choice has to be made between constitutive and illustrative accounts of the person and work of Christ and that any account of atonement that falls short of a constitutive account is not actually a doctrine of atonement.

8

. . .

Atonement as Reconciliation

Karl Barth

Our introductory chapter claimed that any adequate treatment of the doctrine of atonement must engage and integrate all three levels of knowing and being: (1) narrative/symbol, (2) history, and (3) ontology. At the first level, the metaphors or symbols of atonement (e.g., sacrifice, judgment, military victory, ransom) receive their interpretation from the context of the narrative structure of biblical texts and should not be read in a flat-footed, literalist manner. At the second level, the metaphors and narratives refer beyond themselves to the history of God's covenant with Israel; of the incarnation, life, death, and resurrection of Jesus of Nazareth; and of the appropriation of Jesus's atoning work through the Holy Spirit in the church. At the third level, both symbol and history refer beyond themselves to the ontological realities of the triune God, the incarnate Christ, and the renewed creation. In this manner, we come to know *who* God is by *what* God has done. The history of salvation reveals the economic Trinity: God as the Father of Jesus Christ, Jesus of Nazareth as the incarnate Son of the Father, and the Holy Spirit as God's presence in the church—all of which makes known to us the immanent Trinity who is eternally Father, Son, and Holy Spirit. The work of Jesus Christ cannot be separated from his person as the Second Person of the Trinity become a human being. And the efficacy of Christ's atoning work graciously mediated through the church and the sacraments presupposes an ontology of union between reconciled humanity and the risen Christ made possible by the presence of the Holy Spirit.

The introductory chapter also distinguishes between atonement theologies that treat the person and work of Jesus Christ as constitutive of and necessary to human salvation and those that treat it as illustrative of a general salvation available elsewhere or everywhere. Constitutive theologies understand "Jesus saves" to mean that the incarnation, life, death, and resurrection of Jesus actually and uniquely provide salvation for all human beings who have ever lived or ever will. Illustrative theologies understand the historical figure of Jesus to be an important moral example or illustration of divine presence. This second approach generally understands Jesus to be a way of salvation for Christians, but only one way among many other paths to salvation (however defined). Jesus of Nazareth might be favorably compared to such figures as Moses, Socrates, or Buddha as a spiritual guide or moral example for others but not regarded as the unique Savior or Redeemer of the entire human race from sin.

In our examination of various metaphors and models of the atonement throughout, we have tried to trace the extent to which different theologians have succeeded or failed to integrate these three levels of knowing and being. We consider those theologies that coordinate metaphors or symbols of salvation with accounts both of Jesus's person as the incarnate Son of God and of his work as constitutive of salvation through his whole earthly life (incarnation, teaching and mission, crucifixion, resurrection, ascension, and second coming) as more adequate because they more comprehensively and faithfully integrate the essential subject matter of Christian faith. Less adequate accounts, by contrast, treat the metaphors or symbols in ways informed only by his incarnation and cross (satisfaction) or only by his teaching and death (exemplarism).

This chapter will examine the atonement theology of the twentieth-century Reformed theologian Karl Barth as found primarily in his *Church Dogmatics* IV/1. Barth's contribution is indispensable because he so capably integrates symbol/metaphor, history, and ontology. Barth's account is one of those masterful texts that deserves to be included among such theological classics as Athanasius's *On the Incarnation* and Augustine's *Confessions*.

The Methodological Presuppositions of Barth's Theology

Our account of Barth's atonement theology begins with two statements that succinctly summarize his contribution. First, Barth's entire theology can be summarized in the statement "God is in himself who he is in his revelation." This goes beyond merely affirming a correspondence between the economic and immanent Trinity. Rather, Jesus Christ as the Word incarnate is not merely a reflection of God, nor even a communication of information about God, but is God's very self-revelation. In Christ, God himself is personally present.[1]

Second, according to Barth, the doctrine of the atonement is itself the "heart of the message received by and laid upon the Christian community and therefore the heart of the Church's dogmatics." The "center" of the Christian message is that in God's atoning work in Jesus Christ, God is with us: "'God with us' is the centre of the Christian message—and always in such a way that it is primarily a statement about God and only then and for that reason a statement about us men" (CD IV/1, 3, 5). Barth's theology of the atonement is an account of how these two statements fit together.

Throughout Barth's career, he was concerned with the relationship between knowledge and reality—not as a philosopher who was concerned to formulate an epistemology or metaphysics but as a theologian whose methodology was patterned on Anselm's *fides quaerens intellectum*.[2] Barth insists that God's revelation in Christ faithfully communicated not only Christ's significance for us (*propter nos*) but also who God is in himself (*in se*).[3]

Accordingly, Barth's theological career began with a rejection of the epistemological "turn to the self" that characterized nineteenth-century liberal Protestant theology. Barth identifies Ludwig Feuerbach's assertion—namely, that talk about God is only talk about human aspiration—as the definitive critique of all theology that followed Schleiermacher.[4] In the end, the liberal Protestant combination of rationalism and subjectivism was not speaking of God at all but only "speaking of man in a loud voice."[5]

Barth is equally critical, however, of the notion of God as a kind of "naked sovereignty," an "absolute World-ruler as such, and in general," an absolute power (*potentia absoluta*) who "rules absolutely." Such a God might well be a "false god," an "idol," and the "exact opposite of the true God" (CD II/2, 49–51). Barth is convinced that such an understanding of God characterized much of Reformed Protestant orthodoxy. Modern atheism, he believes, finds its origins in a revolt against such a God. The God of liberal Protestantism was only a projection of human subjectivity, but the God of absolute sovereignty is not the God who has been revealed in Jesus Christ either (II/2, 53–54).[6]

1. Barth, CD IV/1, 204. See T. F. Torrance, *Karl Barth*, 84.

2. Barth, *Anselm*.

3. A. Torrance, "Trinity," 73.

4. Feuerbach, *Essence of Christianity*; Busch, *Great Passion*, 58–60; Hart, "Revelation," 39; Hart, *Regarding Karl Barth*, 8; A. Torrance, "Trinity," 72–73; Mangina, *Karl Barth*; T. F. Torrance, *Karl Barth*, 30–31; Tietz, "Barth's Historical and Theological Significance," 10–11.

5. Barth, *Word of God and the Word of Man*, 196.

6. Busch, *Great Passion*, 112–13.

Barth's theology is positively characterized by the following motifs:[7]

1. The distinction between God and the world: Against the immanentism of nineteenth-century Protestant theology, which moved from the subjectivity of human experience, piety, or morality to language about God, Barth insists that divine transcendence renders impossible any move from human experience to knowledge of the divine. Theology must begin with the transcendent God. Accordingly, Barth refers to God as "wholly other."[8] God is not one object among many objects in the world, so it is not possible to speak of God using ordinary human language (*CD* I/2, 750).[9]

2. Actualism: While it is impossible to move from humanity to God, God *has* made the move from himself to humanity. The human subject does not determine the possibilities of what can be known about God; rather, God has made himself known through an act of sheer divine grace.[10] Barth uses the language of "act," of "event, "occurrence," and "happening," to describe the personal *living* God who is "being in act," who has spoken and acted concretely to make himself known in his revelation (*CD* IV/1, 6).[11] The fact that God speaks affirms the personalist dimension of revelation: "God's Word means that God speaks. . . . It is *the* truth as it is God's speaking person" (I/1, 136).[12]

3. Particularism: Barth's theology consciously moves from the particular to the general (rather than vice versa), beginning with the particular narratives of the biblical witness. Barth neither begins with a general account of the nature of God or the universe nor asks questions about the conditions under which knowledge of God might be possible. Rather, it is God's activity in Word and event that establishes what is possible.[13] God has taken the initiative to make himself known to particular witnesses (prophets and apostles) in the economy of salvation, not to everyone. This means that faith and theology are always a "response," a "following after" (*nachfolgen*).[14]

7. Hunsinger, *How to Read Karl Barth*, 29–30.

8. Barth, *Humanity of God*, 42; Hart, *Regarding Karl Barth*, 9; Tietz, "Barth's Historical and Theological Significance," 12; Schwöbel, "Theology," 20–21.

9. Hart, *Regarding Karl Barth*, 10.

10. Busch, *Great Passion*, 61–63; Schwöbel, "Theology," 2.

11. Hunsinger, *How to Read Karl Barth*, 30–32; Hart, "Revelation," 45.

12. Hart, "Revelation," 8.

13. Busch, *Great Passion*, 68.

14. Hunsinger, *How to Read Karl Barth*, 32–35; Busch, *Great Passion*, 68; Hart, "Revelation," 47–48; Bruce, "Revelation," 62.

4. Objectivism: According to Barth, true knowledge of God is objective knowledge (*CD* II/1, 12, 13, 49).[15] This objective knowledge has two aspects: knowledge of God and salvation in Jesus Christ. God's revelation in history demands an identity in eternity; otherwise, God's revelation would not be a true self-revelation. If God has revealed himself as triune in history, then God must be triune in himself.[16] Because God communicates his Word to us, and in so doing conveys his truth to us, divine revelation is a *rational* event grounded in God's own being.[17] Knowledge of God occurs not when we apply our prior conceptions to God (which is self-projection) but when we allow our concepts to be corrected in the light of divine revelation.[18] In his reading of Scripture, Barth focused on the objective "subject matter" (*die Sache*) of the text, the incarnate Jesus Christ who lived, died, and rose again.[19]

5. Mediation: That the uncreated God has communicated himself within the sphere of creation means that knowledge of God is always mediated through created realities and most especially through the humanity of Jesus Christ. Our knowledge of God is thus always indirect and never immediate. In the incarnation, God has "cross[ed] the boundary between Himself and us" (*CD* I/2, 31).

The Ontological Presuppositions of the Atonement

Adam Johnson has written that "treatments of the doctrine of the atonement . . . share a conspicuous absence of sustained theological reflection on the role of the doctrine of God as a whole (the doctrines of the Trinity, divine attributes and election)." Bruce McCormack likewise refers to a "weakness of Protestant theology . . . a decided lack of interest in 'ontological questions' within the realm of dogmatics." Both point to Barth's treatment of the atonement as an exception to this weakness. If the preceding motifs provide the methodological background for Barth's doctrine of the atonement, his discussion of the following doctrines provides the atonement's ontological presuppositions.[20]

---

15. Busch, *Great Passion*, 72–76.
16. Hunsinger, *How to Read Karl Barth*, 35–39.
17. T. F. Torrance, *Karl Barth*, 45–46.
18. Busch, *Great Passion*, 76.
19. Tietz, "Barth's Historical and Theological Significance," 11.
20. Johnson, *God's Being in Reconciliation*, 9; McCormack, "Ontological Presuppositions," 346; Hunsinger distinguishes between "ontology$_1$" (a "systematic framework within which theology was constrained to operate") and "ontology$_2$" ("a field of inquiry pertaining to the material covered and the sorts of things and relations one describes in it"). Barth rejects ontology

Revelation and Scripture

As noted above, the revelation of God means that God speaks. Barth ties the relation between revelation as divine act and speech to his theology of Scripture through his threefold account of the divine Word: (1) the Word of God revealed (the incarnate Word), (2) the Word of God written (Holy Scripture), and (3) the Word of God preached (church proclamation).[21] First, as the Word incarnate, Jesus Christ is the personal presence of God himself: "God was with us, with us His enemies. . . . He was with us as one of us. His Word became flesh of our flesh, blood of our blood" (*CD* I/1, 115).

Second, prophets and apostles, the writers of Scripture (the Word of God written), are witnesses to this event of revelation, but they are not themselves revelation (*CD* I/1, 113; 112–14). Rather, the Bible as canon is the church's witness to God's revelation in the incarnate Word. Barth's description of canonical Scripture in *CD* I/1 anticipates what he later writes about the atonement:

> The prophetic and apostolic word is the word, witness, proclamation and preaching of Jesus Christ. The promise given to the Church in this Word is the promise of God's mercy which is uttered in the person of Him who is very God and very Man and which takes up our cause when we could not help ourselves at all because of our enmity against God. The promise of this Word is thus Immanuel, God with us. . . . Holy Scripture is the word of men who yearned, waited and hoped for this Immanuel and who finally saw, heard and handled it in Jesus Christ. (I/1, 107–8)

Third, the Word of God preached in the church's gathered worship is human "talk about God on the basis of God's own direction" (*CD* I/1, 90). Christian proclamation has in common with Scripture that it points away from itself to God's revelation in Jesus Christ. There is a fundamental difference, however, between the "absolutely constitutive significance" of Holy Scripture and the church's proclamation in word and sacrament: "The apostolic succession of the Church must mean that it is guided by the Canon, that is, by the prophetic and apostolic word as the necessary rule of every word that is valid in the Church" (I/1, 103, 104).[22]

---

as a "controlling system" (ontology$_1$), but he is willing to use ontology in the "looser sense" of ontology$_2$. Hunsinger, *Reading Barth with Charity*, 2.

21. Mangina, *Karl Barth*, 33–36, 39–43, 45–48; Hart, *Regarding Karl Barth*, 28–47.

22. Barth is clear that the Word as church proclamation not only is "preaching" but also includes sacrament (*CD* I/1, 56). In his last series of public lectures, Barth reformulated his threefold distinction as "The Word," "The Witnesses," and "The Community." Barth, *Evangelical Theology*, 15–47.

The Trinity

Barth departed from the traditional pattern of Western theology by placing the doctrine of the Trinity at the beginning of his *Church Dogmatics*. In
so doing, he set the stage for a trinitarian revival in theology that continues
today. For Barth, the "root of the doctrine of the Trinity" is the "fact" of
divine revelation; in revelation, "God's Word is identical with God Himself"
(*CD* I/1, 304). To know Jesus Christ is to know God as the Son of God, who
does not merely make this impression on us but truly is the Son (I/1, 415),
who "can reveal the Father and reconcile us to the Father because He reveals
Himself as the One He is" (I/1, 414).[23]

Revelation thus has a trinitarian structure: the God who has made himself known in the particular concrete history of Jesus Christ, who himself
summarizes God's history with Israel, is imparted to us by the Holy Spirit,
witnessed to by Scripture, and proclaimed in the church as it aligns itself with
that witness. The reality of the God whom we encounter as Father, Son, and
Holy Spirit in revelation (the economic Trinity) is this reality from all eternity
(the immanent Trinity; *CD* I/1, 479–80).[24] The triune God is thus the essential
"subject matter" of theology, both the "ontic" and the "noetic" basis of the
revealed Word, the beginning and end of the theological task, "the essential
grammar of God's engagement with humanity and the possibility of theological objectivity."[25]

However, the doctrine of the Trinity is a matter not only of revelation but
also of restoration and reconciliation. Everything that Barth writes about
knowledge of and fellowship with God makes clear that we cannot reach
God through our own epistemological or moral efforts. Restoration between
God and humanity has come in Jesus Christ through the Holy Spirit (*CD* I/1,
409–10):[26] Johnson writes, "The work of the incarnate Son reconciles us to
God because Jesus Christ is himself God and not another or different god
from the Father with whom we are reconciled."[27]

The correlation between the doctrine of the Trinity and God's work of
reconciliation is evident throughout *CD* IV/1, which contains Barth's definitive
discussion of the atonement. The volume begins, "The whole being and life
of God is an activity, both in eternity and in worldly time, both in Himself
as Father, Son and Holy Spirit, and in His relation to man in all creation.
. . . But here he wills and works a particular thing: not one with others, but

23. Molnar, "Barth on the Trinity," 23–25.
24. Busch, *Great Passion*, 43.
25. A. Torrance, "Trinity," 73–77; Busch, *Great Passion*, 43.
26. Molnar, "Barth on the Trinity," 26.
27. Johnson, *God's Being in Reconciliation*, 69.

one for the sake of which He wills and works all others" (*CD* IV/1, 7). In the atonement, the triune God has made himself the God of humanity (IV/1, 38). Atonement means that humanity has been allowed to participate in the life of this triune God: "In this event God allows the world and humanity to take part in the history of the inner life of His Godhead" (IV/1, 215).

Divine Perfections and Election

In his discussion of God's perfections, Barth affirms the traditional perfections of aseity, simplicity, immutability, impassibility, and timelessness. God is "perfect" and "self-sufficient." The perfections are intrinsic to God's "simple being" *ad intra*—that is, they do not arise from God's relation to the world.[28] However, such language does not imply some kind of divine nature independent of or prior to the triune persons. There is a trinitarian pattern to the divine perfections, and the perfections of God do not describe a God other than the triune God.[29]

In terms of the order of knowledge, we come to know the divine perfections through God's revelation in Jesus Christ, not through *a priori* speculation. Jesus Christ is the ultimate basis and warrant for the predicates we attribute to God. We know what love is through the person and work of Christ. The fullness of the perfections is seen in the incarnation of the Son of God in Jesus Christ (*CD* IV/1, 39).[30]

Crucial for Barth's understanding of the relation between God and God's creatures is what George Hunsinger refers to as the principle of "divine antecedence": "Everything that God does in time finds its antecedent ground in eternity."[31] God's being and essence do not change with creation; whatever God does *ad extra*, he does in accord with his antecedent being. Barth's understanding seems to be that the God who is transcendently immutable and impassible is also transcendently free to change in relation to creation: "The God who is impassible is free in love to embrace temporal change without losing his essential constancy as the triune God."[32]

Key to Barth's understanding is the "dialectic" between love and freedom: the being of the triune God is the one who loves in freedom (*CD* II/1, 257).

28. Barth, *CD* II/1, 332; IV/1, 213; IV/2, 133, 346; Hunsinger, *Reading Barth with Charity*, 129; Johnson, *God's Being in Reconciliation*, 101.

29. Johnson, *God's Being in Reconciliation*, 100; Long, *Saving Karl Barth*, 141; Hunsinger, *Reading Barth with Charity*, 129–31.

30. Johnson, *God's Being in Reconciliation*, 107, 113.

31. Hunsinger, *Reading Barth with Charity*, 8. See also Johnson, *God's Being in Reconciliation*, 37–38

32. Hunsinger, *Reading Barth with Charity*, 132, 133.

Love is intrinsic to God's being; indeed, God's being is always act in love, and we know this from God's love in Jesus Christ. However, God also loves in complete freedom; we know this from the divine sovereignty shown in Christ's death and resurrection.[33] How are God's love and freedom related? Barth grounds divine freedom and love in the divine aseity and the relations between the divine persons: "God's being as He who lives and loves is being in freedom. In this way, freely, He lives and loves. And in this way, and in the fact that He lives and loves in freedom, He is God, and distinguishes Himself from everything else that lives and loves. . . . This is the freedom of the divine life and love" (II/1, 301).

A crucial implication of this love-freedom dialectic is that creation is not necessary. God would still be triune and would still be love without the creature (CD II/2, 6).[34] The God who loves necessarily within the Trinity loves the world in complete freedom. God's freedom entails that he may enter into a covenant with his creatures but is not required to do so. Conversely, God's love entails that he would not be free to renounce such a covenant afterward. God's triune covenantal love draws the creature into union with God in Christ, and that covenantal union is irrevocable (II/1, 274–75, 280; II/2, 7).[35]

According to Barth, the beginning of God's acts *ad extra* is God's decision to unite himself to humanity in the person of his Son, to be Jesus Christ. Jesus is thus the primary object of God's election. In his election to be Jesus, God has decided to be "for us" and not "against us."[36] Before there was a creation, God planned to co-exist with humanity, to love it. God was under no compulsion; this decision was consistent with his trinitarian love as the one who eternally loves.[37] "In the beginning, . . . before there was any reality distinct from God which could be the object of the love of God or the setting for His acts of freedom, God anticipated and determined within Himself (in the power of His love and freedom, of His knowing and willing) that the goal and meaning of all His dealings with the as yet nonexistent universe should be the fact that in His Son He would be gracious towards man, uniting Himself with him" (CD II/2, 101).

Election is a key theme in Barth's discussion of the atonement: "In this free act of the election of grace the Son of the Father is no longer just the eternal Logos, but as such, as very God from all eternity He is also the very God and

33. Tseng, *Karl Barth's Infralapsarian Theology*, 216–17.
34. Tseng, *Karl Barth's Infralapsarian Theology*, 216–17; Molnar, "Barth on the Trinity," 23; Busch, *Great Passion*, 124–25.
35. Tseng, *Karl Barth's Infralapsarian Theology*, 218–21.
36. Gibson, "Barth on Divine Election," 49–50.
37. Busch, *Great Passion*, 126–27.

very man he will become in time" (*CD* IV/1, 66).[38] This understanding of divine favor is crucial to Barth's perspective. As we will see below, Barth uses a judicial model of the atonement but insists that even God's judgment must be interpreted in terms of God's unconditional prior love.

God with Us: Atonement and Creation

Barth's initial discussions of atonement pursue a variation of a traditional Reformed understanding of penal substitution.[39] However, Barth modifies his approach in *CD* IV/1. In what follows, we will examine *CD* IV/1 both because it marks a shift in Barth's thought and because it represents Barth's most mature and complete account of the atonement.

Barth introduces atonement in *CD* IV/1 with the declaration that atonement is about *Immanuel*, "God with us," which is at the "center" of "the whole complex of Christian understanding and doctrine," the "heart of the Christian message" (IV/1, 4, 6). (Barth refers to Isa. 7:14; 8:8, 10; and Matt. 1:23; see *CD* IV/1, 5–6.) He proceeds to outline this heart of the Christian message in seven points.

First, "God with us" is a "report" or "event," not a state. Barth distinguishes between God's general activity in creation and providence and God's special activity in Christ. "God with us" means that God "does not will to be God without us, that He creates us rather to share with us and therefore with our being and life and act His own incomparable being and life and act." This is the "very heart" of the Christian message (*CD* IV/1, 6–7).

Second, what God does in creation and providence is aimed at this particular act of "God with us." "God wills and works all things, but here He wills and works a particular thing: not one with others, but one for the sake of which He wills and works." This act is the *telos* (organizing goal) of *all* of God's acts both in himself and in the history of his acts in the created world (*CD* IV/1, 7–8).[40]

Third, Barth speaks of "salvation" as "beyond creation" and as "union with God." This salvation is "participation in the being of God" and is "more than creation": "Salvation, fulfilment, perfect being means . . . being which has a part in the being of God, from which and to which it is: not a divinised

---

38. A key point of controversy in the current discussion is whether Barth places election in the doctrine of God rather than the doctrine of creation or soteriology because it is "first and foremost" a "self-determination." Johnson, *God's Being in Reconciliation*, 36–37.

39. Barth, *CD* II/1, 393–406; *CD* II/2, 489–97; Barth, *Dogmatics in Outline*, 101–23.

40. In this passage, Barth specifically mentions the Trinity as an act of God in himself.

being but a being which is hidden in God, and in that sense (distinct from God and secondary) eternal being." This salvation is not proper to created being but is "grace" because it comes to the creature freely from God (CD IV/1, 8, 10). It reveals the glory of God, which consists in God's "free love" together with the "dignity of man"—a dignity that God invests in humanity but is not proper to it (IV/1, 10).

Fourth, "God with us" is God's original plan for humanity. It is "the most primitive relationship between God and man, that which was freely determined by God Himself before there was any created being. In the very fact that man is, and that he is man, he is as such chosen by God for salvation; that eschaton is given him by God" (CD IV/1, 10).

Fifth, sin now enters the picture. "God with us" "means God with us men who have forfeited the predetermined salvation, forfeited it with a supreme and final jeopardising even of our creaturely existence." In rejecting God's purposes, humanity has turned its back on participation in God's being, thereby denying its entire reason for being, its teleological goal. However, God deals graciously and savingly with fallen humanity: "But it is with this lost son in a far country, with man as he has fallen and now exists in this sorry plight, that God has to do in this redeeming event" (CD IV/1, 10, 11).

Sixth, "God with us" means incarnation. God himself in his own person has become human in order to fulfill his redemptive will. Where humanity has refused and failed, God himself has intervened *as* human. Because God is God (freedom and love), God can exercise his power by suffering for us the consequences of our transgression, the "wrath" and "penalty" to "satisfy" himself (CD IV/1, 12). Here Barth uses the language of "penal substitution," but it will become clear that he considerably modifies the traditional position.

In the incarnation, God in Christ becomes his own human partner "in our place" and so "satisfies us" as well, achieving "peace" between God and humanity. But God does more than restore the original creation. God's "gracious answer" to human failure is his "participation in our being," which results in our "participation" in God's being in eschatological fullness. Jesus Christ does not merely redeem our being but gives himself as the gift of its fulfillment (CD IV/1, 13–14).

Seventh, "God with us" therefore includes "we with God." Salvation "does not mean the extinguishing of our humanity, but its establishment." In Christ, we are summoned to our true being—we are made free for God. God's grace becomes in us "something specifically human," "action in the truest sense of the word." Our faith, love, and hope are found in "that one man," who answers for us and enables us to believe, love, and hope in freedom (CD IV/1,

14–15). Barth concludes that these "seven points" say "almost everything that needs to be said about 'God with us'" (IV/1, 16).

The preceding demonstrates that Barth's doctrine of atonement is grounded in his doctrine of creation. It has affinities with approaches we have seen in theologians like Irenaeus and Aquinas. However, unique to Barth's approach is his connection between atonement and election. The man Jesus Christ—not simply the Logos as the Second Person of the Trinity—is the foundation of election from all eternity. In his discussion of "God with us," Barth is clear that salvation was God's goal for humanity from all eternity.

Barth's position appears to have certain affinities with that of Duns Scotus: even if there had been no human sin, God would still have become incarnate in Jesus Christ. Yes, the atonement is at the heart of Christian faith and is God's response to human sin. However, from all eternity, Jesus Christ is the Creator and the source of human union with God. Therefore, even if humanity had not sinned, Jesus still would have accomplished his task as mediator, bringing humanity into union with God. The purpose of the atonement is not merely to combat sin but to fulfill God's original will for creation:

> What takes place in Jesus Christ, in the historical event of the atonement accomplished by Him in time, is not simply one history among others, and not simply the reaction of God against human sin. It stands at the heart of the Christian message and the Christian faith because here God maintains and fulfils his Word as it was spoken at the very first. . . . For in Jesus Christ we do not have to do with a second and subsequent, but with the first and original content of the will of God, before and above which there is no other will—either hidden or revealed in some other way. (CD IV/1, 47–48)[41]

The Covenant as the Presupposition of Reconciliation

One of the distinctive features of Barth's theology, and his discussion of the atonement, is the attention he devotes to Israel as God's covenant partner. Consistent with what we have seen thus far, Barth insists that the covenant is not part of a "general concept" of God but refers to God's unique relationship with a specific people.

Barth begins his section titled "The Covenant as the Presupposition of Reconciliation" by stating that Jesus Christ is "God with us" in the reconciliation between God and humanity in fulfillment of God's covenant. Barth asserts that "covenant" is the Old Testament term for the "basic relationship between God and his people." In the promise "I will be your God and you will

---

41. Hunsinger, foreword to Tseng, *Karl Barth's Infralapsarian Theology*, 10.

be my people" (Jer. 7:23; cf. 11:4; 30:22; etc.), "my people" refers specifically to the twelve tribes of Israel (*CD* IV/1, 22).

The Old Testament covenant is a covenant of grace in which God chooses a particular people and they in turn choose God. The covenant is an "event of a divine and human choice" in which the God of the covenant is a personal, living, acting God and Israel as a nation exists only in this history with God (*CD* IV/1, 23). While God's covenant is with Israel, Israel's mission is to the "nations" (Isa. 60). God has chosen this people to be his representative through whom his redemptive will is to be declared to all humanity (*CD* IV/1, 28).

The new covenant of Jeremiah (Jer. 31:32–33) does not replace the Mosaic covenant but is a revelation of the purpose of the first covenant: "I will be your God and you will be my people." Israel was disobedient to the first covenant, but Jeremiah and Ezekiel speak of a "new spirit" and a "law written in their hearts." In the New Testament, Paul writes of a "new covenant" of the "Spirit" rather than the "letter" and a "circumcision of the heart." In the new covenant, God "remits guilt" but also creates the "freedom of obedience"; the new covenant negates Israel's unfaithfulness but not God's faithfulness (*CD* IV/I, 32–34).

Following his discussion of covenant in the Old Testament, Barth provides a systematic reflection on the meaning of covenant for atonement. From the beginning, God's plan was to make himself the covenant partner of humanity and humanity the covenant partner of God, and this is accomplished in Jesus Christ. Jesus is elect Israel as well as the mediator of the covenant. "Jesus Christ is the atonement. . . . He is the maintaining and accomplishing and fulfilling of the divine covenant as executed by God Himself." Jesus is the "servant who stands before God as the representative of all nations" and who "stands among the nations as the representative of God, bearing the judgments of God" (*CD* IV/1, 34–35). God's promise to Israel—"I will be your God and you will be my people"—has become an "event" in Jesus Christ (IV/1, 37, 38).

God's covenant with humanity is thus a covenant of grace. Since humanity cannot atone for its transgression, atonement can take place only "from God, in the freedom of God, and not of man, in the freedom of the grace of God to which we have no claim" (*CD* IV/1, 39). In atonement God does not merely give "out of his fullness" but gives *himself* in the incarnation (IV/1, 40). The fulfillment of the covenant—both in historical proclamation in the Old Testament and in historical existence in the New Testament—is achieved in the "mediator," the eternal Word of God, God himself in historical identity with Jesus of Nazareth. In the incarnation of the Word in time,

God has kept his covenant, both with himself and with all humanity, in this particular man (IV/1, 67).

This historic "particularity" of the human Jesus thus proceeds directly from the "one elect people of Israel" as the "consummation of election": "The Word did not simply become any 'flesh.' . . . It became Jewish flesh. . . . The pronouncements of the New Testament Christology . . . relate always to a man who is seen to be not a man in general, a neutral man, but the conclusion and sum of the history of God with the people of Israel, the One who fulfills the covenant made by God with this people" (CD IV/1, 166). As the incarnate Son of God, Jesus Christ took the place given to the people of Israel in their own relation to God: "Where in the Old Testament we find Israel, or the king of Israel, in the New Testament we find the one Israelite Jesus. He is the object of the same electing will of the Creator, the same merciful divine faithfulness. He is bound to the same obedience and service of God" (IV/1, 170). Israel and its kings and priests were only "provisional representatives" of the incarnate Son of God, who "in His unity with the Israelite . . . exists in direct and unlimited solidarity with the representatively and manifestly sinful humanity of Israel. . . . He accepts personal responsibility for all the unfaithfulness, the deceit, the rebellion of this people and its priests and kings" (IV/1, 170, 172).

The Hypostatic Union as the Ontological Basis of the Atonement

Barth crucially refuses to separate Christology (ontology) from atonement (economy). Barth departs from the traditional approach, which distinguishes between the doctrines of (1) the person of Christ and (2) the work of Christ, followed by (3) a doctrine of the two "states" of humiliation and exaltation. Barth complains that the traditional approach does not lead to a faithful exposition of the "subject matter" of the New Testament. The New Testament has no "special Christology," no "Christ in Himself" abstracted from the nation of Israel, Jesus's disciples, the world, and the work that Jesus does on their behalf (CD IV/1, 124). While Barth strongly affirms the validity of the Chalcedonian Definition, which he describes as "normative for all subsequent development" and "factually right and necessary," he insists that "there can be no question of a doctrine of the two natures which is autonomous, a doctrine of Jesus Christ as God and man which is no longer or not yet related to the divine action which has taken place in Him, which does not have this action and man as its subject matter" (IV/1, 133).[42]

42. On the Chalcedonian dimension of Barth's Christology, see Hunsinger, "Karl Barth's Christology."

Barth thus discusses atonement in the light of Christology, focusing on Jesus Christ as the mediator between God and humanity. The atonement is the fulfillment of the covenant but is neither God's gracious being in itself (the triune God) nor the work of grace in itself (the being of humanity to whom God is gracious). Rather, the atonement is the middle point between these two—namely, Jesus Christ, the one person who includes within himself both the sovereign act of God and the being of reconciled humanity. He is not a third theme, distinct from the first two (God and humanity), but the one theme that expounds the first two. In Jesus Christ as mediator between God and humanity, God's reconciling and humanity's reconciliation are a single event (CD IV/1, 122, 123, 125–26).

Barth states that there are three "christological aspects" of Jesus's "active person" and "personal work," which are necessary for an understanding of the doctrine of the atonement (CD IV/1, 128). First, Jesus Christ is "very God," acting for us human beings, God himself become human. Jesus Christ is the revealer of God as he is himself God. As God, Jesus Christ is the Son of God the Father and, with the Father, is the source of the Holy Spirit, united in one essence with the Father by the Spirit (IV/1, 128–29).

That Jesus Christ is God and Creator means that he is able to become a creature. As we saw above, the aseity of the Son of God does not prevent but actually permits him to exist in time and to become temporal. God's omnipotence is so great that in Christ, he can become weak and impotent (CD IV/1, 129). He is able to give himself up to creaturely limitation and suffering (IV/1, 130).

Second, Jesus Christ is truly human. The reconciliation of the world takes place in the "person" of a man whose personal identity is that of God. Jesus is a human being like all other human beings, subject to human limitations and suffering. He is not partly God and partly human but altogether human. He is human in virtue of his deity, whose glory consists in his humiliation (CD IV/1, 130). He is "bound by sin" but free from committing it.[43] He is mortal and has actually died, "but in dying He is superior to death, and at once and altogether rescued from it, so that (even as a man like us) He is triumphant and finally alive" (IV/1, 131).

Third, Jesus Christ is one. The unity of the one divine person is the source of the first two christological aspects: "He is the 'God-man,' that is, the Son of God who as such is this man, this man who as such is the Son of God" (CD IV/1, 135). The New Testament knows only the one person, Jesus Christ,

---

43. Barth departs from the tradition in asserting that the Son assumed a fallen human nature (CD I/2, 151); Price, "Barth on the Incarnation," 139.

both God and human without division or distinction, the mediator between God and humanity: "He Himself is the Mediator and pledge of the covenant . . . in that He fulfils it—from God to man and from man to God. . . . Jesus Christ is the actuality of the atonement" (IV/1, 136).

The Way of the Son of God into the Far Country

As noted above, a central theme in Barth's theology is that God is *in se* what he is in his revelation; conversely, what God has been revealed to be in history, he is *in se*. Barth devotes two sections to God's revelation in Christ as historical event: "The Way of the Son of God into the Far Country" (*CD* IV/1, 157–210) and "The Judge Judged in Our Place" (IV/1, 211–83). Barth begins by affirming that "the atonement is history. . . . It is indeed truth, but truth actualised in a history and revealed in this history as such—revealed, therefore, as history." Atonement is the "very special history of God with man, the very special history of man with God" (IV/1, 157–58).

Barth's discussions of the three "christological aspects" deal with who Jesus is: Jesus Christ is fully God, Jesus Christ is fully human, Jesus Christ is one. Yet each of these descriptors also says something about what Jesus *does* in reconciliation: Jesus Christ is *God* acting, Jesus Christ is *man* obeying, Jesus Christ is *man obeying as God*. In "The Way of the Son of God into the Far Country," Barth discusses three further aspects of the "mystery of reconciliation" that correspond to the three earlier christological aspects.

The first aspect of the mystery of reconciliation is the "condescension" in which God is gracious to humanity in Jesus Christ. In the incarnation, all of humanity's limitations and weaknesses become God's limitations and weaknesses. The Son of God "goes into the far country, into the evil society of this being which is not God and against God" (*CD* IV/1, 158). In the atonement, the Son of God takes the form of a Servant who is the true Lord. He wills to be obedient to the Father, becomes a servant to all, and reconciles humanity to God in his death and in the power of his resurrection (IV/1, 159).

As Jesus Christ, God is thus not only the electing Creator but also the elect creature. Jesus as the Son of God incarnate exists in solidarity with the sinful and representative humanity of Israel. He accepts responsibility for all of Israel's unfaithfulness and therefore stands under the wrath and judgment of God. In solidarity with the humanity of Israel, God in Christ has made the guilt of humanity his own, bearing God's own rejection and condemnation, bearing the "divinely righteous consequences of human sin," allowing the divine sentence to be fulfilled on himself (*CD* IV/1, 170, 175).

The second aspect of the mystery of reconciliation is that God remains God even in his humiliation. The divine being does not change; it is not diminished, transformed into something else, or "admixed" with something else (*CD* IV/1, 183). Jesus humbled himself, but he did not cease to be who he is: "God gives Himself, but He does not give Himself away" (IV/1, 179–80, 183, 185). For God to become incarnate in Christ is not a disunity but the power and freedom of divine love (IV/1, 186–88).

The third aspect of the mystery of reconciliation is that Christ's obedience as the Son of God incarnate is "grounded in the being of God Himself." Barth here affirms one of the more controversial aspects of his Christology: that there is obedience within the inner trinitarian life of God. Within God, there is a first who rules and a second who obeys in humility; there is also a third, the Holy Spirit. Jesus Christ as human who is obedient in humility to the Father corresponds to what he is as God. In rendering obedience, Jesus Christ does what "only God can do" (*CD* IV/1, 193, 200–204, 209–10).[44]

The Judge Judged in Our Place

Barth writes at the beginning of "The Judge Judged in Our Place" that it had been necessary to discuss the person of Jesus Christ before discussing his work (*CD* IV/1, 211). He now begins the discussion of Christ's work by repeating Anselm's question: "Why did He become a servant? Why did the Son of God concretely render obedience in this way? . . . In other words: *Cur Deus homo?*" (IV/1, 211–12).

Barth's initial response has echoes of exemplarist, incarnational, and satisfaction models of atonement. Reminiscent of exemplarist models, he appeals first to divine self-revelation: God wills the outward revelation of the inward riches of his deity. For the sake of his own glory, God willed to proclaim that he does not will to be God without creation. As the image of the Father, the Son is the original model for everything that God does in the world. Before anything else, the atonement includes the self-proclamation of God's glory (*CD* IV/1, 212).

However, divine self-revelation is not sufficient as an explanation for the incarnation. Because of the sin of humanity, the world would have been lost apart from God taking up its cause. Although nothing would be lacking in the triune life if God had not done so, God magnifies his glory through reconcili-

---

44. This is one of the more problematic aspects of Barth's theology. See Hunsinger, *Reading Barth with Charity*, 91–97, 115–19.

ation, "hastening to the help of the world as its loyal Creator, by taking up its cause. In doing what He does for His own sake, He does it, in fact, *propter nos homines, et propter nostram salutem* [for us humans, and for our salvation]" (*CD* IV/1, 212).

Barth also echoes the incarnational models already seen in patristic theologians such as Irenaeus and Athanasius. In order for sinful humanity to "participate" in the triune life, God's history must be played out in world history: "*Cur Deus homo?* . . . Because the great and self-sufficient God wills to be also the Saviour of the world" (*CD* IV/1, 214). Reminiscent of Irenaeus's notion of recapitulation, Barth writes that in "giving himself up," God humbled himself in order to change our status "from within, in order to turn it for good" (IV/1, 215–16).

While Barth echoes exemplarist and participationist models of atonement, the chief model that he expounds here is forensic judgment, echoing both Anselmic satisfaction and Reformed penal substitution models. God's restoration of order and peace, and of satisfaction, resembles Anselm (*CD* IV/1, 19, 217). Divine wrath, punishment, and substitution/exchange echo Calvin (IV/1, 19, 74, 223):

> It was to fulfil this judgment on sin that the Son of God as man took our place as sinners. He fulfils it—as man in our place—by completing our work in the omnipotence of the divine Son, by treading the way of sinners to its bitter end in death, in destruction, in the limitless anguish of separation from God, by delivering up sinful man and sin in His own person to the non-being which is properly theirs. . . . We can say indeed that He fulfils this judgment by suffering the punishment which we have all brought on ourselves. (IV/1, 253)

However, Barth does not appropriate satisfaction or penal substitution models of atonement in a manner that imposes them *a priori* on the biblical witness. As noted above, Barth insists that theological concepts can only be understood through careful attention to their biblical context. It is not for us to judge ahead of time how God will judge the world: "How God will fulfil the sentence to which man has fallen inescapably victim is a matter for Him to decide. . . . He can exercise grace even with His judgment and in execution of it" (*CD* IV/1, 221).

In that light, Barth notably does not derive his notion of judgment or justice from a generally accepted account of the meaning of the terms but from their use in the narrative context of Scripture. Barth looks to the Old Testament, specifically to the judges of the Old Testament, who first and foremost brought *salvation*. This is true in the New Testament as well. Because Jesus

Christ is Savior, he is also Judge, and vice versa: "If He were not the Judge, He would not be the Saviour. He is the Saviour of the world in so far as in a very definite (and most astonishing) way He is also its Judge" (CD IV/1, 217).

Accordingly, and related, Barth departs from both the traditional satisfaction and the penal substitution model in that the standard of justice is not of an abstract preconceived justice, but the personal character of Jesus Christ himself, who is the divine Judge (CD IV/1, 217). Because Jesus Christ is God himself incarnate as a human being, the judgment of Jesus Christ is the judgment of God. Because Jesus is the divine measure of righteousness and justice, there can be no higher standard against which humanity can measure itself. There can be no higher standard "because this Judge is the measure of all righteousness, because any right which man might seek apart from Him or set up and assert side by side with Him could only be wrong, because conversely any right being or action on the part of man can consist only in His bowing before the judgment of this Judge and recognising and accepting His sentence as just whatever it may be" (IV/1, 219).

Jesus Christ is the "true Judge," not only because he is God's Son but also because in the "abasement" of the incarnation in which he becomes our brother and in the obedience that he renders to his Father is found the "divine accusation against every man and the divine condemnation of every man" (CD IV/1, 220). However, rather than condemning humanity, God fulfills his judgment against humanity by giving to us the pardon we unsuccessfully try to give ourselves (IV/1, 221). Why did the Son of God become human? In order for God to judge the world so as to show grace in the execution of what Barth calls "this strange judgment": "to pronounce us free in passing sentence, to free us by imprisoning us, to ground our life in our death, to redeem and save us by our destruction" (IV/1, 222–23).

Methodologically, Barth makes the interesting move of articulating his doctrine of the atonement as judgment through a narrative summary of the account of Jesus's history in the Synoptic Gospels.[45] Barth refers to these narratives as both "history" and "story." Thus, the significance of what it means for Jesus to be Judge, the meaning of the atonement, is to be found through the historical recounting itself (CD IV/1, 223).

The story has three distinct parts. The first part tells of the sayings and acts of Jesus in his entry into and life in Galilee. In this setting, Jesus stands in "marked contrast to the whole world of men. He belongs to it, . . . but He is a stranger within it" (CD IV/1, 224). It is in the light of his life and teaching that Jesus is shown to be the Judge of humanity (IV/1, 225). As revealed by

45. Ford, *Barth and God's Story*, 33–46.

his two temptations (in the wilderness and in Gethsemane), Jesus is distinguished from the rest of humanity precisely in his unwavering obedience to the Father (IV/1, 272).

The second part of the story/history begins with Jesus's entry into Jerusalem, concluding with the Last Supper and Gethsemane. Jesus is no longer the subject but the object of what happens. There is a "reversal of roles" in that those who were judged in the first part of the story now become those who judge Jesus. "The Judge allows Himself to be judged" (CD IV/1, 226–27).

The third part of the story/history is the Easter story, which tells us that God has acknowledged Jesus of Nazareth, this "strange Judge who allowed Himself to be judged, by raising Him from the dead" (CD IV/1, 227). In raising Jesus, God the Father vindicates his Son's role as Judge by reversing the guilty verdict by which he had been crucified. The resurrection is thus the "great verdict of God." It is God's acceptance of the Son of God acting as our representative, in which the "divine wrath" is fulfilled as "divine grace": "It is its acceptance as the act of His obedience which judges the world, but judges it with the aim of saving it" (IV/1, 309).

This three-part story/history is the "mystery" of both God's mercy and his righteousness. God reconciled the sinful world to himself not from without but from within, not as an act of "arbitrary kindness" but by accepting the world in its sinful place—by doing right where humanity had done wrong—thus making peace in what Barth referred to as a "neat and tidy job" (CD IV/1, 237). Barth insists that the meaning of God's action in Jesus's cross and resurrection is inherently meaningful in itself: "The Gospel story says this factually. It does not offer any theological explanation. It says hardly anything about the significance of the event. But in telling us what it has to tell, and in the way it does, it testifies that we are dealing with the event which at bottom cannot bear any other theological explanation than that which we have tried to give it in actual agreement with every Church which is worthy of the name of Christian" (IV/1, 239–40).

Implications of the Atonement

What then does the creedal affirmation mean that the Son of God became incarnate "*for us* and our salvation"? The following is a brief summary of material that Barth treats at far greater length.

First, Jesus Christ's saving work is constitutive, not merely illustrative, of human salvation from sin. In his person, Jesus Christ is the eternal God who has given himself in his Son to be human. In his mission, Jesus Christ is the Judge who in this passion takes the place of those who ought to be judged (*CD* IV/1, 246). God himself suffered and died in his Son, resulting in reconciliation with God. In Christ, God himself is for us (IV/1, 250–51). Because Jesus is the Son of God incarnate, his word of forgiveness is *God's* divine word of forgiveness.

Second, that Jesus Christ is "for us" means that he has taken our place as Judge. We no longer have to convince ourselves that we are innocent, nor do we have to prove ourselves right and others wrong (*CD* IV/1, 231–33): "It is no longer necessary that I should pronounce myself free and righteous. It is no longer necessary that even if only in my heart I should pronounce others guilty. . . . I am not the Judge. Jesus Christ is Judge. The matter is taken out of my hands. And that means liberation" (IV/1, 234).

Third, Jesus's death and resurrection are inextricably connected. Any theology of atonement that focuses exclusively on the cross is inadequate. The death and resurrection of Jesus "are not two acts of God, but one" (*CD* IV/1, 342). The risen Jesus Christ is "for us" as the Word of God's "Yes" to humanity and the world even in the "No" of the cross. The "No" pronounced in the cross of Jesus Christ can only be heard in the redemptive form of the "Yes" pronounced in his resurrection (IV/1, 351).

Fourth, the resurrection of Jesus Christ, the Holy Spirit, and the church are closely correlated. The resurrection is both Jesus's vindication as Judge and the guarantee of his continuing presence in the church through the Holy Spirit: "He not only did represent us, He does represent us. He not only did bear the sin of the world, He bears it" (*CD* IV/1, 313–14). Jesus Christ's action in his resurrection is "the true and direct bridge from once to always, from Himself in His time to us in our time" (IV/1, 315).

Likewise, the Holy Spirit cannot be separated from either the doctrine of the atonement or the death and resurrection of Jesus Christ. The being and work of Jesus Christ is the being and work of his Spirit—the subjective appropriation of the grace of Jesus Christ and the reconciliation of the world to God. The Holy Spirit is the one eternal God present to the creature, giving himself to it so that it can recognize and embrace God and his work. Jesus died and rose for all, but the hand of God has touched the church specifically through the presence and activity of the Holy Spirit (*CD* IV/1, 147–48).

Barth criticizes historic Protestantism at this point: "older Protestantism" was mistaken in orienting the doctrine of atonement to the individual Christian's experience of grace (*CD* IV/1, 150). The reality of the church should be addressed before the question of individual salvation. The theme of atonement is the reconciliation of the world to God in Jesus Christ, and only in this context does the theme of individual reconciliation come: "It is the Church which in this particularity is ordained to the ministry of reconciliation and the witness of the grace of God in relation to the rest of the world" (IV/1, 150; see also 149).

Barth on Penal Substitution

Throughout his account of the atonement, Barth uses forensic imagery of "judgment": Jesus Christ is the "Judge Judged in Our Place." He does not hesitate to use language of "substitution," "satisfaction," and "punishment" in his account. However, as we have seen, Barth radically transforms traditional concepts while retaining traditional language.[46] What is crucial for Barth is that we cannot know ahead of time (*a priori*) what concepts such as "judgment" mean without listening to how they are used in the biblical text.

Toward the end of "The Judge Judged in Our Place," Barth writes that he adopted the forensic metaphor as a "framework" because of "its particularly good basis in the Bible." However, he notes that there are "other standpoints and terminologies" that "might equally be considered" (*CD* IV/1, 273–74). He then provides an alternative summary of how the "cultic" metaphor of sacrifice (Jesus as the "Lamb of God") could be pursued to develop a doctrine of the atonement (IV/1, 275–83). From this discussion it is clear that Barth was not exclusively committed to the forensic metaphor.

As noted above, Barth's initial discussion of atonement employs imagery of enlightenment and revelation (exemplarism) and restoring created order (Anselm) even while using forensic imagery. Barth uses other imagery as well: Sin is the obstacle that must be removed and overcome in order for reconciliation to take place (Christus Victor); Jesus Christ fulfills judgment on sin by treading the way of sinners to the bitter end in death, thus delivering sinful humanity in his own person from the non-being that should be theirs (recapitulation).

What then of penal substitution language? Barth is clear that atonement is not the appeasing of divine wrath or the fulfilling of a requirement of righteousness that must take place before forgiveness is possible. The New Testament does not speak of a divine enmity against humanity that is removed by the atonement. Rather, the "wrath of God" is "solely a description of the corruption of man to which God has given him up." God does not need reconciliation with human beings; we need reconciliation with God (*CD* IV/1, 74).

Barth also recognizes that the concept of atonement as punishment has little support in Scripture. However, punishment language cannot be evaded: "If Jesus Christ has followed our way as sinners to the end to which it leads,

---

46. Hunsinger, "Karl Barth's Christology," 136.

in outer darkness, then we can say with that passage from the Old Testament [Isa. 53] that He has suffered this punishment." Nonetheless, we cannot make this a "main concept" as in some older accounts, "especially those which follow Anselm of Canterbury." "Punishment" cannot mean "that by His suffering our punishment we are spared from suffering it ourselves, or that in so doing He 'satisfied' or offered satisfaction to the wrath of God. The latter thought is quite foreign to the New Testament" (CD IV/1, 253).

Instead, "the passion of Jesus Christ is the judgment of God in which the Judge Himself was the judged. And as such it is at its heart and centre the victory which has been won for us, in our place, in the battle against sin" (Christus Victor). The "passion of the Son of God" become human is the divine action that destroys evil "at its very root." The activity of the second Adam "reversed and overthrew the activity" of the first and in so doing brought in a new humanity, "founded a new world and inaugurated a new aeon" (recapitulation) (CD IV/1, 254). If Barth retains the language of judgment and punishment, he reinterprets it through metaphors that more closely resemble the logic of Christus Victor, recapitulation, or incarnational models.[47]

Barth goes on to write that the passion of Christ is not grounded in a desire for retribution on God's part but flows out of the radical nature of divine love, which could "satisfy" itself only in the outworking of "divine wrath" by "removing" sinful humanity. Barth suggests that this would be the place for what he refers to as the "doubtful concept" that God has done what is "satisfactory." God has done that which is "sufficient to take away sin," to "restore order between himself and creation," to bring in the "new man," to "redeem man from death" (CD IV/1, 254–55).

Why did God become human? Barth provides the following summary: "He took our place as Judge. He took our place as the Judged. He was judged in our place. And He acted justly in our place. It is important to see that we cannot add anything to this." Barth concludes that everything in theology depends on the theology of the cross (theologia crucis): "Everything depends upon the fact that the Lord who became a servant, the Son of God who went into the far country, and came to us, was and did all this for us; that He fulfilled, and fulfilled in this way, the divine judgment laid upon Him" (CD IV/1, 273).

In the end, Barth does not embrace a single "theory of the atonement."[48] While he employs a forensic model, he acknowledges that this is but one metaphor. Barth is more than willing to appropriate metaphors from a variety of

47. Smythe, "Karl Barth," 249–50; Johnson, God's Being in Reconciliation, 123–24. On substitution in Barth's theology, see Johnson, "Barth on the Atonement."
48. Johnson, "Barth on the Atonement," 157.

atonement models to make the argument that the atonement is "constitutive" rather than merely illustrative of salvation.

Conclusion

What is most remarkable about Barth's theology of atonement is its comprehensiveness. For Barth, the atonement is the center of theology because it touches on and is related to every area and facet of theology.

Like patristic and medieval figures such as Irenaeus and Aquinas, Barth grounds the doctrine of the atonement in creation. Even prior to creation and the fall into sin, the triune God intended to share the love between the Father, Son, and Holy Spirit with human beings. Barth uses the language of "participation" and *telos* to speak of a union of God with humanity that is entirely gratuitous, of which humanity is incapable in itself, and which was God's intention for humanity in the original creation even apart from sin. The election of humanity in Jesus Christ means that from all eternity, God graciously intended to make human beings his covenant partners.

Barth discusses atonement within the context of both Testaments, viewing the New Testament as a fulfillment of the Old Testament covenant. Who Jesus is and what Jesus does can only be understood as the fulfillment of Old Testament promise.

Barth ties together ontology and soteriology, correlating the Trinity and the person of Jesus Christ to Christ's reconciling work. Because Jesus Christ is truly God and truly human, the one mediator between God and humanity, he is able to save sinful humanity by reconciling us to God. Because Jesus Christ is the incarnate Son who willingly and freely obeys his Father, he is able to undo the disobedience of sinful humanity.

Barth's method of "following after" (*nachfolgen, a posteriori*) means that he rejects any doctrine of the atonement that interprets the work of Christ through *a priori* metaphors imposed on the biblical material. Rather, he follows the narrative text of Scripture to interpret the logic of atonement metaphors through the lens of the Gospel accounts. He insists that the Jesus who saves us now must be the same Jesus who lived, died, and rose from the dead in first-century Palestine.

For Barth, the crucifixion, the resurrection, and the presence of the Holy Spirit in the church are inseparably related. The doctrine of the atonement does not end with Jesus's death on a cross outside first-century Jerusalem. Because Jesus is still alive and the Holy Spirit has been given to the church, what Jesus did there and then is an ongoing reality here and now.

Barth's primary metaphor is forensic: "The Judge Judged in Our Place." Yet when Barth speaks of "judgment," "punishment," the "wrath of God," or "satisfaction," he explains these metaphors through a logic reminiscent of patristic incarnational and Christus Victor models. Atonement does not bring about a change in God—moving God from wrath to love or from judgment to forgiveness. Rather, from beginning to end, the atonement is a revelation of God's love.

Finally, Barth insists that the atonement is good news. The atonement is the "Yes" of God in Jesus Christ that has reversed the "No" of human sinfulness. The atonement is not only judgment but also re-creation that restores humanity to its original goal of "participation" in the life of the triune God and points to the eschatological future of a new creation. Consequently, the church's worship, proclamation, and mission are witnesses to the good news: that in Jesus Christ the triune God has loved and elected fellowship with humanity from all eternity, that God originally expressed this love through creation, and that Jesus Christ as the incarnate Son of God has come to share in our humanity in order to restore fallen creation to the circle of the triune love even when we had refused it. As Barth insists, God does not need reconciliation, but we do.

9

. . .

Atonement Today

Our concluding chapter will have three sections. The first will examine current debates about the doctrine of the atonement, specifically among evangelicals. The second will discuss the alternative approach of Thomas F. Torrance. The third will conclude with an overview of crucial aspects necessary for a theologically adequate doctrine of the atonement.

Evangelical Controversy

C. H. Dodd's 1935 book *The Bible and the Greeks* challenges the notion that atonement should be interpreted as propitiation. Dodd argues that the Greek terms translated as "atonement" are better understood to mean "purify" or "purge" and are better translated as "expiation." Propitiation refers to a personal object (God is propitiated), while expiation refers to an impersonal object (one expiates an altar or place of worship). Dodd finds no examples in the LXX translation of the Old Testament in which *hilaskesthai* (atone) is used in reference to God as the grammatical object. In his commentary on Romans, Dodd argues that *hilastērion* should be translated as "expiation" (not "propitiation") and that Jesus's death was not a satisfaction of divine wrath.[1]

Dodd's thesis met resistance, primarily from evangelical defenders of atonement as penal substitution. Australian Leon Morris wrote several books

1. Dodd, *Bible and the Greeks*; Dodd, *Epistle of Paul to the Romans*.

on the atonement, largely directed against Dodd's position.[2] *The Cross of Christ*, by evangelical Anglican author John Stott, is described by Alister McGrath as "the most respected and authoritative evangelical writing on this most important of subjects."[3] Another influential defense of atonement as penal substitution appeared in an essay by J. I. Packer titled "What Did the Cross Achieve?"

In recent decades, an echo of the controversy between Dodd and his challengers has arisen among evangelicals concerning penal substitution as an adequate theological model for atonement. Stephen Chalke asserts in *The Lost Message of Jesus* that "the cross isn't a form of cosmic child abuse—a vengeful Father, punishing his Son for an offence he hasn't committed." The resulting controversy eventuated in an "atonement debate" among evangelical scholars regarding penal substitution.[4] What follows will provide summary and assessment of three books by evangelical authors active in this ongoing debate.

Pierced for Our Transgressions is perhaps the most vigorous evangelical defense of penal substitution in the recent debate.[5] The authors provide a brief answer to the question "What is penal substitution?" and make clear that they are defending an uncompromising version of the model. In giving his Son, God the Father "spared sinful people from condemnation, death, and punishment," but did not spare his own Son. God the Son "veiled his glory in a human body," lived a "perfect human life," "took our sin and guilt upon himself," and on the cross suffered the "infinite torment of the wrath and fury of his Father," after which he rose from the dead and will return to rule. Thus, God "turned aside his own righteous wrath against sinful humanity" and triumphed over the powers of evil "by punishing evil in the person of the Son." God was "faithful to his promise that sin will be punished," demonstrating his justice by "punishing sin and acquitting the righteous," and God demonstrated his love for sinners by reconciling those who were his enemies.[6]

The authors do not regard penal substitution as simply a metaphor or one of several possible models of atonement. Penal substitution is the normative literal description of God's saving work in Jesus Christ in light of which all

2. Morris, *Apostolic Preaching*; Morris, *Cross in the New Testament*; Morris, *Glory in the Cross*; Morris, *Atonement*.
3. McGrath, foreword to the 2006 edition of Stott, *Cross of Christ*, 9.
4. Chalke and Mann, *Lost Message of Jesus*, 182; Tidball, Hilborn, and Thacker, *Atonement Debate*.
5. Jeffery, Ovey, and Sach, *Pierced for Our Transgressions*.
6. Jeffery, Ovey, and Sach, *Pierced for Our Transgressions*, 103–4.

other metaphors or models should be understood. Insofar as Jesus is the "perfect man," succeeding where Adam failed, penal substitution provides the context for the notion of "recapitulation"; by punishing evil in order to defeat Satan, Jesus in the penal substitution model provides victory over sin (Christus Victor); "reconciliation" is the consequence of the imputation of our guilt to Christ; when Jesus gave his life as a "ransom for many," he paid the price of God's "righteous wrath" and our deserved "punishment."[7]

The book consists of two main parts: part 1 makes a positive case for penal substitution while part 2 responds to critics. Part 1 has three main sections: Chapter 2 provides a biblical case for penal substitution. Chapters 3 and 4 provide a "theological framework" and address the "pastoral importance" of penal substitution. Chapter 5 makes an argument that penal substitution did not begin with the Reformation but can be found in the writings of the church fathers and Aquinas.

Mark Baker and Joel Green's *Recovering the Scandal of the Cross* provides a clear alternative to *Pierced for Our Transgressions*.[8] The authors criticize the penal substitution model for the following reasons:

1. Penal substitution is not taught in Scripture. Baker and Green claim that in the Bible God is the source, not the object, of atonement. Sacrifice in the Old Testament includes elements of cleansing, forgiveness of sins, and substitution, but sacrifice is neither an averting of divine wrath nor a satisfaction or penalty. The New Testament speaks of Jesus's death in terms of sacrifice, exchange, and substitution but not penal satisfaction. Paul's discussion of divine wrath in Romans has both present and future dimensions that indicate "how seriously God takes sin." However, Paul's theology of the cross "lacks any developed sense of divine retribution." The death of Christ is rather the expression of God's love in which God's righteousness "wipes away human hostility toward God." Thus, atonement deals with the human problem of sin, not a divine problem of wrath. The problem is not that God needs to be reconciled to the world but that the world is estranged from God.[9]

2. Penal substitution (especially as popularly interpreted) leads to a problematic theology of the Trinity in which the Father and the Son are opposed to each other and Jesus dies to save us from God the Father

7. Jeffery, Ovey, and Sach, *Pierced for Our Transgressions*, 133, 142, 143.
8. Baker and Green, *Recovering the Scandal of the Cross*. The first edition of Baker and Green's book was a major target of criticism in *Pierced for Our Transgressions*.
9. Baker and Green, *Recovering the Scandal of the Cross*, 72–84, 81, 82.

rather than from our sin. Baker and Green are aware that defenders of the doctrine regard this as a caricature, and they respond at length to the more theologically sensitive presentations of writers such as I. Howard Marshall, J. I. Packer, and Kevin Vanhoozer. In the end, however, they find the "essential logic" of penal substitution problematic.[10]

3. The doctrine of penal substitution arose within the culture of Western modernity and reflects the values of modern Western culture, both in its individualism and in its echoes of modern Western understandings of law. Penal substitution does not communicate well in postmodern and global settings.[11]

The authors insist that the New Testament contains a variety of atonement metaphors, none of which should be considered exclusively normative. The New Testament presents Jesus's death through five constellations of images drawn from the ancient Mediterranean world: the law court (justification), commerce (redemption), personal relationships (reconciliation), worship (sacrifice), and battleground (triumph over evil). Together these create a "melange of voices."[12] The metaphors do not stand on their own but must be interpreted within the "multiple narrative contexts in the New Testament" to discern "an interpretive pattern."[13]

Baker and Green also argue that a theology of the atonement should focus not on Jesus's death alone but on his entire, life, death, and resurrection. In addition, Jesus's mission must be understood within the context of Israel as the covenant people of God. Jesus's life of faithfulness, his crucifixion, and his resurrection are all stages in a single drama of salvation.[14]

A central theme of Baker and Green's book is that the cross is primarily an expression of God's love and graciousness rather than God's judgment. Both Old and New Testaments bear witness to God's wrath as a "corollary of God's righteousness," but divine wrath is "relationally based, not retributively oriented." The atonement is God's initiative, a demonstration of divine love with universal significance for all persons without distinction. One of the book's primary criticisms of penal substitution is that it undermines the primacy of divine love by implying that God's justice or wrath must be satisfied before God's love can be expressed.[15]

10. Baker and Green, *Recovering the Scandal of the Cross*, 170–90.
11. Baker and Green, *Recovering the Scandal of the Cross*, 44–49, 120.
12. Baker and Green, *Recovering the Scandal of the Cross*, 41, 52–111.
13. Baker and Green, *Recovering the Scandal of the Cross*, 28, 26.
14. Baker and Green, *Recovering the Scandal of the Cross*, 26, 60, 100, 186.
15. Baker and Green, *Recovering the Scandal of the Cross*, 68–72, 82, 138–39.

The atonement is also not merely a theory or doctrine but provides a model for how Christians should live in a cruciform fashion. The cross not only is an "invitation to salvation" but also "defines the nature of salvation and the life of salvation." The cross is the foundation on which the identity and practices of the church are built. The cross grounds the faith, formation, and life of the people of God.[16]

Finally, cultural context is a major theme of Baker and Green's book. The authors claim that the atonement metaphors of the New Testament were drawn from first-century Mediterranean culture, and that later historic atonement models also reflect the cultures of their times. As Platonic idealism thought of human nature as a universal in which all human beings participate, so recapitulation portrayed the incarnate Christ as infusing humanity with immortality and redemption. The Christus Victor model of ransom worked well in a culture in which slaves could be ransomed. Anselm's satisfaction model uncritically interpreted the atonement within medieval categories of honor and satisfaction without allowing God's relation with Israel or God's character revealed in Christ to shape his argument. Abelard's moral influence model is not only subjective and individualist but neglects the "community-forming" nature of Christ's work. Finally, penal substitution (especially as developed by Hodge) "ends up with a God who can only operate within certain legal confines as determined by a particular concept of justice" derived from "Western judicial systems."[17]

N. T. Wright's *The Day the Revolution Began: Reconsidering the Meaning of Jesus's Crucifixion* has numerous similarities to the work of Baker and Green. However, it is more of a biblical theology with reflections on contemporary implications. Wright contrasts two different understandings of atonement throughout the book. The first is "the great heaven-and-hell scheme of Western eschatology" and its "works contract."[18] This schema clearly corresponds to penal substitution, and Wright criticizes it for not thinking through the implications of creation, the resurrection, and the new creation. Penal substitution focuses "not on God's kingdom coming to earth as in heaven, but on my sin, my heavenly (that is nonworldly) salvation." In this schema, "the cross has nothing to do with social and political evil."[19]

Wright complains that modern Christians have made three errors in this approach: they have (1) "Platonized" eschatology, substituting "heaven" for new creation; (2) moralized anthropology, substituting moral performance

16. Baker and Green, *Recovering the Scandal of the Cross*, 88–89.
17. Baker and Green, *Recovering the Scandal of the Cross*, 142–91.
18. Wright, *Day the Revolution Began*, 28, 76.
19. Wright, *Day the Revolution Began*, 35, 36.

for a biblical notion of human vocation; and (3) "paganized" soteriology, substituting the idea that God kills Jesus to "satisfy his wrath" for a biblical soteriology.[20]

In contrast to this first interpretation, Wright insists that atonement in the Bible is not about "going to heaven" but about "new heavens" and a "new earth." Like Baker and Green, Wright states that the New Testament "meets us with complex and puzzling information about the cross in both outline and detail." Replacing "going to heaven" with "new heavens and new earth" has direct consequences for understanding the human problem and the divine solution. Atonement is broader than the cross; it includes the work of Jesus "not only in his crucifixion, but also in his resurrection and particularly in his ascension." Atonement can also be extended "backward" to speak of Jesus's cosmic work and Israel, as he is the one who would "save his people from their sins."[21]

The bulk of Wright's book is a narrative retelling of a covenantal and community-oriented notion of salvation traced through the Old Testament, the Gospels and Acts, and Paul's Letters. In the Old Testament, God's plan to deal with sin is "focused on the people of Israel." In the New Testament, Jesus as Messiah "stands in for Israel" to fulfill the divine plan and restore creation. Jesus's death must then be seen in connection to the "entire" Old Testament narrative. Wright interprets multiple biblical metaphors within a common narrative framework: "What look to us like detached images actually mean what they mean in relation to one another *within this story*."[22]

Wright's reading of the Old Testament contrasts a "covenant of vocation" with what he calls the "works contract." The vocation is that of being a genuine human being with tasks to perform as part of the Creator's purpose for the world. Humans were created to worship the Creator, and this included proper flourishing in the world to bear God's image as "vice regents." The human plight is that humans have abrogated their vocation, giving their authority to non-human forces. Thus, human vocational failure is also the moral failure of worshiping the creature rather than the Creator. Wright focuses on Old Testament themes of Passover, priesthood, and "return from exile" within the contexts of this vocational covenant.[23]

Wright's New Testament discussion echoes these Old Testament themes throughout. The multiple metaphors associated with Jesus's death must be interpreted in connection to the entire Old Testament narrative. Outside of

20. Wright, *Day the Revolution Began*, 147.
21. Wright, *Day the Revolution Began*, 66, 68, 69.
22. Wright, *Day the Revolution Began*, 68, 94.
23. Wright, *Day the Revolution Began*, 76–78, 100–104.

the story, they will be interpreted in terms of the "works contract."[24] Wright devotes four chapters to the earthly Jesus, the Gospels, and Acts. All four Gospels tell the story of Jesus as Israel's God having returned at last. Jesus is "Emmanuel," "God with us." The Gospels speak not of an "angry father lashing out at an innocent" but "of someone embodying the love of God himself, acting as the personal expression of that love all the way to his death."[25] They all agree that in Jesus "something has happened" to overthrow the powers of evil. "Echoing the combination of themes that Jesus himself drew together, the evangelists in their different ways saw the great victory over the powers of evil being won by means of taking away sin."[26] Wright agrees that the Gospels think of Jesus as a substitute: Jesus takes upon himself "the weight of Israel's sins, and thereby of the world's sins." However, Jesus's death is not a "dogmatic formula": "The story is the reality. . . . The gospels invite us to make this story our own, to live within the narrative."[27]

Wright's discussion of Paul's Epistles echoes these Old Testament and Gospel themes. Paul shared the early Christian vision that the goal of the "covenant of vocation" was that humans who found salvation in Christ would become participants in the new creation in worship, here and now, not in "heaven."[28] Jesus's resurrection means that those who belong to Jesus are part of the "new creation," "God's Israel." God sends Jesus and the Spirit to create a new world in which the power of evil has been dealt with.[29]

As he does elsewhere, Wright claims that the primary problem in Romans is not simply "sin" but "ungodliness," a "failure of worship," which results in "injustice." The traditional reading of Romans misses that Paul is dealing not with sin in itself but with the idolatry that lies behind sin. The point of Jesus's death as Messiah (representative of Israel) is that it demonstrates the faithfulness of God to his covenant plan. Romans 6–8 is thus "an extended exposition of the new Passover and Exodus."[30] Justification anticipates the final verdict where there is no condemnation for those "in the Messiah Jesus." In the metaphors of "justification" and "redemption," Paul is not invoking either a "law court" metaphor or a "slave market" metaphor but thinking of the restoration of true worship—God cleanses people from sin so that true worship is possible.[31] Thus, the meaning of the cross in the New Testament

---

24. Wright, *Day the Revolution Began*, 94.
25. Wright, *Day the Revolution Began*, 200–201.
26. Wright, *Day the Revolution Began*, 208–9.
27. Wright, *Day the Revolution Began*, 217, 223, 224.
28. Wright, *Day the Revolution Began*, 228–33.
29. Wright, *Day the Revolution Began*, 235, 237.
30. Wright, *Day the Revolution Began*, 268, 272.
31. Wright, *Day the Revolution Began*, 308, 316, 320, 321.

is "not a system, but a story; not a theory, but a meal and an act of humble service; not a celestial mechanism for punishing sin and taking people to heaven, but an earthly story of a human Messiah who embodies and incarnates Israel's God and who unveils his glory in bringing his kingdom to earth as in heaven."[32]

We will evaluate these three representative books in terms of our three categories of (1) metaphor/symbol/narrative, (2) history, and (3) ontology, associated with the three levels of knowing and being (*ordo cognoscendi* and *ordo essendi*).

Metaphor

Perhaps the most significant difference between *Pierced for Our Transgressions* and the other two books concerns the distinction between metaphors, models, and doctrines. Our claim throughout this book has been that Scripture uses numerous metaphors to describe the work of Christ: legal metaphors (judgment and forgiveness), financial metaphors (redemption), rescue from slavery (ransom), and military metaphors (conquest and victory). Proper interpretation demands that these metaphors be considered not simply in themselves but within a narrative context that often challenges literalist readings. For example, metaphors of victory and conquest are inherently paradoxical in that Jesus conquers sin through death and resurrection, not violence.

Models go beyond metaphors to look for theological connections between metaphors. Different models can assess the same metaphors in different ways. For example, Christus Victor, satisfaction, and penal substitution variously bring together metaphors of judgment, redemption, and victory to provide different accounts of the relationship between atonement and justice. Finally, doctrines of the atonement attempt to correlate various models in order to provide comprehensive theological explanations of the atonement.[33]

The most fundamental disagreement between *Pierced for Our Transgressions* and the other two texts is that the authors of the former regard the biblical imagery of judgment and divine wrath not as one metaphor among others but as a straightforward literal account of how atonement functions in Scripture. They then draw a rather straight line from a literal reading of the metaphor to penal substitution as both a model *and* a theological explanation. In short, atonement effectively *is* penal substitution. In line with this conflation of metaphor and theological explanation, the authors tend to embrace a methodology that parallels the "deductive rationalism" already noted in

---

32. Wright, *Day the Revolution Began*, 415.
33. Crisp, "Methodological Issues."

figures such as Hodge—as seen in their arguments from biblical texts and their analysis of justice.

The authors of *Pierced for Our Transgressions* and Wright display clear hermeneutical differences in relating the New Testament passion narratives to Old Testament figures of the Passover, the Day of Atonement, and the Suffering Servant of Isaiah. *Pierced for Our Transgressions* makes the following argument: (1) the Passover sacrifice, the scapegoat, and the Suffering Servant are all examples of substitutionary sacrifices; (2) because these sacrifices involve punishment, they are all examples of *penal* substitution; (3) insofar as the New Testament interprets Jesus's death as the fulfillment of these Old Testament sacrifices, the atonement necessarily must be a case of penal substitution.[34]

By contrast, Wright interprets Jesus's Last Supper narrative in terms of the imagery of Passover and sacrifice but insists that "reference to sacrifice carries no suggestion that the animals were being somehow 'punished' in the place of the Israelites." Wright's interpretation of Romans 3:23–25 draws on "new Passover" and "new exodus" imagery to suggest that *hilastērion* should be translated neither as "expiation" nor as "propitiation" but as "mercy seat," corresponding to the lid over the ark in the Jewish temple. Wright insists that Jewish sacrifices were not about punishment but about cleansing and purgation. The point of interpreting Jesus's death through images of Passover and Day of Atonement is that God has purified his people through the blood of Jesus so that sins can be forgiven and the covenant renewed. Similarly, Jesus as the "punishment that has made us whole" (Isa. 53:5) makes sense not as a "moralistic works contract" but as Jesus's fulfillment of the Servant's vocation, taking upon himself the consequences of Israel's sin so that Israel and the world may be rescued.[35]

Pierced for Our Transgressions offers a deductive argument drawn from the interpretation of the three Old Testament sacrificial images in terms of penal substitution. It then applies that conclusion directly to its New Testament fulfillment. Wright's argument instead draws inductively on a reading of both Testaments in terms of notions of covenant faithfulness and rescue from idolatry. It then draws the narrative and symbolic connections between them.

The deductive approach of *Pierced for Our Transgressions* is also evident in their response to the objection that "Biblical justice is about restoring relationships, not exacting retribution." The authors devote several pages to

34. Jeffery, Ovey, and Sach, *Pierced for Our Transgressions*, 34–67.
35. Wright, *Day the Revolution Began*, 189.

defending the retributive theory that those who do wrong must not be allowed to do so with impunity, "and it is right therefore that offenders suffer a certain penalty."[36] At no point do they show awareness of any alternative categories of justice, such as restorative justice, which agrees that those who do wrong must face consequences but addresses justice primarily in terms of restored relationships, not punishment.[37]

In contrast to such a deductive approach, Baker and Green as well as Wright agree that (1) the legal metaphors are metaphors and not literal descriptions; (2) the New Testament contains numerous metaphors, none of which should be given priority over the others; and (3) the metaphors can only be interpreted through a close examination of the narrative structure of the biblical texts. Of the three books, *Recovering the Scandal of the Cross* contains the lengthiest discussion of metaphor itself, while Wright makes his case by reading the metaphors through the interpretive lens of an overarching biblical narrative. Wright's book contains the most thorough biblical exegesis, with Baker and Green providing the most complete reflection on theological method.[38]

History

Of the three books, Wright's provides the most thorough discussion of the relationship between the Testaments while also arguing that the complete life of the earthly Jesus (including a close reading of the Gospels) is necessary for a doctrine of the atonement. By contrast, *Pierced for Our Transgressions* appeals to the Old Testament primarily for examples of penal substitution and focuses in the Gospels on the ransom imagery of Mark 10:45 and Jesus's crucifixion (Mark 15:33–34). The authors' argument parallels the deductive approach already seen: Jesus's reference to "the cup that I drink" (10:38) is read in light of Old Testament references to the "cup" of divine wrath; the darkness surrounding Jesus's crucifixion also echoes Old Testament passages concerning God's wrath. In both cases, the inference is drawn that God poured out his wrath on Jesus on the cross. To the response that penal substitution neglects the resurrection of Jesus, the authors reply primarily in terms of epistemological attestation: the resurrection confirms that Jesus was from God and demonstrates his victory over death.[39]

36. Jeffery, Ovey, and Sach, *Pierced for Our Transgressions*, 249–63.
37. Zehr, *Changing Lenses*.
38. Baker and Green, *Recovering the Scandal of the Cross*, 117–23.
39. Jeffery, Ovey, and Sach, *Pierced for Our Transgressions*, 67–73, 213–14.

Ontology

None of the three books discusses ontology at length—specifically the Chalcedonian Definition that Jesus Christ is one divine person with both divine and human natures. The most explicit discussions of the doctrine of God and the Trinity occur in *Pierced for Our Transgressions* concerning (1) the relationship between the Father and the Son in atonement and (2) the relationship between divine love and divine wrath. The authors answer the objection that penal substitution implies a "division between the members of the Trinity" by claiming that the members of the Trinity have different "roles" and can act in different ways. They argue that the Son can propitiate the Father and the Father can exact punishment on the Son.[40] However, the authors do not indicate whether this is a distinction of roles within the economic Trinity (as traditionally understood) or a distinction of roles (and therefore of *wills*) within the immanent Trinity. This ambiguity risks positing something like the eternal contract between the Father and the Son found in Hodge and veering toward anthropomorphism and tritheism.

Concerning the question of whether biblical references to divine wrath are metaphorical or literal, the authors of *Pierced for Our Transgressions* reply that divine wrath cannot be "merely metaphorical" because God acts "in a wrathful way." They appeal to a "unity of divine attributes" to suggest that "holiness, righteousness, and love" can be "perfectly consonant," but their use of the term "attribute" leaves certain questions unresolved.[41] If divine wrath is not a metaphor, is it simply a description of a divine action toward sinful creatures or is wrath inherent to the divine nature itself? The term "attribute" implies the latter. Is wrath then a divine perfection without which God could not be God? And if wrath is inherent to the divine nature, would wrath be expressed between the divine persons apart from creation? Would the Father be eternally angry with the eternal Son? If this seems implausible, does an attribute of divine wrath demand the creation of a world (and particularly a sinful world) against which wrath could be expressed? Would this not make the existence both of creation and of evil ontological necessities in order for the divine attribute of wrath to be expressed?

The more coherent (and historic) alternative would be to acknowledge that wrath is not a divine attribute, property, or perfection but rather a metaphor that describes God's exercise of justice in the face of evil. The traditional position is that insofar as justice presupposes the existence of evil, justice itself cannot be a divine attribute (since evil does not exist necessarily) but is rather

40. Jeffery, Ovey, and Sach, *Pierced for Our Transgressions*, 131–32.
41. Jeffery, Ovey, and Sach, *Pierced for Our Transgressions*, 294.

a description of the way in which divine goodness or love exercises itself in the face of *contingent* evil. Neither divine justice nor wrath would therefore be attributes of God; rather, they are metaphors corresponding to the divine perfection of God's essential goodness. To claim otherwise would necessitate evil.

Thomas F. Torrance

In previous chapters, we argued that one of the strengths of the atonement theologies of Aquinas and Barth lay in their integration of knowing and being, of ontology and epistemology—that their theologies held together the three levels of metaphor/narrative, history, and ontology. The late Thomas F. Torrance accomplished a similar task in his discussion of the atonement, which we offer here as a positive example of a recent approach.[42]

Epistemology and Ontology

A distinctive feature of Torrance's theology is his insistence on the interrelation between knowledge and being, between epistemology and ontology. In contrast to ancient and modern dualisms that create breaches between knowledge and reality, Torrance advocates a critical realism in which the contingency and intrinsic intelligibility of created realities are grounded in inherent "ontorelations." God's revelation in Jesus Christ has taken place freely within the intelligible structures of space and time that God has created; Jesus therefore provides trustworthy knowledge of who God is in himself.[43] Torrance posits a "stratified structure" from which knowledge of God arises that parallels the orders of knowing and being we have been employing in this book. The first level of knowledge Torrance designates the "evangelical and doxological." This is the "basic level of experience and worship" in which we encounter God through the gospel and the life and mission of the church. The second level is the "theological" in which God has revealed himself as Father, Son, and Holy Spirit—the "Economic Trinity"—within the "structures of space and time." Finally, the "higher theological and scientific level" moves from the "Economic Trinity" to the "Ontological" or "Immanent" Trinity.[44] This interconnection between ontology and epistemology is central to Torrance's discussion of the following:

42. For an introduction to ontology in Torrance's theology, see Colyer, *How to Read T. F. Torrance*. For Torrance's discussion of the atonement, see Purves, *Exploring Christology and Atonement*, 199–250.
43. T. F. Torrance, *Reality and Evangelical Theology*, 9–20; T. F. Torrance, *Space, Time, and Resurrection*, 1–26; T. F. Torrance, *Mediation of Christ*, 11–19.
44. T. F. Torrance, *Ground and Grammar of Theology*, 156–59.

1. The Trinity: The Christian doctrine of God follows from God's self-revelation in Jesus Christ. While Jesus Christ as God incarnate is the center of divine revelation, it is through the Holy Spirit that God has enabled sinful and redeemed human beings to participate in the eternal communion of the Father and the Son: "What God is in his historical self-manifestation to us in the Gospel as Father, Son and Holy Spirit, he is revealed to be inherently and eternally in himself."[45]

2. Creation: The created universe is distinguished by the characteristics of contingency, existence, and rationality. In contrast to the eternal and necessary existence of the triune God, created realities are contingent not only in the sense that they might have existed differently but also in the sense that God has freely created the universe out of nothing (*creatio ex nihilo*). An infinite difference thus distinguishes the necessary existence of the triune Creator from the contingency of creation. The only reason that can be posited for the existence of creation is God's loving will to create a reality other than himself. While creation is contingent, created realities have an authentic and real existence—they possess their own creaturely integrity. Finally, created realities have an intrinsic contingent rationality—that is, created realities are inherently knowable. They exist in relation to other created realities but above all in relational dependence on their Creator.[46]

3. Anthropology: The human being has been created in the image of God as male and female, essentially social beings who were made to be in communion with God and with one another. As the image of God, humanity reflects God's glory, and the human being is the "Priest of Creation." Sin has broken the bond of communion both between God and humanity and between man and woman. Ruptured relations between the sexes lead to ruptured relationships with other human beings as well as with nature. The rebellion of sin is the refusal to keep within the limits of creatureliness and to fit within God's restored order of creation.[47]

4. Christology: Torrance's theology directly correlates the Trinity and Christology. Knowledge of God the Father and of Jesus Christ the incarnate Son of the Father arise together, and we know both through

---

45. T. F. Torrance, *Christian Doctrine of God*, 1–2.

46. T. F. Torrance, *Christian Doctrine of God*, 203–34; T. F. Torrance, *Divine and Contingent Order*, 1–61.

47. T. F. Torrance, *Incarnation*, 38–39, 72; T. F. Torrance, *Ground and Grammar of Theology*, 1–6.

the Spirit of God, who anointed Christ and has been sent to the church following Jesus's resurrection. Our knowledge of Father and Son comes through God's self-revelation as the person of Jesus Christ, the mediator between God and humanity.[48]

Jesus Christ's atoning work cannot be separated from his divine person since it is as God incarnate that Christ accomplished salvation.[49] The doctrine of Christ is expressed in the hypostatic union: that Jesus Christ is true divine nature and true human nature in one person. Without ceasing to be God, the Son of God exists as the man Jesus, who is fully and truly human. As one whose personal identity is fully God, Jesus lived as fully human. Jesus had a fully human mind, will, and body.[50] It is because Jesus Christ is fully God become human that his word of forgiveness is the very forgiveness of God.[51]

Another crucially related theme in Torrance's Christology is the incarnate Christ's "vicarious humanity." In the incarnation, Jesus Christ has assumed our humanity and has transformed it from within. This means not only that in Christ God has come among us, that in our humanity God is acting on our behalf but also that Jesus Christ's human obedience to the Father is humanity's response to God, and through his response Jesus has restored our fallen human nature.[52]

5. Participation: The incarnation does not mean that relations between God and humanity have been restored in an extrinsic manner—as a merely forensic declaration. Rather, through the gift of the Holy Spirit, redeemed men and women are joined in union with Christ's risen humanity in order that they might share in the eternal love of and communion with the triune God. While human beings remain creatures and are preserved in our humanity, through mutual indwelling (perichoresis) between the risen Jesus Christ and us, and through faith and the sacraments, we "participate" in the very being of God as Father, Son, and Holy Spirit.[53]

History

The mystery of Jesus Christ is historical in that the incarnation of the Son of God as the man Jesus took place as a historical event in space and time.[54]

48. T. F. Torrance, *Mediation of Christ*, 63–65.
49. T. F. Torrance, *Incarnation*, 37.
50. T. F. Torrance, *Incarnation*, 83–84.
51. T. F. Torrance, *Mediation of Christ*, 68.
52. T. F. Torrance, *Incarnation*, 184–86; T. F. Torrance, *Mediation of Christ*, 88.
53. T. F. Torrance, *Mediation of Christ*, 74–75.
54. T. F. Torrance, *Incarnation*, 6.

The gospel is concerned with the oneness of Jesus Christ on the one hand with God the Father, and on the other with the nation of Israel as God's covenant people.[55] The incarnation of God in Jesus Christ has a "prehistory" in that God selected one of the peoples of humanity to be the instrument of his redemptive purpose in order eventually to reveal himself to all people and to save all humanity.[56] Despite Israel's persistent sinful rebellion, God's election of Israel created a "community of reciprocity" in which the corporate interaction of Israel and God took place. This revelation of God through Israel provided permanent structures of thought and speech, including the covenant structures of temple, prophet, priest, and king.[57] While God's covenant with Israel took place in a particular history, its essential purpose led to universal blessing and redemption of all humanity through the prophetic, priestly, and kingly ministry of Jesus Christ.[58]

The person of Jesus Christ cannot be separated from his atoning work nor his atoning work from his person. The atoning work of Jesus includes his entire earthly life, beginning with his birth at Bethlehem and concluding with his resurrection and ascension. Jesus Christ's atoning work takes place "within the one person of Christ, and of the unity of his deity and humanity in that one person."[59] In the virgin birth of Jesus, the incarnation took place in the midst of our humanity, re-creating it. The virgin birth is the pattern for the gospel of grace; what took place once for all uniquely in Jesus Christ happens in every instance to those who are reborn through the Spirit and share in his birth.[60]

In his earthly mission, Jesus restored humankind to the divine image. Jesus lived a life of faithfulness and obedience to the Father and Creator. In the incarnation, Jesus's prayer became a redemptive activity as Jesus prayed in our place, relying completely on God, fulfilling the covenant between God and humanity, and exercising vicarious obedience to the Father.[61] Jesus not only represented humanity toward God but also represented God to humanity, showing God's compassion and mercy to the lost sheep of Israel.[62] As the presence of God's kingdom, Jesus shared the undeserved grace of God with humanity at the same time that his presence was God's judgment on sin. God's judgment of sin in Christ is not shown by Jesus's condemnation

---

55. T. F. Torrance, *Mediation of Christ*, 14–15.
56. T. F. Torrance, *Incarnation*, 37, 41.
57. T. F. Torrance, *Mediation of Christ*, 22–25, 27–33; T. F. Torrance, *Incarnation*, 41–50.
58. T. F. Torrance, *Incarnation*, 50–56.
59. T. F. Torrance, *Incarnation*, 37.
60. T. F. Torrance, *Incarnation*, 94–96, 99–102.
61. T. F. Torrance, *Incarnation*, 114–21.
62. T. F. Torrance, *Incarnation*, 129–38.

of sinners, however, but in his taking that responsibility on himself. In Jesus, God entered into our alienated existence in the midst of evil in order to reclaim us for himself.[63]

As shepherd-priest, Jesus entered into solidarity with sinners in order to redeem them by taking their sin upon himself. Jesus's entire life and work led inevitably toward the cross, where God executed judgment not through violence but by entering as a human being into guilt and suffering from within, by allowing human evil to overcome him. Christ's atoning work was not a transaction; rather, as God's presence in love, Jesus represented God's judgment, enduring to its end the conflict between God's love and humanity's rejection of that love. On the cross, Jesus the incarnate God—the mediator—bore God's judgment on humanity while standing in solidarity with humanity.[64]

Finally, there can be no discussion of atonement without mention of Jesus's resurrection. The resurrection is not merely the completion of Jesus's saving work but "belongs to the ontological structure of the mediator himself."[65] The resurrection is the positive side to God's judgment on sin. Any doctrine of satisfaction properly belongs with the resurrection, which is not divine satisfaction in death but the satisfaction of the Father in the Son who has made atonement. The resurrection is the fulfillment of justification in making actual what has been declared.[66] The resurrection of Jesus Christ means that we have a "real sharing in the union of the Son with the Father," a "*communion or koinonia* of the Spirit who is mediated to us from the Father through the Son, and who is the Love of God poured into our hearts."[67]

Metaphor and Symbol

Torrance begins the second half of his two-volume set on *Incarnation* and *Atonement* by insisting that there can be no "theory" of the atonement: "The innermost mystery of atonement and intercession remains mystery: it cannot be spelled out." Rather, any discussion must bring together "conjunctive statements" based on a synthesis found in the person of Jesus Christ the mediator. The approach must be *a posteriori*, following Christ, seeking to be conformed to the truth of Christ.[68] In its fullest sense, the atonement embraces the "entire life and work of Christ." Atonement involves (1) God's self-giving to restore communion between God and humanity through assuming humanity into

63. T. F. Torrance, *Incarnation*, 139–40, 241, 244–45
64. T. F. Torrance, *Incarnation*, 137, 148, 150–53.
65. T. F. Torrance, *Atonement*, 212.
66. T. F. Torrance, *Atonement*, 215, 223–24.
67. T. F. Torrance, *Space, Time, and Resurrection*, 70 (emphasis original); see also 61–74.
68. T. F. Torrance, *Atonement*, 2, 4–5.

union with God; (2) fulfillment of divine judgment on sin to remove obstacles between God and humanity; and (3) the establishing of covenant communion through incarnation and atonement accomplished by Jesus Christ as mediator, God and man in one person, acting as God from God's side and as human from the side of humanity.[69]

Torrance frames his discussion through consideration of three Old Testament terms for redemption: *padah*, *kipper*, and *goel*. *Padah* emphasizes the *nature* of the redeeming act. It is "redemption from slavery," from "divine judgment," from "alien oppression," redemption from the authority of evil. *Kipper* has to do with the *act* of "redemption as the actual wiping out of sin and guilt." God "atones," "blots out sin," "pardons" the guilty. *Goel* is redemption through a "kinsman-redeemer." The focus is on the *person* of the redeemer.[70]

In the New Testament, all three concepts come together. *Padah* is redemption by the "mighty hand" of Christ—the "dramatic aspect of the atonement." *Kipper* is redemption through Christ's expiatory sacrifice—the "cultic-forensic aspect of the atonement." (Cultic aspects include priesthood, sacrifice, and worship, while forensic aspects correspond to justification and juridical elements.) *Goel* is redemption through restored personal union and communion with God—the "ontological aspect of the atonement."[71]

Torrance argues that these three concepts have been reflected in different historic theories of the atonement. The dramatic aspect has been reflected in Christus Victor theories. The cultic-forensic has been echoed in models that emphasize either sacrifice or priesthood—for example, "eucharistic sacrifice" or, alternatively, satisfaction or penal substitution. The ontological aspect can be found in incarnational models that focus on deification or, alternatively, in exemplarist models.[72]

Torrance proposes that the three concepts also correspond to the *triplex munus* or three offices of Christ. The office of prophet corresponds to "incarnational assumption" or *goel*, to Christ's "passive obedience." The office of priest corresponds to Christ as sacrifice for sin, or *kipper*. Finally, the office of king corresponds to Christ's "active obedience," in which redemption takes place through the holiness of Jesus's entire life, or *padah*.[73]

Much of Torrance's *Atonement* volume consists of lengthy discussion of four notions of atonement in the New Testament: "The Priesthood of Christ,"

69. T. F. Torrance, *Atonement*, 9.
70. T. F. Torrance, *Atonement*, 27–50.
71. T. F. Torrance, *Atonement*, 50–53.
72. T. F. Torrance, *Atonement*, 53–56.
73. T. F. Torrance, *Atonement*, 59–60.

"Atonement as Justification," "Atonement as Reconciliation," and "Atonement as Redemption." Torrance makes the case that all three Old Testament concepts appear in New Testament accounts of each of the four notions of Christ's saving work. *Goel* is linked to Jesus's life and ministry as the Son of God become human, his life leading up to the cross, his ascension, and his high priesthood, where he advocates for us before the Father. *Padah* appears in breaking the powers of sin and death and triumphing over the powers of evil in Jesus's resurrection, in the kingly ministry of Christ. *Kipper* emphasizes Christ's work as priest and judge, a priest who is also a sacrifice and a judge who takes the place of the judged.[74]

Space prevents a detailed discussion of Torrance's account, but a few key elements are worth highlighting. Concerning Christ's priesthood, Torrance is clear that sacrifice is not a matter of appeasing God. God is the subject, not the object, of the atoning action. Old Testament sacrifices were *witnesses* to God's forgiveness, not attempts to "placate or propitiate God."[75] Indeed, it is God who both propitiates and expiates in the sacrifice of Jesus. Expiation refers to the act through which reconciliation is effected, while propitiation refers to "personal healing and personal reconciliation." Torrance claims that the biblical notion is distinct in that God both initiates and fulfills the action: "God *himself* draws near—*he* propitiates himself. . . . He is the God who, in his holy love, judges humanity but who draws near in so doing. . . . He is also the man who in our place draws near to God and so submits himself to divine judgment, offering himself in sacrifice to God."[76]

In his discussion of propitiation and expiation, Torrance moves away from an "external forensic" notion of divine judgment toward a more patristic focus on atonement as incarnation, or in his own words, "ontological union." Crucial to his understanding of Christ's self-offering is the notion of "vicarious repentance," that Jesus's prayer is "identical with his personal being," that Jesus prays not only with words but with the "self-offering" of his life. In the New Testament, propitiation is therefore not forensic "but is drawn into the personal Father-Son relationship." Torrance states that "we cannot think of Christ being punished by the Father in our place and the New Testament nowhere uses the word *kolazō*, punish, of the relation between the Father and the Son."[77]

Similarly, in "Atonement as Justification," Torrance uses the expression "substitutionary atonement" in reference to the "expiation of sin," and states

74. T. F. Torrance, *Atonement*, 62.
75. T. F. Torrance, *Atonement*, 19, 141.
76. T. F. Torrance, *Atonement*, 68–69.
77. T. F. Torrance, *Atonement*, 71–72.

that Jesus "bore our guilt, and was judged as a malefactor." However, he insists that this is not a matter of "humanity propitiating God": "How could God, God of all grace and love, allow himself to be propitiated by man, as if he needed to be propitiated before he could be gracious and forgiving? On the contrary, God is himself always *subject* throughout this act of atonement."[78]

That Torrance interprets New Testament language of divine judgment in terms of onto-relational union is evident in two ways. First, Torrance uses the expression "enhypostatic atonement" to emphasize that atonement is not an extrinsic legal transaction but a work of God in which "God in Christ acts *as man* as well as God." Second, in answering the question "How could Christ die for us?" Torrance appeals to ontological union: since humanity was created in the image of God and by the Word of God, it is in the Word that we have our true humanity. In the incarnation, the "Word made flesh" is the true source of our humanity and thus was able to represent all humanity. "It was thus that Christ, true God took upon himself our flesh and became true man, and as such made atonement."[79]

This personal dimension of atonement becomes further evident in Torrance's section "Atonement as Reconciliation." As noted above, the focus of atonement is "ontological" (*goel*). Torrance writes that "what the New Testament calls reconciliation [is] the re-creating of the bond of union between God and humanity and humanity and God, a bond which is ontological and personal, which involves our human being and knowing."[80] Torrance emphasizes that atonement takes place in the hypostatic union through exchange and participation. Reconciliation is accomplished "in the person of the incarnate Son." Jesus Christ is himself the God of the covenant, who has taken upon himself the humanity of those who have broken the covenant. He is both the turning of God to humanity and the turning of humanity to God.[81] Reconciliation is thus the "full outworking of the hypostatic union." It begins with the union of God and humanity at the birth of Jesus, continues with his identification of himself with our sin that leads to and undergoes the judgment of the cross, and leads to the assumption and exaltation of our humanity in the resurrection of Jesus to share in the eternal life of God himself. Reconciliation is the "wonderful exchange" in which "Christ took our place, that we might have his place."[82] It is both objective and subjective in that the atonement as an act of God toward humanity is not sufficient in

---

78. T. F. Torrance, *Atonement*, 120–22.
79. T. F. Torrance, *Atonement*, 121–23, 126.
80. T. F. Torrance, *Atonement*, 137.
81. T. F. Torrance, *Atonement*, 148.
82. T. F. Torrance, *Atonement*, 149–51.

itself to save. Rather, atonement "must be worked through the heart and mind of men and women, until they are brought to acquiesce in the divine judgement on sin and are restored in heart and mind to communion with God."[83]

Finally, "Atonement as Redemption" emphasizes the eschatological and teleological aspects of atonement. Again, all three Hebrew concepts are present in redemption. *Kipper* is present in those passages of Scripture that refer to redemption by expiation, *goel* in passages that stress the person of Jesus Christ provides our redemption, and *padah* in those passages that emphasize God's mighty act of grace in the breaking in of God's eschatological kingdom.[84] But the primary emphasis of redemption would be the *padah* or Christus Victor dimensions of atonement. Redemption is God's mighty act in delivering us from the slavery of evil to the liberty of being God's children. It is closely connected with Jesus's resurrection, Pentecost, and the church as the Holy Spirit is poured out on the church after Jesus's resurrection to incorporate the church into Christ's body to make the church the body of Christ. Redemption is also re-creation, beginning with the church but with cosmic dimensions as well, proclaiming a new humanity that is universal—thus the missionary call of the church—and looking forward to the redemption of space and time when all of creation will be renewed with the eschatological return of Christ.[85]

A comparison of Torrance's atonement theology with the three books discussed above shows certain commonalities. Torrance does not minimize what he calls the cultic-forensic aspects of the atonement and is willing to use language of "sacrifice," "substitution," and "bearing judgement" in reference to the cross of Christ. At the same time, he challenges any merely extrinsic or judicial interpretation of the judgment metaphor, rejecting the notion that the atonement might involve the "punishing" of the Son by the Father or that Jesus's death would be the condition of the Father's forgiveness. Torrance rejects any notion of conciliating or placating God as a "heathen concept."[86] Any change taking place in atonement would be on the part of sinful humanity, as God is the subject and not the object of "propitiation." Torrance seems to use the expression "propitiation" in order to make clear that atonement is not an impersonal removal of sin but a personal and ontological act that takes place within the union of God and humanity in Jesus Christ. One statement nears an explanation of propitiation: "When in reconciliation God actually takes upon himself the sentence of rejection and bears it instead of mankind, then

---

83. T. F. Torrance, *Atonement*, 158.
84. T. F. Torrance, *Atonement*, 175.
85. T. F. Torrance, *Atonement*, 177–81, 193–200, 308–14.
86. T. F. Torrance, *Atonement*, 141.

God takes all his own righteous enmity against sin and absorbs it in himself."[87] Absorption is a metaphor, not an explanation, but Torrance is clear that the New Testament does not provide explanations: "Atonement by blood means the substitution of life for life. But why that should constitute an explanation in God's sight is not explicitly said, except that it is God's gracious will. The atonement knows no *why*, no ultimate *why* except God himself."[88]

Torrance would thus agree with Baker, Green, and Wright that no single metaphor or image defines the atonement. Instead, Torrance identifies three interrelated images or metaphors and shows how all three are crucial to the various New Testament discussions of the work of Christ. Distinctive to Torrance's approach is his focus on ontology. The "onto-relational" realities of the Trinity, creation, the incarnation, and the participation of redeemed humanity in the life of the Trinity provide the most significant structures for a doctrine of the atonement. Thus, Torrance's approach corrects Philip Melanchthon's famous saying that "To know Christ is to know his benefits."[89] Torrance reverses this: through his benefits, Christ is known in himself. Unless the Christ whom we know through his benefits is the same Christ who is in himself truly God and truly human, the Second Person of the Trinity come to us as a human being, he can be of no benefit to us.

Concluding Reflections

If the symbols, metaphors, and narratives that speak of God's salvation in Jesus Christ are normative for our understanding of God's purposes, and if God has truly acted in a constitutive manner to bring about salvation in the life, crucifixion, and resurrection of the earthly Jesus, then God's revelation in Christ is a true revelation of God's own being and character, and theology cannot refuse to speak of who God and Christ must be in themselves. Metaphor and history lead inevitably to ontology. If God's revelation in the history of Israel, in the life, death, and resurrection of Jesus Christ, and in the presence of the Holy Spirit in the church is a true revelation of God's character, then God must be triune—Father, Son, and Holy Spirit—in himself from all eternity.

Conversely, if the metaphors that speak of God's action in Christ are merely instrumental and projectionist, if we are free to choose other metaphors and symbols more to our tastes, and if God's revelation in Jesus is illustrative rather than constitutive of our salvation, then it follows just as inevitably

87. T. F. Torrance, *Atonement*, 155.
88. T. F. Torrance, *Atonement*, 88.
89. Melanchthon, preface to *Loci Communes*, 21–22.

that God's action in Christ cannot provide a true or definitive revelation of God's being and character.

The doctrine of atonement thus has implications for our general approach to Scripture and for other areas of theology. Specifically, the symbolic and narrative character of Scripture point beyond themselves in the direction of both history and ontology. The symbols and narratives refer first to the historical Jesus "who died for our sins," then also to God who was reconciling the world to himself in Jesus Christ (2 Cor. 5:19). Whether we understand God's saving work in Christ to be constitutive or illustrative of salvation has implications not only for what we understand about the earthly Jesus but also for how we read the canonical texts and what we understand to be true of God's very nature. If the biblical symbols and narratives are human projections, they tell us not so much about what God has done in Christ but about our own concerns and aspirations. On the other hand, to assign normative value to the metaphors and symbols of Scripture that refer to God's atoning work in Jesus Christ does not give us license to decide ahead of time (a priori) that we know what those symbols mean. Only by entering into the narrative logic of the canonical Scriptures do we discover the meaning of the symbols, a narrative logic that subverts a selective literalism. Readings that impose a specific understanding of the atonement based on an a priori deduction about what metaphors of judgment or sacrifice must mean are as misleading, and in their own way as reductionist, as illustrative readings. In contradistinction to both illustrative and literalist approaches, atonement metaphors must be read in light of the incarnation, crucifixion, and resurrection of Jesus and of the revelation of the triune God witnessed to in Scripture. The metaphors do not terminate either in themselves or in our own religious imaginations but point beyond themselves to the God we confess as Father, Son, and Holy Spirit, the God who has truly come near to us in the cross and resurrection of Jesus Christ.

Both trinitarian personalism and the doctrine of creation are thus necessary presuppositions of atonement theology. Creation is not necessary, but a matter of sheer grace. It is the gratuitous sharing of the eternal knowing and loving between the Father, Son, and Holy Spirit with other creatures. The triune God creates not out of need or loneliness but out of generosity.

A corollary of the radical contingency of creation is the distinction between God and creatures. Language of theosis, divinization, or participation does not erase the distinction between God and creature. Rather, it acknowledges that because there is an infinite gap between God and creatures, creatures may infinitely share in God's knowing and loving, while remaining infinitely dependent on a gracious gift that comes from outside themselves.

Accordingly, an adequate atonement theology must not neglect Christian anthropology. To be created in the image of God as male and female means that one is fundamentally oriented toward communion—communion with other human beings but also with God. To be a human being means to have a teleological orientation toward a knowing and loving union with God, an orientation that is entirely gratuitous but (given our creation in God's image) also intrinsic to our humanity. It is not lost even in the fall into sin. The doctrines of creation and the fall must be understood dialectically then, not sequentially. A constitutive doctrine of the atonement assumes that all human beings have been created to know and love God, have fallen into sin, and have been redeemed by Christ, whether they acknowledge it or not.

God's election of and covenant with Israel as the people of God provides the essential historical, symbolic, and canonical background to both Christology and ecclesiology. We can only know that "God is with us" (Immanuel) if we first know that God was with Israel. An atonement theology that neglects the relationship between Israel and Jesus and between Israel and the church will necessarily tend toward individualism and timelessness.

The doctrine of the incarnation provides the ontological counterweight to the doctrine of the Trinity. Jesus Christ is a divine person with both divine and human natures. We must speak of the identity of the incarnate, crucified, and risen Lord Jesus Christ as the Second Person of the Trinity. It is because the personal identity of Jesus Christ is that of God that he is able to save. Accordingly, the revelation of God in Christ is the self-revelation of God, and relation with the incarnate Lord draws us into relation with God himself. The word of grace and forgiveness that Jesus brings to us is God's word of forgiveness. The life and regeneration that Christ communicates to us is the life of God, not merely that of a God-like or God-filled creature.

An adequate doctrine of the atonement must hold together both the person and work of Jesus Christ in his entire earthly mission: Jesus's incarnation, his teaching and "mighty works," his death on the cross, his resurrection, ascension, and second coming. In following Anselm, Western theology particularly risks associating atonement solely with Jesus's death in such a manner that his humanity has no significance for our salvation either before his crucifixion or after his resurrection. The personal identity of Jesus Christ as the Second Person of the triune God needs to be correlated with the continuing humanity of Jesus Christ in his resurrection and ascension.

The threefold office of prophet, priest, and king (triplex munus) spells out the theological significance of various atonement metaphors and models across Jesus's entire mission. The office of prophet points to the significance of Jesus's entire earthly mission. The office of priest points to Jesus's crucifixion.

The office of king points to Jesus's resurrection as not merely confirmatory but essential to the atonement. The threefold office makes clear that atonement is not a matter of Jesus's death alone. Various models of the atonement speak to the significance of Jesus's earthly life, death, and resurrection together.

Exemplarist and incarnational models focus on Jesus's earthly life, teaching, and mighty works. However, in light of the incarnation, Jesus cannot be reduced to an illustrative example but is rather the ontological exemplar of atonement. Jesus's life of vicarious "repentance" echoes the theme of "recapitulation" (Irenaeus). The notion of Jesus's "vicarious humanity" (Torrance) means that Jesus is both substitute and representative. Jesus's anointing by the Holy Spirit at his baptism points to Jesus as the ontological exemplar of the Christian's own participation "in Christ" through the church's incorporation as the body of Christ into Jesus's risen humanity. In incarnational atonement models, Jesus's death means undergoing the full consequences of sin and death, while Jesus's resurrection is a restoration of creation anticipating eschatological renewal on the last day.

By the same token, in Christus Victor models, Jesus's entire life is understood to be a battle against the "forces of evil": law, death, and the devil. Jesus's death is his nonviolent conquest of evil; Jesus's resurrection defeats death and restores the creation order.

Finally, in models that focus on priestly and forensic judgment metaphors, Jesus's holy life of obedience and submission to God is an implicit judgment on human sinfulness. In Jesus's death, God takes the judgment of sinners on himself. In Jesus's resurrection, God vindicates not only Jesus's own righteousness but also sinners for whom Jesus's death and resurrection leads to justification. Themes of judgment and substitution are present, but such language is interpreted through the lens of incarnational theology. The atoning work of Jesus is not only the punishment of sin but also its removal, and this is accomplished not simply through divine power in Jesus's death and resurrection but by working itself out to its conclusion though the whole incarnate life of Christ.

In that light, if the atonement is truly to address the situation of fallen humanity, a mere word of enlightenment or a forensic declaration of pardon from guilt is insufficient. The fallen human situation requires transformation from within. What is needed is not enlightenment and pardon alone but re-creation and transformation, an undoing of evil itself.

Accordingly, the humanity of Jesus is as central to the doctrine of atonement as is his divinity. To overcome the effects of sin on human nature, Jesus must act from within, taking on himself the consequences of our human sinfulness and transforming evil to good. At the same time, if God's revelation in Jesus is to be a true communication of his life (and not only a divine Word) to human beings, then that life must be communicated in a manner in which human beings can share. Salvation and redemption consist in a participation in the crucified and risen humanity of Christ.

The resurrection, ascension, and enduring humanity of Jesus are thus essential to atonement. In Jesus Christ, God not only experiences the effects of sin but also undoes them—that is, he transforms and re-creates our fallen human nature through our participation in the resurrection life of his Son. Resurrection is necessary to re-create human nature and communicate to us the divine life. By participating in the renewed divine image that has been re-created in the humanity of the incarnate and risen Jesus Christ, human nature is restored to the divine image. The ascension means that Jesus Christ continues to act as mediator on behalf of sinful and restored humanity in his permanent vicarious humanity. The worship of the church is a participation in the ascended Christ's own worship on our behalf. To speak of union with Christ, dwelling in Christ, or the risen Christ's presence *in the church* or *through the sacraments* is to speak of Jesus Christ's continuing mediation as the Son of God permanently become human and embodied, not simply as the Second Person of the Trinity or in his divine nature.

"Grace," then, describes not only forgiveness of sin but our participation in God's saving action in the life, death, and resurrection of Jesus Christ. The primary understanding of salvation and grace in the New Testament is that of incorporation into the risen Christ. Grace is God's communication of his own life to redeemed human beings through union with the risen humanity of the incarnate Lord.

How exactly is God's saving life and love communicated to us? It seems sufficient to suggest that we are personally or relationally united to the risen Christ through the agency of the Holy Spirit. The modern Western rediscovery of Orthodox eucharistic theologies has led to an emphasis on a Spirit-mediated understanding of Christ's eucharistic presence and, by implication, of the mediation of grace in general. The mission of the Holy Spirit brings us into contact with the risen Christ not simply in his divinity as the Second Person of the Trinity but also in his risen humanity. Grace is mediated to redeemed human beings in a trinitarian manner—from God the Father, through the mediation of the risen Christ, by the agency of the Holy Spirit, the Spirit who makes the humanity of the risen Christ present to us to remake our humanity in the divine image.

As the election of Israel is essential to the doctrine of the atonement, so is ecclesiology. As a worshiping community, the church is both the body of Christ and a communion of persons in communion with the crucified and risen Christ. The church is the post-resurrection community of the people of God who also share in the triune life. In the church's worship, the sacraments are both a participation in Jesus's once-for-all sacrifice and also a sharing in his resurrected life. Baptism is initiation into Christ's crucified and risen life (Rom. 6:3–4). The Eucharist is a continuing communion with Christ (1 Cor. 10:16) through the presence of the Holy Spirit. The church exists not for itself alone but to share in the mission of the Son and the Holy Spirit—that is, to proclaim to all people that they have been created, have fallen, and have been redeemed by Christ and that they also are called to participate in Jesus Christ's atoning life, death, and resurrection.

Finally, atonement has a teleological dimension. The doctrine of atonement does not simply look back to Jesus Christ's once-for-all death on the cross but looks forward to the eschatological acquittal and renewal of all creation: the vision of and full sharing in the mutual knowledge and love of the Father, Son, and Holy Spirit, when we shall see the triune God face to face and know fully as we are fully known (1 Cor. 13:12).

Bibliography

Primary Sources

Anselm of Canterbury. *Proslogion*. In *Anselm of Canterbury: The Major Works*, edited by Brian Davies and G. R. Evans, 82–104. Oxford: Oxford University Press, 1998.

———. *Why God Became Man (Cur Deus Homo)*. In *Anselm of Canterbury: The Major Works*, edited by Brian Davies and G. R. Evans, 260–356. Oxford: Oxford University Press, 1998.

Aquinas, Thomas. *Commentary on John*. Translated by James A. Weisheipl, OP, and Fabian R. Larcher, OP. Steubenville, OH: Emmaus Academic, 2013.

———. *The Literal Exposition on Job: A Scriptural Commentary Concerning Providence*. Translated by A. Damico. Atlanta: Scholars Press, 1989.

———. *Summa contra Gentiles*. Translated by Laurence Shapcote, OP. Steubenville, OH: Emmaus Academic, 2019.

———. *Summa Theologiae*. Edited by John Mortenson and Enrique Alarcón. Translated by Laurence Shapcote, OP. Lander, WY: The Aquinas Institute for the Study of Sacred Doctrine, 2012.

———. *De Veritate*. Translated by Robert W. Mulligan, SJ. Chicago: Regnery, 1952.

Athanasius. *Against the Arians (Contra Arianos)*. In vol. 4 of *Nicene and Post-Nicene Fathers*, Series 2. Edited by Philip Schaff and Henry Wace. Peabody, MA: Hendrickson, 1995.

———. *Against the Pagans (Contra gentes)*. In vol. 4 of *Nicene and Post-Nicene Fathers*, Series 2. Edited by Philip Schaff and Henry Wace. Peabody, MA: Hendrickson, 1995.

———. *Festal Letters (Epistulae festales)*. In vol. 4 of *Nicene and Post-Nicene Fathers*, Series 2. Edited by Philip Schaff and Henry Wace. Peabody, MA: Hendrickson, 1995.

———. *On the Incarnation (De Incarnatione)*. In vol. 4 of *Nicene and Post-Nicene Fathers*, Series 2. Edited by Philip Schaff and Henry Wace. Peabody, MA: Hendrickson, 1995.

———. *The Letters of Athanasius Concerning the Holy Spirit (To Serapion)*. Translated by C. R. B. Shapland. London: Epworth, 1951.

———. *On the Councils of Ariminum and Seleucia (De Synodis)*. In vol. 4 of *Nicene and Post-Nicene Fathers*, Series 2. Edited by Philip Schaff and Henry Wace. Peabody, MA: Hendrickson, 1995.

Augsburg Confession. In *The Book of Concord: The Confessions of the Evangelical Lutheran Church*. Edited by Richard Kolb and Timothy J. Wengert. Translated by Charles P. Arand. Minneapolis: Fortress, 2000.

Augustine of Hippo. *Homilies on the First Epistle of John*. Vol. 14 of The Works of St. Augustine. Edited by Daniel E. Doyle, OSA, and Thomas Martin, OSA. Translated by Boniface Ramsey. Hyde Park, NY: New City Press, 2008.

———."On the Fortieth Day, the Ascension of the Lord." Sermon 263. In *Sermons (230–272B) on the Liturgical Seasons*. The Works of Saint Augustine: A Translation for the 21st Century, part 3, vol. 7. Translated by Edmund Hill, OP. Edited by John E. Rotelle, OSA. New Rochelle, NY: New City Press, 1993.

———. On the Trinity. In vol. 3 of *Nicene and Post-Nicene Fathers*, Series 1. Edited by Philip Schaff. Peabody, MA: Hendrickson, 1995.

Aulén, Gustaf. *Christus Victor: An Historical Study of the Three Main Types of the Idea of Atonement*. Translated by A. G. Hebert. Rev. ed. New York: Macmillan, 1969. Originally published 1931.

———. *The Drama and the Symbols: A Book on Images of God and the Problems They Raise*. Translated by Sydney Linton. Philadelphia: Fortress, 1970.

———. *The Faith of the Christian Church*. Translated by Eric H. Wahlstrom. Philadelphia: Fortress, 1960.

Baker, Mark D., and Joel B. Green. *Recovering the Scandal of the Cross: Atonement in New Testament and Contemporary Contexts*. 2nd ed. Downers Grove, IL: InterVarsity, 2011.

Barth, Karl. *The Doctrine of God*. Vol. II/1 of *Church Dogmatics*. Translated by G. W. Bromiley and T. F. Torrance. Edinburgh: T&T Clark, 1957.

———. *The Doctrine of God*. Vol. II/2 of *Church Dogmatics*. Translated by G. W. Bromiley and T. F. Torrance. Edinburgh: T&T Clark, 1957.

———. *The Doctrine of Reconciliation*. Vol. IV/1 of *Church Dogmatics*. Edited by T. F. Torrance and G. W. Bromiley. Translated by G. W. Bromiley. Edinburgh: T&T Clark, 1956.

———. *The Doctrine of the Word of God*. Vol. I/1 of *Church Dogmatics*. Edited by T. F. Torrance and G. W. Bromiley. Translated by G. W. Bromiley. Edinburgh: T&T Clark, 1975.

———. *Dogmatics in Outline*. Translated by G. T. Thomson. New York: Harper & Row, 1959.

———. *Evangelical Theology: An Introduction*. Translated by Grover Foley. Grand Rapids: Eerdmans, 1963.

———. *The Humanity of God*. Translated by John Newton Thomas and Thomas Wieser. Richmond: John Knox, 1960.

———. *The Word of God and the Word of Man*. Translated by Douglas Horton. New York: Harper, 1957.

Bernard of Clairvaux. *Tractatus contra quaedam capitula errorum Petri Abaelardi ad Innocentium II pontificem*. Patrologia Latina 182. Turnhout: Brepols, 1998.

Calvin, John. *Institutes of the Christian Religion*. Edited by John T. McNeill. Translated by Ford Lewis Battles. 2 vols. Philadelphia: Westminster, 1960.

The Canons and Decrees of the Council of Trent. Edited and translated by J. Waterworth. London: Dolman, 1848.

Clement of Rome. *1 Clement*. In *Early Christian Fathers*. Translated by Cyril C. Richardson. Library of Christian Classics. Philadelphia: Westminster, 1953.

Cyril of Jerusalem. *Catechetical Lectures*. In vol. 7 of *Nicene and Post-Nicene Fathers*, Series 2. Edited by Philip Schaff and Henry Wace. Peabody, MA: Hendrickson, 1995.

Eusebius of Caesarea. *Demonstration of the Gospel*. 2 vols. Translated by W. J. Ferrar. London: SPCK, 1920.

The Gospel of Nicodemus. In vol. 8 of *Ante-Nicene Fathers*. Edited by Alexander Roberts and James Donaldson. Peabody, MA: Hendrickson, 1994.

Gregory of Nazianzus. "The Second Oration of Easter" (Oration 45). *Orationes*. In vol. 7 of *Nicene and Post-Nicene Fathers*, Series 2. Edited by Philip Schaff and Henry Wace. Peabody, MA: Hendrickson, 1995.

Gregory of Nyssa. "The Great Catechism." In vol. 5 of *Nicene and Post-Nicene Fathers*, Series 2. Edited by Philip Schaff and Henry Wace. Peabody, MA: Hendrickson, 1995.

The Heidelberg Catechism. http://www.rcus.org/heidelberg-catechism-2011.

Hodge, Charles. *Systematic Theology*. 3 vols. Grand Rapids: Eerdmans, 1991.

Ignatius of Antioch. *To the Trallians*. In *Early Christian Fathers*. Translated by Cyril C. Richardson. Library of Christian Classics. Philadelphia: Westminster, 1953.

Irenaeus of Lyons. *Against Heresies*. In vol. 1 of *Ante-Nicene Fathers*. Edited by Alexander Roberts and James Donaldson. Peabody, MA: Hendrickson, 1994.

———. *Demonstrations of the Apostolic Preaching.* Edited by Johannes Quaesten and Joseph C. Plumpe. Translated by Joseph P. Smith. Ancient Christian Writers 16. New York: Paulist Press, 1952.

Jeffery, Steve, Michael Ovey, and Andrew Sach. *Pierced for Our Transgressions: Recovering the Glory of Penal Substitution.* Wheaton: Crossway, 2007.

John of Damascus. *An Exact Exposition of the Orthodox Faith.* In vol. 9 of *Nicene and Post-Nicene Fathers,* Series 2. Edited by Philip Schaff and Henry Wace. Peabody, MA: Hendrickson, 1995.

Julian of Norwich. *Showings.* Translated by Edmund Colledge, OSA, and James Walsh, SJ. New York: Paulist Press, 1978.

Knell, Matthew. *The Immanent Person of the Holy Spirit from Anselm to Lombard: Divine Communion in the Spirit.* Eugene: Wipf & Stock, 2009.

Luther, Martin. "The Large Catechism." In *The Book of Concord: The Confessions of the Evangelical Lutheran Church.* Edited by Richard Kolb and Timothy J. Wengert. Translated by Charles P. Arand. Minneapolis: Fortress, 2000.

———. *Lectures on Galatians 1535 Chapters 1–4.* Edited by Jaroslav Pelikan and Walter A. Hansen. Vol. 26 of *Luther's Works.* American ed. Edited by Jaroslav Pelikan and Helmut T. Lehmann. St. Louis: Concordia, 1963.

McFague, Sallie. *Models of God: Theology for an Ecological Nuclear Age.* Philadelphia: Fortress, 1987.

Melanchthon, Philip. *Loci Communes.* In *Melanchthon and Bucer.* Translated by Lowell J. Sater. Edited by Wilhelm Pauk. Library of Christian Classics 19. Philadelphia: Westminster, 1969.

Methodius. "Three Fragments from the Homily on the Cross and Passion of Christ." In vol. 6 of *Ante-Nicene Fathers.* Edited by Alexander Roberts and James Donaldson. Peabody, MA: Hendrickson, 1994.

Origen. *Against Celsus.* In vol. 4 of *Ante-Nicene Fathers.* Edited by A. Cleveland Cox. Peabody, MA: Hendrickson, 1994.

———. *Commentary on the Gospel of John.* In vol. 9 of *Ante-Nicene Fathers.* Edited by A. Cleveland Cox. Peabody, MA: Hendrickson, 1994.

———. *Commentary on the Gospel of Matthew.* In vol. 9 of *Ante-Nicene Fathers.* Edited by Allan Menzies. Peabody, MA: Hendrickson, 1994.

Peter Abelard. *Apologia Contra Bernardum.* Edited by E. M. Buytaert. Opera Theologica I, Corpus Christianorum Continuatio Mediaevalis 11. Turnhout: Brepols, 1969.

———. *Commentary on the Epistle to the Romans.* Translated by Steven R. Cartwright. Fathers of the Church Mediaeval Continuation 12. Washington, DC: Catholic University of America Press, 2011.

———. *Historia calamitatum: Consolation to a Friend.* Edited by Alexander Andrée. Toronto Medieval Latin Texts 32. Toronto: Pontifical Institute of Mediaeval Studies for the Centre for Medieval Studies, 2015.

Rashdall, Hastings. "Christ as Logos and Son of God." *The Modern Churchman* 23, no. 11 (February 1934): 643–51.

———. *Christus in Ecclesia: Sermons on the Church and Its Institutions.* Edinburgh: T&T Clark, 1904.

———. *Conscience and Christ: Six Lectures on Christian Ethics.* London: Duckworth, 1916.

———. "The Creeds." *The Modern Churchman* 4, no. 4 (July 1914): 204–14.

———. *Doctrine and Development: University Sermons.* London: Methuen, 1898.

———. "Fighting Against God." *The Modern Churchman* 1, no. 12 (March 1912): 696–706.

———. *God and Man.* Oxford: Blackwell, 1930.

———. *The Idea of Atonement in Christian Theology.* London: Macmillan, 1919.

———. "Miracles and the Divinity of Christ." *The Modern Churchman* 1, no. 7 (October 1911): 373–89.

———. *Philosophy and Religion: Six Lectures Delivered at Cambridge.* New York: Scribner's Sons, 1910.

———. "Theism or Pantheism?" *The Modern Churchman* 6, no. 7 (October 8, 1916): 395–404.

———. *The Theory of Good and Evil: A Treatise on Moral Philosophy.* 2nd ed. 2 vols. London: Oxford University Press, 1924.

Robinson, John A. T. *Honest to God*. London: SCM, 1963.

———. *The Human Face of God*. Philadelphia: Westminster, 1973.

1662 Book of Common Prayer, The. International ed. Downers Grove, IL: IVP Academic, 2021.

Thirty-Nine Articles of Religion, The. http://anglicansonline.org/basics/thirty-nine_articles.html.

Tidball, Derek, David Hilborn, and Justin Thacker, eds. *The Atonement Debate: Papers from the London Symposium on the Theology of the Atonement*. Grand Rapids: Zondervan, 2008.

Torrance, Thomas F. *Atonement: The Person and Work of Christ*. Downers Grove, IL: IVP Academic, 2009.

———. *The Christian Doctrine of God: One Being Three Persons*. Edinburgh: T&T Clark, 1996.

———. *Divine and Contingent Order*. Oxford: Oxford University Press, 1981.

———. *The Ground and Grammar of Theology*. Belfast: Christian Journals, 1980.

———. *Incarnation: The Person and Life of Christ*. Downers Grove, IL: InterVarsity, 2008.

———. *The Mediation of Christ*. Grand Rapids: Eerdmans, 1983.

———. *Reality and Evangelical Theology: The Realism of Christian Revelation*. Downers Grove, IL: InterVarsity, 1982.

———. *Space, Time and Resurrection*. Grand Rapids: Eerdmans, 1976.

Weaver, J. Denny. *The Nonviolent Atonement*. Grand Rapids: Eerdmans, 2011.

Wesley, John. *Explanatory Notes upon the New Testament*. Vol. 2. Repr., Peabody, MA: Hendrickson, 1986.

———. "God's Love to Fallen Man." Sermon 59 in *The Sermons of John Wesley*, ed. Thomas Jackson. New York: Nelson & Phillips, 1872. http://wesley.nnu.edu/john-wesley/the-sermons-of-john-wesley-1872-edition/sermon-59-gods-love-to-fallen-man/.

———. "The Witness of Our Own Spirit." Sermon 12 in *The Sermons of John Wesley*, ed. Thomas Jackson. New York: Nelson & Phillips, 1872. http://wesley.nnu.edu/john-wesley/the-sermons-of-john-wesley-1872-edition/sermon-12-the-witness-of-our-own-spirit/.

———. *The Works of John Wesley*. Vol. 7. Edited by Franz Hildebrandt and Oliver Beckerlegge. Nashville: Abingdon, 1983.

White, Vernon. *Atonement and Incarnation: An Essay in Universalism and Particularity*. Cambridge: Cambridge University Press, 1991.

Wright, N. T. *The Day the Revolution Began: Reconsidering the Meaning of Jesus's Crucifixion*. New York: HarperCollins, 2016.

Secondary Sources

Althaus, Paul. *The Theology of Martin Luther*. Translated by Robert C. Schultz. Philadelphia: Fortress, 1966.

Anatolios, Khaled. *Athanasius*. London and New York: Routledge, 2004.

———. *Athanasius: The Coherence of His Thought*. London: Routledge, 1998.

Barth, Karl. *Anselm: Fides Quaerens Intellectum; Anselm's Proof of the Existence of God in the Context of His Theological Scheme*. Translated by Ian W. Robertson. Richmond: John Knox, 1960.

Baxter, Richard. *The Saints' Everlasting Rest*. London: T. Nelson and Sons, 1856.

Behr, John. *Irenaeus of Lyons: Identifying Christianity*. Oxford: Oxford University Press, 2013.

———. *The Way to Nicaea*. Vol. 1 of Formation of Christian Theology. Crestwood, NY: St. Vladimir's Seminary Press, 2001.

Boersma, Hans. "Redemptive Hospitality in Irenaeus: A Model for Ecumenicity in a Violent World." *Pro Ecclesia* 11, no. 2 (Spring 2002): 207–26.

Bond, H. Lawrence. "Another Look at Abelard's Commentary on Romans 3:26." In *Medieval Readings of Romans*, edited by W. S. Campbell, P. S. Hawkins, and B. D. Schildgen, 11–32. New York: T&T Clark International, 2007.

Borg, Marcus. *The Heart of Christianity: Rediscovering a Life of Faith*. New York: HarperCollins, 2003.

Boyd, Gregory. *God at War: The Bible and Spiritual Conflict*. Westmont, IL: IVP Academic, 1997.

Bruce, Matthew J. A. "Revelation." In *Wiley Blackwell Companion to Karl Barth Volume I: Barth* and *Dogmatics*, edited by George Hunsinger and Keith L. Johnson, 59–70. Hoboken, NJ: Wiley Blackwell, 2020.

Burns, J. Patout. "The Concept of Satisfaction in Medieval Redemption Theory." *Theological Studies* 36, no. 2 (June 1975): 285–304.

Busch, Eberhard. *The Great Passion: An Introduction to Karl Barth's Theology*. Translated by G. W. Bromiley. Grand Rapids: Eerdmans, 2004.

Campbell, John McLeod. *The Nature of the Atonement*. Grand Rapids: Eerdmans, 1996.

Cessario, Romanus. "Aquinas on Christian Salvation." In *Aquinas on Doctrine: A Critical Introduction*, edited by Thomas G. Weinandy, Daniel A. Keating, and John P. Yocum, 117–37. London: T&T Clark, 2004.

Chalke, Stephen, and Alan Mann. *The Lost Message of Jesus*. Grand Rapids: Zondervan, 2003.

Christensen, Michael J. "John Wesley: Christian Perfection as Faith Filled with the Energy of Love." In *Partakers of the Divine Nature: The History and Development of Deification in the Christian Traditions*, edited by Michael J. Christensen and Jeffrey A. Wittung, 219–31. Grand Rapids: Baker Academic, 2007.

Cobb, Peter G. "The Liturgy of the Word in the Early Church." In *The Study of Liturgy*, edited by Cheslyn Jones, Geoffrey Wainwright, and Edward Yarnold, SJ, 179–88. New York: Oxford University Press, 1978.

Collins, Kenneth. *Theology of John Wesley: Holy Love and the Shape of Grace*. Nashville: Abingdon, 2007.

Colyer, Elmer M. *How to Read T. F. Torrance: Understanding His Trinitarian and Scientific Theology*. Downers Grove, IL: InterVarsity, 2001.

Crisp, Oliver D. "Methodological Issues in Approaching the Atonement." In *T&T Clark Companion to the Atonement*, edited by Adam J. Johnson, 315–33. London: Bloomsbury T&T Clark, 2017.

Daly, Robert J. *Christian Sacrifice: The Judaeo-Christian Background Before Origen*. Washington, DC: The Catholic University Press of America, 1978.

———. *The Origins of the Christian Doctrine of Sacrifice*. Philadelphia: Fortress, 1978.

Davies, Brian. *The Thought of Thomas Aquinas*. Oxford: Oxford University Press, 1992.

Dawn, Marva J. "Powers and Principalities." In *Dictionary for Theological Interpretation of the Bible*, edited by Kevin J. Vanhoozer, 609–12. Grand Rapids: Baker Academic, 2005.

Dodd, C. H. *The Bible and the Greeks*. London: Hodder & Stoughton, 1935.

———. *The Epistle of Paul to the Romans*. London: Collins, 1959.

Donovan, Mary Ann. *One Right Reading? A Guide to Irenaeus*. Collegeville, MN: Liturgical Press, 1997.

Dorrien, Gary J. "Idealistic Orderings: Hastings Rashdall, Post-Kantian Idealism, and Anglican Liberal Theology." *Anglican and Episcopal History* 82, no. 3 (September 2013): 289–317.

———. *Kantian Reason and Hegelian Spirit: The Idealistic Logic of Modern Thought*. Chichester, West Sussex: Wiley Blackwell, 2012.

Dunn, James. *The Theology of Paul the Apostle*. Grand Rapids: Eerdmans, 1998.

Edmondson, Stephen. *Calvin's Christology*. Cambridge: Cambridge University Press, 2004.

Emery, Gilles, OP. *The Trinitarian Theology of St. Thomas Aquinas*. Translated by Francesca Aran Murphy. Oxford: Oxford University Press, 2007.

Erb, Peter C., ed. *The Pietists: Select Writings*. Classics of Western Spirituality. Mahwah, NJ: Paulist Press, 1983.

Erdman, Rachel. "Sacrifice as Satisfaction, Not Substitution: Atonement in the *Summa Theologiae*." *Anglican Theological Review* 96, no. 3 (Summer 2014): 461–80.

Fairweather, Eugene R. "Incarnation and Atonement: An Anselmian Response to Aulén's *Christus Victor*." *Canadian Journal of Theology* 7 (1961): 167–75.

Fee, Gordon D. "Paul and the Metaphors for Salvation." In *The Redemption: An Interdisciplinary Symposium on Christ as Redeemer*, edited by Stephen T. Davis, Daniel Kendall, SJ, and Gerald O'Collins, SJ, 43–67. Oxford: Oxford University Press, 2006.

Feiss, Hugh, ed. *On Love: A Selection of Works of Hugh, Adam, Achard, Richard, and Godfrey of St. Victor*. New York: New City Press, 2012.

Feuerbach, Ludwig. *The Essence of Christianity.* Translated by George Eliot. New York: Harper & Brothers, 1957.

Finger, Thomas. "*Christus Victor* and the Creeds: Some Historical Considerations." *Mennonite Quarterly Review* 72, no. 1 (January 1998): 31–51.

Ford, David F. *Barth and God's Story: Biblical Narrative and the Theological Method of Karl Barth in the Church Dogmatics.* Eugene, OR: Wipf & Stock, 1985.

Gibson, David. "Barth on Divine Election." In *Wiley Blackwell Companion to Karl Barth Volume I: Barth and Dogmatics*, edited by George Hunsinger and Keith L. Johnson, 47–58. Hoboken, NJ: Wiley Blackwell, 2020.

Gondreau, Paul. "The Humanity of Christ, the Incarnate Word." In *The Theology of Thomas Aquinas*, edited by Rik Van Nieuwenhove and Joseph Wawrykow, 252–76. Notre Dame: University of Notre Dame Press, 2005.

Greer, Rowan. "The Christian Bible and Its Interpretation." In *Early Biblical Interpretation*, edited by James Kugel and Rowan Greer, 163–76. Philadelphia: Westminster, 1986.

Gunton, Colin. *The Actuality of Atonement.* Grand Rapids: Eerdmans, 1989.

Harnack, Adolf von. *History of Dogma.* 7 vols. Translated by Neil Buchanan. Boston: Little, Brown, 1896–1905.

Harper, Brad. "*Christus Victor*: Postmodernism, and the Shaping of Atonement Theology." *Cultural Encounters* 2, no. 1 (Winter 2005): 37–51.

Hart, David Bentley. "A Gift Exceeding Every Debt: An Eastern Orthodox Appreciation of Anselm's *Cur Deus Homo*." *Pro Ecclesia* 7, no. 3 (Summer 1998): 333–49.

Hart, Trevor. *Regarding Karl Barth: Toward a Reading of His Theology.* Downers Grove, IL: InterVarsity, 1999.

———. "Revelation." In *The Cambridge Companion to Karl Barth*, edited by John Webster, 37–56. Cambridge: Cambridge University Press, 2000.

Healy, Nicholas M. "Introduction." In *Aquinas on Scripture: An Introduction to His Biblical Commentaries*, edited by Thomas Weinandy, Daniel Keating, and John Yocum, 1–20. London: T&T Clark, 2005.

Hochban, John I, SJ. "St. Irenaeus on the Atonement." *Theological Studies* 7, no. 4 (December 1946): 525–57.

Hogg, David S. *Anselm of Canterbury: The Beauty of Theology.* Burlington, VT: Ashgate, 2004.

Holsinger-Friesen, Thomas. *Irenaeus and Genesis: A Study of Competition in Early Christian Hermeneutics.* Winona Lake, IN: Eisenbrauns, 2009.

Hoskyns, Sir Edwin, and Noel Davey. *The Riddle of the New Testament.* London: Faber & Faber, 1931.

Hunsinger, George. Foreword to *Karl Barth's Infralapsarian Theology: Origins and Development, 1920–1953*, by Shao Kai Tseng, 9–14. Downers Grove, IL: InterVarsity, 2016.

———. *How to Read Karl Barth: The Shape of His Theology.* New York: Oxford University Press, 1991.

———. "Karl Barth's Christology: Its Basic Chalcedonian Character." In *The Cambridge Companion to Karl Barth*, edited by John Webster, 127–42. Cambridge: Cambridge University Press, 2000.

———. *Reading Barth with Charity: A Hermeneutical Proposal.* Grand Rapids: Baker Academic, 2015.

Johnson, Adam J. "Barth on the Atonement." In *Wiley Blackwell Companion to Karl Barth Volume I: Barth and Dogmatics*, edited by George Hunsinger and Keith L. Johnson, 147–58. Hoboken, NJ: Wiley Blackwell, 2020.

———. "A Fuller Account: The Role of 'Fittingness' in Thomas Aquinas' Development of the Doctrine of the Atonement." *International Journal of Systematic Theology* 12, no. 3 (July 2010): 302–18.

———. *God's Being in Reconciliation: The Theological Basis of the Unity and Diversity of the Atonement in the Theology of Karl Barth.* New York: Bloomsbury T&T Clark, 2012.

Jones, Paul Davydd. "The Fury of Love: Calvin on the Atonement." In *T&T Clark Companion to the Atonement*, edited by Adam J. Johnson, 213–35. London: Bloomsbury T&T Clark, 2017.

Kelly, J. N. D. *Early Christian Doctrines.* Rev. ed. New York: HarperCollins, 1978.

Kerr, Fergus. *After Aquinas: Versions of Thomism.* Malden, MA: Blackwell, 2002.

Keshgegian, Flora A. "The Scandal of the Cross: Revisiting Anselm and His Feminist Critics." *Anglican Theological Review* 82, no. 3 (Summer 2000): 475–92.

Lane, Anthony S. *Bernard of Clairvaux: Theologian of the Cross.* Cistercian Studies 248. Collegeville, MN: Liturgical Press, 2013.

Langford, Thomas A. *In Search of Foundations: English Theology, 1900–1920.* Nashville: Abingdon, 1969.

Lawson, John. *The Biblical Theology of Saint Irenaeus.* London: Epworth, 1948.

Leinhard, Marc. *Luther: Witness to Jesus Christ; Stages and Themes of the Reformer's Christology.* Minneapolis: Augsburg, 1982.

Leithart, Peter J. *Athanasius.* Grand Rapids: Baker Academic, 2011.

Levering, Matthew. *Christ's Fulfillment of Torah and Temple: Salvation According to Thomas Aquinas.* Notre Dame, IN: University of Notre Dame Press, 2002.

Lindstrom, Harald. *Wesley and Sanctification.* Wilmore, KY: Francis Asbury, 1998.

Long, D. Stephen. *Saving Karl Barth: Hans Urs von Balthasar's Preoccupation.* Minneapolis: Fortress, 2014.

Luby, Daniel J. "The Perceptibility of Grace in the Theology of John Wesley: A Roman Catholic Consideration." PhD diss., University of St. Thomas, 1994.

Maddox, Randy L. *Responsible Grace: John Wesley's Practical Theology.* Nashville: Kingswood, 1994.

Mangina, Joseph L. *Karl Barth: Theologian of Christian Witness.* Louisville: Westminster John Knox, 2004.

Markham, Ian S. "Revisionism." In *Oxford Handbook of Systematic Theology,* edited by John Webster, Kathryn Tanner, and Iain Torrance, 600–616. Oxford: Oxford University Press, 2007.

Marshall, Bruce. "*Quod Scit Una Uetula*: Aquinas on the Nature of Theology." In *The Theology of Thomas Aquinas,* edited by Rik Van Nieuwenhove and Joseph Wawrykow, 1–35. Notre Dame: University of Notre Dame Press, 2005.

McCormack, Bruce L. "The Ontological Presuppositions of Barth's Doctrine of the Atonement." In *The Glory of the Atonement: Biblical, Historical and Practical Perspectives: Essays in Honor of Roger Nicole,* edited by Charles E. Hill and Frank A. James, 346–66. Downers Grove, IL: InterVarsity, 2004.

McGrath, Alister. Foreword to the 2006 edition of *The Cross of Christ,* by John R. W. Stott, 9–12. Downers Grove, IL: InterVarsity, 2006. Originally published 1986.

———. "The Moral Theory of the Atonement: An Historical and Theological Critique." *Scottish Journal of Theology* 38, no. 2 (1985): 205–20.

McIntyre, John. *Anselm and His Critics: A Re-Interpretation of the* Cur Deus Homo. Edinburgh: Oliver & Boyd, 1954.

Merriell, D. Juvenal, C. O. "Trinitarian Anthropology." In *The Theology of Thomas Aquinas,* edited by Rik Van Nieuwenhove and Joseph Wawrykow, 123–42. Notre Dame: University of Notre Dame Press, 2005.

Moberley, Robert. *Atonement and Personality.* London: John Murray, 1901.

Molnar, Paul D. "Barth on the Trinity." In *Wiley Blackwell Companion to Karl Barth Volume I: Barth and Dogmatics,* edited by George Hunsinger and Keith L. Johnson, 23–34. Hoboken, NJ: Wiley Blackwell, 2020.

Morgan, Jonathan. "*Christus Victor* Motifs in the Soteriology of Thomas Aquinas." *Pro Ecclesia* 21, no. 4 (Fall 2012): 409–21.

Morris, Leon. *The Apostolic Preaching of the Cross.* Grand Rapids: Eerdmans, 1955.

———. *The Atonement: Its Meaning and Significance.* Downers Grove, IL: InterVarsity, 1983.

———. *The Cross in the New Testament.* Grand Rapids: Eerdmans, 1965.

———. *Glory in the Cross: A Study in Atonement.* Grand Rapids: Baker, 1979.

Nes, Solrunn. *The Mystical Language of Icons.* Grand Rapids: Eerdmans, 2004.

O'Collins, Gerald, SJ. *Jesus Our Redeemer: A Christian Approach to Salvation.* Oxford: Oxford University Press, 2007.

O'Collins, Gerald, SJ, and Michael Keenan Jones. *Jesus Our Priest.* Oxford: Oxford University Press, 2010.

Osborn, Eric. *Irenaeus of Lyons.* Cambridge: Cambridge University Press, 2001.

———. "Irenaeus of Lyons." In *The First Christian Theologians*, edited by G. R. Evans, 121–26. Malden, MA: Blackwell, 2004.

Ovey, Michael J. "Appropriating Aulén? Employing *Christus Victor* Models of the Atonement." *Churchman* 124, no. 4 (Winter 2010): 297–330.

Oxenham, Henry Nutcome. *The Catholic Doctrine of the Atonement.* 3rd ed. London: W. H. Allen, 1881.

Packer, J. I. "What Did the Cross Achieve? The Logic of Penal Substitution." *Tyndale Bulletin* 25 (1974): 3–46.

Pelikan, Jaroslav. *The Emergence of the Catholic Tradition.* Vol. 1 of A History of the Development of Doctrine. Chicago: University of Chicago Press, 1971.

———. Foreword to *Christus Victor: An Historical Study of the Three Main Types of the Idea of Atonement*, by Gustaf Aulén. Translated by A. G. Hebert, xi–xix. Repr., New York: Macmillan, 1969. Originally published 1931.

Peters, Ted. "The Atonement in Anselm and Luther: Second Thoughts About Gustaf Aulén's *Christus Victor.*" *Lutheran Quarterly* 24 (1972): 301–14.

Peterson, Brandon. "Paving the Way? Penalty and Atonement in Thomas Aquinas's Soteriology." *International Journal of Systematic Theology* 15, no. 3 (July 2013): 265–83.

Peterson, Robert A. *Calvin's Doctrine of the Atonement.* Phillipsburg, NJ: P&R, 1983.

Prestige, G. L. *Fathers and Heretics: Six Studies in Dogmatic Faith with Prologue and Epilogue.* London: SPCK, 1968.

Price, Robert B. "Barth on the Incarnation." In *Wiley Blackwell Companion to Karl Barth Volume I: Barth and Dogmatics*, edited by George Hunsinger and Keith L. Johnson, 137–46. Hoboken, NJ: Wiley Blackwell, 2020.

Pugh, Ben. "'Kicking the Daylights Out of the Devil': The Victory Motif in Some Recent Atonement Theology." *European Journal of Theology* 23, no. 1 (2014): 32–42.

Purves, Andrew. *Exploring Christology and Atonement: Conversations with John McLeod Campbell, H. R. Macintosh and T. F. Torrance.* Downers Grove, IL: InterVarsity, 2015.

Quinn, Philip L. "Abelard on Atonement: 'Nothing Unintelligible, Arbitrary, Illogical, or Immoral about It.'" In *Reasoned Faith*, edited by Eleonore Stump, 348–64. Ithaca, NY: Cornell University Press, 1993.

Rahner, Karl. *The Trinity.* Translated by Joseph Donceel. New York: Seabury, 1974.

Ramsey, Arthur Michael. *From Gore to Temple: The Development of Anglican Theology between* Lux Mundi *and the Second World War, 1889–1939.* London: Longmans, Green, 1960.

Rayner, Margaret J. "Hastings Rashdall on Immortality." *Modern Believing* 48, no. 2 (April 2007): 53–62.

Rodger, Symeon. "The Soteriology of Anselm of Canterbury: An Orthodox Perspective." *Greek Orthodox Theological Review* 34, no. 1 (1989): 19–43.

Root, Michael. "Necessity and Unfittingness in Anselm's *Cur Deus Homo.*" *Scottish Journal of Theology* 40, no. 2 (May 1987): 211–30.

Schmiechen, Peter. *Saving Power: Theories of Atonement and Forms of the Church.* Grand Rapids: Eerdmans, 2005.

Schweitzer, Albert. *The Quest of the Historical Jesus: A Critical Study of Its Progress from Reimarus to Wrede.* Translated by W. Montgomery. London: Adam & Charles Black, 1910.

Schwöbel, Christoph. "Theology." In *The Cambridge Companion to Karl Barth*, edited by John Webster, 17–36. Cambridge: Cambridge University Press, 2000.

Smythe, Shannon Nicole. "Karl Barth." In *T&T Clark Companion to the Atonement*, edited by Adam J. Johnson, 237–56. London: Bloomsbury T&T Clark, 2017.

Southern, R. W. *Saint Anselm: A Portrait in Landscape.* Cambridge: Cambridge University Press, 1990.

Stott, John R. W. *The Cross of Christ.* Downers Grove, IL: InterVarsity, 2006. Originally published 1986.

Stump, Eleonore. *Aquinas.* Arguments of the Philosophers. New York: Routledge, 2003.

Sumner, George. "Why Anselm Still Matters." *Anglican Theological Review* 95, no. 1 (2013): 25–35.

Sweeney, Eileen. "Vice and Sin (Ia IIae, qq. 71–89)." In *The Ethics of Aquinas*, ed. Stephen J.

Pope, 151–68. Washington, DC: Georgetown University Press, 2002.

Tietz, Christiane. "Karl Barth's Historical and Theological Significance." In *Wiley Blackwell Companion to Karl Barth Volume I: Barth and Dogmatics*, edited by George Hunsinger and Keith L. Johnson, 9–20. Hoboken, NJ: Wiley Blackwell, 2020.

Torpy, Arthur A. *The Prevenient Piety of Samuel Wesley, Sr.* Pietist and Methodist Studies 30. Lanham, MD: Scarecrow, 2009.

Torrance, Alan. "The Trinity." In *The Cambridge Companion to Karl Barth*, edited by John Webster, 72–91. Cambridge: Cambridge University Press, 2000.

Torrance, James B. Introduction to *The Nature of the Atonement*, by John McLeod Campbell, 1–34. Grand Rapids: Eerdmans, 1996.

Torrance, Thomas F. *Karl Barth, Biblical and Evangelical Theologian.* Edinburgh: T&T Clark, 1990.

———. *Scottish Theology: From John Knox to John McLeod Campbell.* Edinburgh: T&T Clark, 1996.

Torrell, Jean-Pierre, OP. *Christ and Spirituality in St. Thomas.* Translated by Bernard Blankenhorn, OP. Washington, DC: Catholic University of America Press, 2011.

———. *Saint Thomas Aquinas Volume 1: The Person and His Work.* Translated by Robert Royal. Washington, DC: Catholic University of America Press, 2005.

———. *Saint Thomas Aquinas Volume 2: Spiritual Master.* Translated by Robert Royal. Washington, DC: Catholic University of America Press, 2003.

Tseng, Shao Kai. *Karl Barth's Infralapsarian Theology: Origins and Development, 1920–1953.* Downers Grove, IL: InterVarsity, 2016.

Turner, H. E. W. *The Patristic Doctrine of Redemption.* London: Mowbray, 1952.

van Buren, Paul. *Christ in Our Place: The Substitutionary Character of Calvin's Doctrine of Reconciliation.* Grand Rapids: Eerdmans, 1957.

Van Nieuwenhove, Rik. "'Bearing the Marks of Christ's Passion': Aquinas' Soteriology." In *The Theology of Thomas Aquinas*, edited by Rik Van Nieuwenhove and Joseph Wawrykow, 277–302. Notre Dame: University of Notre Dame Press, 2005.

Wallace, Peter J. "History and Sacrament: John Williamson Nevin and Charles Hodge on the Lord's Supper." *Mid-America Journal of Theology* 11 (2000): 171–201.

Walsh, Liam G., OP. "Sacraments." In *The Theology of Thomas Aquinas*, edited by Rik Van Nieuwenhove and Joseph Wawrykow, 326–64. Notre Dame: University of Notre Dame Press, 2005.

Wawrykow, Joseph. "Grace." In *The Theology of Thomas Aquinas*, edited by Rik Van Nieuwenhove and Joseph Wawrykow, 192–221. Notre Dame: University of Notre Dame Press, 2005.

———. "Hypostatic Union." In *The Theology of Thomas Aquinas*, edited by Rik Van Nieuwenhove and Joseph Wawrykow, 222–51. Notre Dame: University of Notre Dame Press, 2005.

Webber, Robert. *Ancient Future Faith.* Grand Rapids: Baker, 1999.

Weinandy, Thomas. *Athanasius: A Theological Introduction.* Hampshire, UK: Ashgate, 2007.

Weingart, Richard E. *The Logic of Divine Love: A Critical Analysis of the Soteriology of Peter Abailard.* Oxford: Oxford University Press, 1970.

Wendel, François. *Calvin: The Origins and Development of His Religious Thought.* Translated by Philip Mairet. Grand Rapids: Baker, 1995.

White, Thomas Joseph. *The Incarnate Lord: A Thomistic Study in Christology.* Washington, DC: Catholic University of America Press, 2015.

Wiendt, Jonathan. "What is Anselm Singing? A Critique of Anselm's Theory of Atonement." *Journal of Theta Alpha Kappa* 29, no. 2 (Fall 2005): 25–39.

Williams, Rowan. "Origen." In *The First Christian Theologians*, edited by G. R. Evans, 132–42. Malden, MA: Blackwell, 2004.

Williams, Thomas. "Sin, Grace, and Redemption in Abelard." In *The Cambridge Companion to Abelard*, edited by Jeffrey Brower and Kevin Guilfoy, 258–78. Cambridge: Cambridge University Press, 2004.

Wingren, Gustaf. *Man and the Incarnation: A Study in the Biblical Theology of Irenaeus.* Translated by Ross Mackenzie. Edinburgh: Oliver & Boyd, 1959.

Wink, Walter. *Naming the Powers: The Language of Power in the New Testament*. Philadelphia: Fortress, 1984.

Witt, William G. "He Was Crucified under Pontius Pilate: He Suffered Death and Was Buried." In *The Rule of Faith: Scripture, Canon, and Creed in a Critical Age*, edited by Ephraim Radner and George Sumner, 92–112. Harrisburg, PA: Morehouse, 1998.

Wood, Darren C. "John Wesley's Use of Atonement." *Asbury Journal* 62, no. 2 (2007): 55–70.

Young, Frances. "The Interpretation of Scripture." In *The First Christian Theologians*, edited by G. R. Evans, 24–38. Malden, MA: Blackwell, 2004.

Zachman, Randall C. "The Christology of John Calvin." In *The Oxford Handbook of Christology*, edited by Francesca Aran Murphy, 284–96. Oxford: Oxford University Press, 2015.

Zehr, Howard. *Changing Lenses: Restorative Justice for Our Times*. 25th anniv. ed. Harrisonburg, VA: Herald, 2015. Originally published 1990.

Author Index

Abailard. *See* Peter Abelard

Althaus, Paul   93n26, 230

Anatolios, Khaled   27n28, 28n30, 28n34, 29nn35–39, 30nn40–41, 31n45, 32n46, 230

Anselm of Canterbury   vii, 5, 12, 30, 46, 46nn26–27, 47, 47n28, 48–50, 50n47, 56–57, 61–63, 63n7, 64, 64nn11–12, 65, 65nn14–15, 66, 66nn16–18, 67, 67n21, 68, 68nn23–24, 69, 69nn25–27, 70, 70nn28–30, 71, 71nn31–35, 72, 72nn36–39, 73–76, 76nn59–60, 77, 77nn63–65, 78–79, 79nn69–70, 80–86, 91, 101–3, 109, 115–16, 118, 124, 126, 134–35, 144, 146–47, 149, 167, 178, 192–93, 198, 205, 223, 227

Anselm of Laon   63

Athanasius of Alexandria   vii, xi–xii, 11, 15–16, 27–36, 27n28, 28nn30–34, 29n39, 31n43, 59, 73, 78–79, 99, 163, 166, 177, 193, 227

Augustine of Hippo   xii, 42, 42n10, 45, 45n21, 71, 77, 92, 92n22, 93, 98, 108, 129, 163, 177, 227

Aulén, Gustaf   vii, ix, xii, 11, 12, 38, 38n1, 39, 39n2, 48, 48nn36–37, 49, 49n41, 50, 50nn46–48, 51, 51nn50–56, 52, 52nn57–61, 53, 53nn62–65, 54, 54nn66–70, 55, 55nn71–75, 56, 56nn76–77, 56nn79–80, 57, 57nn81–84, 58–59, 59nn87–88, 62, 62n4, 74, 80, 101, 101n1, 149, 228

Baker, Mark D.   203, 203nn8–9, 204, 204nn10–15, 205, 205nn16–17, 206, 210, 210n38, 221, 228

Barth, Karl   vii, xii, 7–8, 8n10, 12, 65n13, 80, 140, 149, 176–78, 178nn1–2, 178n5, 179, 179n8, 180, 180n20, 181, 181n22, 182–83, 183n28, 185–85, 185nn38–40, 186–89, 189n42, 190nn43–44, 191–200, 212, 228

Baxter, Richard   151, 151n66, 230

Behr, John   17n9, 230

Bernard of Clairvaux   82–83, 85–86, 86n7, 90n19, 93, 151, 228

Boersma, Hans   17n12, 23n17, 24n21, 26n23, 230

Bond, H. Lawrence   84n3, 85n6, 87n13, 230

Borg, Marcus   172, 172n94, 230

Boso   63–65, 67

Boyd, Gregory   12, 57, 57n85, 230

Bruce, Matthew J. A.   179n14, 230

Burns, J. Patout   62n2, 74n44, 74n46, 231

Busch, Eberhard   178n4, 178n6, 179n10, 179nn13–14, 180n15, 180n18, 182nn24–25, 184n34, 184n37, 231

Calvin, John   vii, xii, 12, 62, 80, 93, 126–41, 144, 146–48, 150–51, 167, 173, 193, 228

Campbell, John McLeod   13, 13n13, 141nn30–31, 147n54, 147n56, 148nn57–58, 231

Cartwright, Steven R.   85n5, 87n13, 229

Cessario, Romanus   102n5, 103n6, 104n10, 108n23, 109nn26–27, 111n34, 117n51, 231

Chalke, Stephen   202, 202n4, 231

Christensen, Michael J.   99n42, 231

Clement of Rome   2, 2n1, 228

Cobb, Peter G.   15n2, 231

237